Essentials of Leadership

A Systematic Approach to Effective Leadership

Bruce E. Beck

The Essentials Group

First Printing: 2018

ISBN-13: 978-1981890668
ISBN-10: 1981890661

The Essentials Group Publisher
11337 Abercairn Ct.
Zionsville, Indiana 46077

To my wife, Kathy, daughters Rachel, Sarah, and Lauren, and son Daniel, son-in-laws Christian and Jon, and, of course, the greatest grandsons in the world. I love you beyond words and thank God every day for you being in my life. Thank you for listening and providing feedback to my verbal processing and ranting about the essentials of leadership.

To my father-in-law, Earl C. Rodgers, the most generous man I have ever known. Thank you for living out your compassion for people and mentoring me to be a better man. You left an incredible legacy of how your faith in the Lord, love of your family, and passion for your community can be the foundation of a life well lived.

Finally, to the greatest leader I have ever known, my dad, Paul E. Beck. Thanks, Dad, for setting such an incredible model of genuine leadership to not only your family but also your community and country. I miss you incredibly and will love you forever.

Table of Contents

The Focus

Writing a book about leadership is a daunting task. Libraries are filled with books on the subject. A search on Amazon or other sites will pull up hundreds of treatises on leadership. I have read many of these, and they offer good insight and perspective. I will reference a number of these resources throughout this book. However, my intent in writing about leadership is twofold: to tell stories of leadership and transformation, and to represent leadership in the context of a dynamic system. My perspective is that leadership is as much a process as it is a title. In our society, the term *leader* is thrown around loosely and used to apply to all sorts of people or businesses in various situations. My view is different. I believe that unique to the term is that *leader* inevitably refers to the idea of setting direction, motivating people to action, and providing vision.

In this book, I will discuss what I call the "essentials" of leadership. These are key elements, attributes, and traits that interact together to define a successful leader. They work together as a dynamic reinforcing system. Understanding the dynamics of this system enables the development and enhancement of an individual's leadership skills.

My goal is to identify essentials for effective leadership and encourage you to think about your own leadership in the context of these essentials. Also, I hope that, as potential leaders are identified, chosen, and coached, an understanding of the dynamics of this model will be useful in developing those leaders beyond their title. My ultimate goal here is to enable leaders to become effective at setting direction, motivating people to action, and providing vision for a new future.

1

The Catalyst

As we work to provide better individual patient outcomes in a challenging global environment, we need outstanding leaders more than ever. Your leadership is critical to our future.

—John Lechleiter, then chairman and CEO of
Eli Lilly, while speaking to the Lilly Senior Man-
agement Group

In 2000, a group of people began a journey together to create a new capability for Eli Lilly and Company. This capability was to establish a Center of Excellence in the corporation for commissioning and qualifying new and existing facilities. Lilly is a Fortune 500 company that is a major pharmaceutical company with a history of over 135 years. It was founded by Colonel Eli Lilly in the 1800s following the American Civil War. The company has been instrumental in bringing to the world life-saving products, such as penicillin, insulin, Prozac, Zyprexa, and Ceclor, just to name a few. Lilly discovers, develops, and manufactures products around the world in a number of research and manufacturing facilities. I was asked to create this Commissioning and Qualification (C&Q) Center of Excellence in response to a serious gap in the company's capabilities.

After forming a team to develop the C&Q capability, we worked together to determine the current industry's best practices and regulatory expectations as critical aspects for defining the best path forward for Lilly. This process became a journey of discovery on many fronts.

In early 2001, the industry was going through a radical change in expectations, which was driven by the regulatory agencies, particularly the Food and Drug Administration (FDA). They were expecting much more documentation and significantly more robust testing and verification of system capabilities. Moreover, they wanted improved discipline in the commissioning-and-qualification approach for new and existing facilities used to manufacture drugs. Quite simply, they raised the bar on expectations, and Lilly and the entire industry had no choice but to respond.

For the uninitiated, commissioning and qualification of pharmaceutical manufacturing facilities can be compared to the testing done by Boeing to test a new airplane. When Boeing rolls a new plane off the production line, they do not simply get a group of people together and say, "Let's go for a ride." They instead spend months testing all of the systems in the plane in a progressive manner until they deem it safe to take a test flight. Ultimately, Boeing and the Federal Aviation Administration (FAA) approve it as airworthy and ready to carry passengers. Commissioning and Qualification essentially accomplishes the same thing for pharmaceutical manufacturing facilities. Manufacturers must verify that drugs can be produced to quality standards in a consistent, controlled manner prior to providing product to the market.

Over a number of months, the newly formed Lilly C&Q team met, explored, and discussed approaches and methods for addressing this gap. Finally, in the fall of 2003, we held a global conference in Indianapolis on the campus of Indiana University–Purdue University Indianapolis (IUPUI) to roll out our proposed direction for Lilly Commissioning and Qualification. Representatives from sites around the world were present, and for five days we reviewed the proposed direction and methods and debated their merit.

As the leader of the conference, I told the delegates on the first day, "We are here to make decisions, and if I had to lock the doors and feed you by sliding food under the door, I would!" The debates were sometimes loud and ardent, but slowly, as the week progressed, this group came together to agree on a path forward. Over fifty representatives left that week, returning to their sites, and began implementing a new approach to commissioning and qualification using the tools and procedures they had agreed upon that week.

As we began to execute and lead teams around the world, it became evident that the methods and procedures we developed were appropriate and added significant value. They not only met the regulatory agency expectations but also provided Lilly with a much better disciplined approach that had many benefits for delivering new assets around the globe. However, as we led teams throughout the world, it also became evident that methods and procedures were not enough for us to be effective. We needed to address the issue and importance of leadership.

We were asking associates to travel worldwide and lead C&Q teams. These teams were often incredibly diverse groups with a wide range of experience. The C&Q leaders had little positional authority with the teams they led. They had to rely on their ability to influence and motivate people. In addition, these teams often had their own ideas and were sometimes not well versed in the corporate C&Q methods and procedures. As I recognized the need to help our staffs improve their leadership abilities, I embarked on a new journey to discover and define what we expected from leaders and needed them to exhibit to be successful.

Part 1

The Leadership Model

2

The Ride Home

It is better to lead from behind and to put others in front, especially when you celebrate victory when nice things occur. You take the front line when there is danger. Then people will appreciate your leadership.

—*Nelson Mandela*

I slumped back into my business class seat and felt the tension of another long European business trip ease out of my body. There was always something about finally bringing a long business trip to an end and knowing I was heading home that allowed me to finally relax. The Continental Airlines 757 climbed to cruising altitude above the skies of Shannon International Airport, and along with the usual sense of tension leaving my body, my thoughts went back to the previous night and the significance of the event I had been a part of only a few hours earlier.

I stood to address the gathering at Jolla's, one of my favorite restaurants in Kinsale, Ireland. I was there to celebrate, along with our Commissioning and Qualification team, the completion of their successful qualification of a new $400 million Lilly biotechnology manufacturing facility called IE42. Our project management group had invited the entire team and their wives, husbands, and significant others to come and participate in the celebration. It was an historic moment, worthy of celebration and a time to stop and reflect upon the significance of their accomplishments.

The team had successfully completed the work at world-class levels of performance for cost, quality, and time. They had come together and become a band of brothers, supporting each other over nearly three years. They had applied a disciplined approach to their work with incredible effort and professionalism while also supporting one another. The results had been outstanding, and the implications significant for Lilly.

As I stood in front of them, I shared with their loved ones the significance of their accomplishments for not only Lilly but also to the world in preparing this new facility for operation. I shared my personal story of having lost my first wife, Jennifer, to cancer a few years before and the devastating impact of this disease on my life and that of my daughter. I explained to them that this facility was to be used to manufacture new novel oncology drugs to fight this dreaded disease. This facility had deep personal meaning to me: it was more than just another project; it was a weapon to be used in fighting a war to save lives. I concluded by thanking the team for their hard work and long hours of sacrifice. I thanked their loved ones for their patience and support and told them they were a vital part of the team and a part of the story. Finally, I closed with these words:

> Years from now when new drugs are being made in this facility—drugs that are saving lives around the world and possibly even one of your own loved one's life—you should remember and know that you had a significant part in making that happen. All the drugs produced from this facility will forever be a part of your story, your legacy. Thank you, and God bless you!

As the plane leveled out at cruising altitude, I reflected on the significance of the IE42 success story in a bigger context. I had formed a C&Q team ten years before to address a huge problem at Lilly. The IE42 project represented the pinnacle of this success story. The results were by all measures outstanding. A disciplined process had been created and implemented. The results spoke for themselves. In a few days I would share, not only the IE42 story, but also the larger story to a room full of vice presidents and senior directors at Lilly.

The disciplined C&Q program, along with superb execution, had proven to be highly effective among many projects. But fundamental to all of the successes was the role of leadership. I began studying leadership over thirty years ago and had the privilege of working with some outstanding leaders at Eli Lilly and Company. As might be expected, I also had some extremely negative experiences with people who were poor leaders. I learned from each experience and applied my learning to lead a variety of manufacturing teams as well as drive a number of major change initiatives. During my last fifteen years at Lilly, I was a director of engineering and responsible for creating the Center of Excellence for Lilly's Commissioning and Qualification. Through my various positions, I have been a student of leadership and its role in organizational success.

In this book I want to share with you what I have learned about leadership. As part of this, I will walk you through a leadership model that I developed and used effectively in leading the Commissioning and Qualification teams at Lilly. Our model evolved as we learned together, but at its core is the concept that *leadership is a system, not a title or abstract idea.* This view is consistent with Peter Senge's view of leadership, which he has written about in his book *The Fifth Discipline: The Art and Practice of a Learning Organization* (Senge, 1990). I build upon Senge's system thinking approach to leadership, and I expand beyond it. In my approach to leadership, I will discuss the *Values, Dimensions, Behaviors*, and *Character Traits of Leaders*. I will show how these four areas interact in a dynamic way to define a leader's capability and effectiveness.

I will use the term *essential* as a descriptor for each element or attribute of my Leadership Model because they all work together to make a leader effective. Because this model is a system, each dimension is reliant upon and impacted by the other. These dimensions are reinforcing loops. If a leader performs well in one dimension, it will reinforce his or her ability to be successful in another. In similar fashion, a failure or weakness in a dimension, value, or trait will also hinder performance in the other dimensions. It is vital that a leader understand these dynamic relationships. They all are essential!

A word of caution: Because I present this material in a structured manner, one could easily interpret it as a linear, step-by-step process of leadership development and execution. But this would be a mistake. The dimensions and traits I describe are a dynamic system of behaviors, attributes, and values, all working together simultaneously. The very nature of a system is that its parts interact and reinforce one another while countering what threatens or seeks to undermine them. As you read this book, you need to recognize that all the parts of my Leadership Model are designed to run simultaneously. Put another way, effective leaders are always conscious of the impact of their decisions and behaviors on those they are trying to lead.

I believe the lessons and principles in this book are transferable to any leadership role regardless of the sector one is in, be it business, military, education, a religious institution, community service, or what have you. Understanding the dynamics of leadership as a system is universally applicable.

***

Several days later after returning from Ireland, I found myself in a Lilly corporate center conference room. I had been asked to give an update on the corporate C&Q program developed several years previously and its impact on the IE42 project. The room did not have an empty seat. It was filled with vice presidents and senior directors from manufacturing as well as engineering and quality. The data I presented was compelling. It clearly showed that the effort had paid off. The C&Q program was nothing but a tremendous success worldwide, and C&Q costs were not just down but also among the lowest in the pharmaceutical industry. Durations to complete the work had been significantly reduced, and the quality of the work had never been higher. New facilities had not just been qualified but had passed FDA "pre-approval inspections" with flying colors and were producing products. As I neared the end of the presentation, I concluded with a slide that represented the foundation for our success. No presentation regarding our C&Q success could be made without telling the whole story. That slide was the Leadership Model, and this is its story.

Leadership Takeaways

- The role of leadership is fundamental to success.

- Leaders are people who know how to set vision, achieve goals, and inspire people to follow and take specific actions.

- The core concept is that leadership is a system, not a title or abstract idea.

- The Leadership Model will address Values, Dimensions, Behaviors, and the Character Traits of Leaders.

- This model is a system, and each dimension is reliant on and impacted by the other.

- Each element is essential to the function of the system.

- The leadership lessons and principles are transferable to any leadership role, regardless of sector.

3

Why Leaders Now?

Leadership is not optional; it is essential. Essential for motivation and direction. Essential for evaluation and accomplishment. It is the one ingredient essential for the success of any organization. Take away leadership and it isn't long before confusion replaces vision.

—Charles R. Swindoll

History would be written in the next twenty-four hours. This was a certainty. Although the outcome was yet to be determined, this event would be either one of the biggest success stories in world history or one of the worst failures.

Not only history would be made, but also direction for the world hung in the balance. After months of intense planning and preparation, D-Day was finally set for June 6, 1941, and Dwight D. Eisenhower, "Ike", was in the "eye of the storm" as the Supreme Allied Commander in charge of the invasion plan and its execution. The decision to go was his and his alone. Carlos D'Este writes in his book, *Eisenhower: A Soldier's Life*, that "No commander in military history faced a more daunting task than the one he did in 1944. Not only was he charged with welding together the largest force ever assembled for an amphibious invasion, but it had to work the first time: There would be no second chance" (D'Este, 2002).

Operation Overlord, the D-Day attack plan, had been in planning for months and involved hundreds of people, including strong personalities and the egos of generals such as George S. Patton and Field Marshall Bernard Montgomery, also called "Monty." In addition, Ike had to engage and navigate through the politics of world leaders such as US President Franklin D. Roosevelt, Great Britain's Prime Minister Winston Churchill, and Charles De Gaulle, the leader of the Free French forces. All these people had their own ideas for the invasion as well as personal agendas. Ike had to find a way through all this to put together a staff of knowledgeable, capable experts and leaders who could develop a viable invasion plan as well as assure that all the logistics, people, and training was in place at the time needed. The complexity of the task was astonishing.

Eisenhower dealt with problem after problem throughout the planning and preparation. The problems ranged from heated strategy disagreements over the use and control of airpower to obtaining enough landing craft to support the invasion. The logistics alone were staggering. The navy had to plan not only the sealift of 156,000 troops but also choreograph the employment of nearly 7,000 Allied naval vessels, 15 of which were hospital ships, and 195,700 naval and merchant marine personnel in the waters off Normandy on D-Day. Eight thousand doctors—who were supplied with 600,000 doses of penicillin, 100,000 pounds of sulfa, and 800,000 pints of plasma—had been assembled to treat the wounded. In all, more than 2.8 million soldiers, sailors, and airmen would be involved in carrying out Operation Overlord (D'Este, 2002, p. 494).

Eisenhower knew that he needed operational control of both tactical and strategic air forces to be successful in Operation Overload. He wrote later in *Crusades in Europe* that "when a battle needs the last ounce of available force, the commander must not be in a position of depending upon request and negotiation to get it... I stated unequivocally that so long as I was in command I would accept no other solution" (Eisenhower, 1948). Eisenhower felt so committed to this position that, in the ensuing internal battle for control between generals and world leaders, he threatened to resign his position and "go home" if not given control of air power.

Eisenhower also dealt with various political struggles in the critical weeks leading up to the invasion. One such instance was his discovery that Prime Minister Churchill insisted on viewing the invasion from a British warship off shore of the landing beaches. Carlos D' Este writes (D'Este, 2002, p. 524):

> Exasperated, Eisenhower forcefully told the prime minister that he would not sanction his presence in harm's way. Not to be outdone by a mere general, Churchill insisted that as minister of defense he had a duty to take part, insisting he would circumvent Eisenhower's authority by going as a crew member; "it is not part of your responsibilities, my dear General," he said, "to determine the exact composition of any ship's company in His majesty's Fleet."... King George VI learned of the prime minister's intentions and put a stop to it. In a letter hand-delivered from Buckingham Palace, the king pointed out that of course he would never presume to interfere in the affairs of his government's principal minister. However, should Churchill carry out his intentions, the king would likewise feel obligated to witness the invasion as the (titular) head of Britain's armed forces.

Churchill gave in grudgingly, but such was the life of Eisenhower in the days leading up to the invasion.

After months of planning and incredible logistical efforts to position and ready almost three million soldiers, sailors, and airmen for the invasion, the final "go" order was being controlled by the weather. There was only a three-day window in early June in which the operation could commence. Three airborne divisions that were to land by parachute and glider the night before the invasion needed moonlight to be successful. This window also had to coincide with the low tides needed for the beach landings. The weather was now the controlling factor.

The weather had everyone on Eisenhower's staff stressed. The invasion force was in position with soldiers on ships at sea, but weather had simply made an invasion on the fifth of June impossible. The delay only increased the stress and uncertainty for everyone. At a late-night meeting on June 4, Eisenhower convened a council of generals, admirals, and air marshals to assess the situation and hear the weather forecast. This was arguably "the most important weather prediction in history." A mistaken forecast for D-Day could turn the entire tide of the war against the Allies.

The weather forecast indicated the worst of the conditions would lift in time. Though not providing perfect conditions, the weather change would offer the Allies an opportunity. After discussions with the invasion commanders, many of the staff left the room, and Eisenhower and a small group remained. Time had run out. A decision had to be made. Historian Stephen Ambrose described the scene this way:

> There was utter silence in the room, the only sounds to be heard were the wind and rain pounding Southwick House. Beetle Smith, a man rarely emotional about anything, was awed by "the loneliness and isolation of a commander at a time when such a momentous decision has to be taken with full knowledge that failure or success rests on his judgment alone. He sat there quietly, not getting up to pace with quick strides as he often does. He was tense, weighing every consideration of weather as he had been briefed to do during the dry runs since April, and weighing them with other imponderables. (Ambrose, 1994)

Ambrose continued:

> Still pondering, Eisenhower said, "The question is, just how long can you hang this operation on the end of a limb and let it hang there? I am quite positive we must give the order. I don't like it but there it is ... I don't see how we can do anything else." With that low-key pronouncement, the invasion of Normandy would take place the morning of June 6th. Based on the most important weather forecast in history. (Ambrose, 1994)

Eisenhower had done all he could do.

In the days leading up to the invasion, Eisenhower had recorded a broadcast to the world to be played on the day of the invasion (D'Este, 2002):

> Soldiers, Sailors and Airmen of the Allied Expeditionary Forces! You are about to embark on the great crusade, toward which we have striven these many months. The eyes of the world are upon you. The hopes and prayers of liberty-loving people everywhere march with you. In company with our brave Allies and brothers-in-arms on other Fronts you will bring about the destruction of the German war machine, the elimination of Nazi tyranny over oppressed peoples of Europe, and security for ourselves in a free world.
>
> Your task will not be an easy one. Your enemy is well trained, well equipped and battle hardened. He will fight savagely … .
>
> I have full confidence in your courage, devotion to duty and skill in battle. We will accept nothing less than full victory!
>
> Good luck! And let us all beseech the blessing of Almighty God upon this great and noble undertaking.

On June 5, Eisenhower had written a different document that reflected little of this same inspiration. He folded it and placed it in his wallet. It was to be used if the unthinkable occurred. It read (D'Este, 2002, p. 527):

> Our landings in the Cherbourg-Havre area have failed to gain a satisfactory foothold and I have withdrawn the troops. My decision to attack at this time and place was based upon the best information available. The troops, the air, and the Navy did all that bravery and devotion to duty

could do. If any blame or fault attaches to the attempt it is mine alone – June 5.

Leadership can be a lonely place and carry many burdens. Eisenhower was the leader the world needed at a critical time in history. The Allies had resources and soldiers, sailors, and airmen to execute an invasion, but critical to success was a leader who could bring people together from different nations and branches of the military. Eisenhower was able to navigate through the politics, egos, and strong opinions to build a plan for invasion. He was able to keep everyone focused on the objective, and through that he built a multinational team to quickly react and address problems as they arose.

If your actions inspire others to dream more, learn more, do more and become more, you are a leader.
—*John Quincy Adams*

General Dwight Eisenhower is a noteworthy example of the value and importance of strong leadership. Today we deal with a vast array of leadership needs. All kinds of endeavors need leadership, including financial institutions, industry, business, the military, governments, and education. Indeed, they all need the kind and quality of leadership Ike exhibited.

The challenges that he dealt with are not so different than what we face today. The effort he faced was complex and involved many different nationalities. It included tremendous logistical challenges of supplying resources across oceans. Communication was always a challenge and had to be managed carefully. It also required sensitivity to cultural ideas and needs. He had to deal with new unproven technology being developed to address problems. Finally, he had to assure that many people not only bought in to the plan but also embraced it and were prepared to execute it. These challenges are still relevant to what leaders face today. Leadership matters, and the lessons of the past can be valuable in guiding us forward.

In November 2014, Roger Trapp wrote in *Forbes* magazine:

The need for leaders is increasingly a preoccupation of business people. Indeed, the need for "leaders at all levels" is one of the 12 critical issues identified in the Global Human Capital Trends 2014 survey published earlier this month by Deloitte University Press, the publishing arm of the professional services firm's leadership center.

In a paper examining the findings, Adam Canwell, Vishalli Dongrie, Neil Neveras and Heather Stockton—who work for Deloitte—point out that leadership "remains the No. 1 talent issue facing organizations around the world," with 86% of respondents to the survey rating it "urgent" or "important." However, the fact that only 13% say they do an excellent job of developing leaders at all levels means that this area has the largest "readiness gap" in the survey.

Trapp concludes:

Organizations have long looked for leaders but the Deloitte team argues that, "21st-century leadership is different." Canwell and his colleagues write: "Companies face new leadership challenges, including developing millennial and multiple generations of leaders, meeting the demand for leaders with global fluency and flexibility, building the ability to innovate and inspire others to perform, and acquiring new levels of understanding of rapidly changing technologies and new disciplines and fields." No wonder organizations are coming up short.

Almost inevitably, the problem is felt to be especially acute today. This is a result of the strengthening of the global recovery, the desire on the part of the companies to expand in new markets and the growing numbers of older leaders choosing to retire. (Trapp, 2014)

The World is Changing—Rapidly

Leaders are needed who can handle and understand a rapidly changing world. Even over just the last thirty years, the technology changes alone are staggering. Several years ago, Wharton School of Business developed the following list of top thirty innovations that have changed the world over the last three decades (Wharton , 2009).

The list includes:

1. Internet, broadband, www (browser and html)
2. PC/laptop computers
3. Mobile phones
4. E-mail
5. DNA testing and sequencing/Human genome mapping
6. Magnetic Resonance Imaging (MRI)
7. Microprocessors
8. Fiber optics
9. Office software (spreadsheets, word processors)
10. Noninvasive laser/robotic surgery (laparoscopy)
11. Open source software and services (e.g., Linux, Wikipedia)
12. Light emitting diodes
13. Liquid crystal display (LCD)
14. GPS systems
15. Online shopping/e-commerce/auctions (e.g., eBay)
16. Media file compression (jpeg, mpeg, mp3)
17. Microfinance
18. Photovoltaic Solar Energy
19. Large scale wind turbines
20. Social networking via the Internet
21. Graphic user interface (GUI)
22. Digital photography/videography
23. RFID and applications (e.g., EZ Pass)
24. Genetically modified plants
25. Bio fuels

26. Bar codes and scanners
27. ATMs
28. Stents
29. SRAM flash memory
30. Anti-retroviral treatment for AIDS

This list represents a dramatic transition for our world regarding business, commerce, travel, computing, healthcare, communication, food, and energy. The twentieth century has often been described as the most innovative century in the history of humankind as we went from creating the first airplane to going to the moon to establishing a full-time space station. Diseases that plagued society and often meant certain death have been eradicated or reduced to manageable health conditions. We went from communication primarily through telegraph and telephone to email, texting, tweeting, and video conferencing. In 1920, half of all Americans lived on farms or in towns of less than 2,500 people. About 25 percent of the labor force still farmed, compared with only 2 percent at the end of the century. Most Americans in 1920 never traveled more than a few hundred miles from where they were born (McCraw, 2000).

In addition to new technology, countries and business climates have also changed dramatically. China opened it doors to commerce, and a transformation began that is still continuing with global impact. Russia has transitioned from the old Soviet economic model to become a global economic player. Brazil continues to grow and lead the southern hemisphere as a powerful economic force and seat of opportunity. Countries such as Vietnam, Indonesia, and India offer significant opportunities as well. In this rapidly changing business climate, leaders are needed who can not only understand these global opportunities but also effectively drive change and position their organization to be successful.

All the signs today indicate that dramatic changes in discovery, innovation, and implementation will continue into the distant future. Changes are occurring so fast that effective leadership is essential to navigate organizations through rapidly changing technology as well as dynamic changing business cultures. Simply stated, management as usual will not get the job done. Organizations that choose to simply manage day-to-day activities and retain their position may find themselves suddenly not just falling behind but out of business. Companies like Kodak, Eastern Airlines, Tower Records, Pan Am Airlines, Polaroid, and Borders Bookstores are just a few that went through painful transitions and even closure due to changes in their industry and in technology. Leadership must provide direction in such an environment and help people not only be successful but also make the changes necessary to have continual success in this rapidly evolving world.

Tamara Lytle wrote an article for the November 27, 2009 *U.S. News and World Report* entitled "Enron, Hurricane Katrina, Examples of Leadership Gone Wrong: Poor crisis leadership was on display after Hurricane Katrina and during the financial crisis." She wrote:

> The collapse of major financial companies starting with Bear Stearns, the stunningly botched reaction to Katrina, the inept federal response to tips about Bernard Madoff's Ponzi scheme, and the financial sleight of hand that brought down Enron are only the latest examples of leadership failure. "We keep making the same stupid mistakes, generation after generation," says William Baker, who holds a doctorate in industrial psychology and is the journalist in residence at Fordham University.
>
> Many of the most stunning leadership disasters have common ingredients, such as executives who lack integrity and build organizational cultures where dissent isn't heard. "Leadership is not position. It's moral authority. Moral authority comes from following universal and timeless principles like honesty, integrity, treating people with respect," says Stephen Covey, author of several bestselling books on leadership and self-improvement, including *The 7 Habits of Highly Effective People*. Baker, author of *Leading With Kindness*, agrees that massive failures often can be traced back to leaders who don't listen.

Part of the problem: The wrong people are often chosen to head organizations. "We go for these effervescent leaders when what's really needed is a dull, focused, plodding [person] building effective groups and organizations," says Timothy Judge, chair of management at the University of Florida business school. It turns out that being an extrovert is highly correlated with being chosen as a leader but not with being a good one, he says. (Lytle, 2009)

Leadership selection and development are challenging. Not only are human resource departments and management struggling to project who can be a future leader in their organization, but people already in leadership positions are often struggling with how to be effective and what this really means. Unfortunately, without proper mentoring and development, leaders can struggle to be effective and sometimes fail miserably. Mentoring is a good thing if the mentor is effective at feedback and provides proper insight. However, I have too often seen mentoring poorly done, and often it is completely nonexistent in organizations. This leaves new leaders with a sense that they are on their own to sink or swim.

In this book I provide tools for not only a mentor but also a leader to assess their effectiveness as a leader. I recognize that leadership is dynamic and that others judge each decision and action a leader makes. It is my hope that this book will provide insight and help in your leadership journey through a rapidly changing world.

Globalization and Diversity

Today's marketplace is quite different than the ones our parents dealt with thirty years ago. As I described previously, China is a huge player in trade and now the world's largest economic power. Countries such as India are developing rapidly and becoming centers for technology support and development. Businesses are opening new operations all over the world to establish presence and take advantage of growing markets. With this globalization comes a need for leadership that can work with diverse cultures. The leader must not only demonstrate sensitivity to cultural differences but also be able to get very diverse groups of people to work together. With the technology capabilities of today, teams may be on opposite sides of the world working on the same project as a virtual team. Leaders find themselves navigating not only diverse teams, but teams literally spread out across the world. Just as Eisenhower had to navigate through different nationalities and military structure and hierarchy on different continents, the leader today must also often deal with similar challenges of diverse cultures and ideas across continents.

Andrea Derler, PhD, who writes and works for Bersin by Deloitte wrote:

> As cultural and business complexity increase so does the demand for a global mindset. So, what is a global mindset? Well, we might be seeking that answer as well, but one thing at least seems for certain: it is the ability to influence individuals, groups, and organizations that have different intellectual, social, and psychological knowledge or intelligence from your own. It is the ability for leaders to 'think and act globally and locally"— replacing yesteryear's "think globally and act locally." It requires leaders to deepen their understanding of local and cultural differences. It requires recognizing situations in which demands from both global and local elements are compelling, while being aware of the diversity across cultures and markets. (Derler, 2011)

Leaders must be able to think and act globally and harness the power of diversity in cultures and thinking. As the world is changing, leadership must be able to navigate organizations through these changes while also assuring them to stay on course and remain grounded to their mission, vision, and values. People are drawn to leaders. As the world becomes more complex and dramatically changes, there is an overpowering need for strong, effective leadership. People want leaders they can follow and believe have a sense of direction and vision. They want leaders who can help them navigate through the changes in culture as well as business. The uncertainties created by change can be managed more effectively with strong leadership. Finally, society as a whole is looking for strong leadership in a world racked with terrorism and war. Social injustices as well as other forms of brokenness are rampant throughout the world. People desperately need and want leadership to help bring about positive, lasting change.

Leaders Need Help

Leadership is not for wimps! Leaders must think globally in a world that has become much more integrated. As Andrea Derler said, leaders must "think and act globally and locally." Leaders have been needed throughout history for specific reasons, just as Eisenhower was needed to lead the invasion of Normandy and the subsequent march across Europe to defeat the Nazi regime. In a world changing so rapidly in technology and business as well as geopolitically, the value and importance of leadership is paramount.

The demands for leadership are great and individuals have been thrust into leadership roles by appointment or situations. As a result, leaders can be easily overwhelmed and are looking for insight on how to effectively lead people and organizations. Organizations also are desperate to find effective leadership to lead them into the future and sustain growth or revive lagging performance. This book is intended to provide structure and a systemic look at leadership. It is intended to provide individuals a roadmap for assessing and developing their own personal leadership muscles. The use of these materials will provide a mirror for personal introspection and guidance as a leader. In addition, the Leadership Model I present can also be used by mentors and managers to frame conversations and coach associates about their leadership strengths and weaknesses. Subsequent conversations can focus on specific dimensions, traits, and behaviors. Finally, organizations can use the tools I describe as a mechanism or roadmap for looking for leaders. This should trigger crucial conversations about desired skills and needs for the organization prior to looking for candidates. The Leadership Model can be used as an assessment tool for evaluating each candidate's strengths and weaknesses and thereby enable an organization to make better choices when choosing new leaders.

Leadership Takeaways

- The need for leaders at all levels is one of the twelve critical issues identified in the Global Human Capital Trends 2014.

- Changes are occurring so fast that effective leadership is essential to navigate organizations through rapidly changing technology as well as dynamic, changing business cultures.

- Not only are human resource departments and management struggling to project who can be a future leader in their organization, but people already in leadership positions are often struggling with how to be effective.

- The leader must not only demonstrate sensitivity to cultural differences but also be able to get very diverse groups of people to work together on teams.

- Leaders must be able to think and act globally and harness the power of diversity in cultures and thinking.

- Organizations are desperate to find effective leadership to lead them into the future and sustain growth or revive lagging performance.

4

The Leadership System

An advanced thinker sees the relations of his topics in such masses and so instantaneously that when he comes to explain to younger minds it is often hard. ... Bowditch, who translated and annotated Laplace's *Méchanique Céleste*, said that whenever his author prefaced a proposition by the words 'it is evident,' he knew that many hours of hard study lay before him.

—William James

Nathaniel Bowditch was born in Salem, Massachusetts on March 26, 1773. At age seven, Nathaniel was sent to the best school in Salem, which was led by a Mr. Watson. It was here that Nathaniel showed a great fondness and aptitude for mathematics. He was quickly solving math problems usually done by much older students. His skills and aptitude were far advanced for his years. By age ten, he had to quit school to help support the family. At twelve, he became an apprentice clerk at a ship chandlery shop. While in this service, he learned the skills of a clerk and bookkeeper but spent his free time reading anything he could get his hands on. He especially enjoyed studying mathematics, a passion he had discovered at a young age.

He continued studying not only mathematics but also a wide variety of other subjects. He devoured books wherever he found them. To his great fortune, the entire scientific library of Dr. Richard Kirwan was captured by a privateer in the English Channel and worked its way through sale to the Salem library. Young Nathaniel was able to take out books and study them at his leisure.

Except for a few lessons he took in bookkeeping, it was believed that he received no other formal instruction after leaving school at age ten. The world was his school, and nature herself his best instructor. He never considered that his lack of formal education was an obstacle to his ability to learn.

As Nathaniel Bowditch grew older, he chose to pursue his ancestor's path of ship mastery. Between 1795 and 1804, he made five voyages as part of a merchant crew. These voyages provided him long periods to continue his pursuits of mathematics, science, and languages. During these trips, he perfected himself in the French language as well as in Italian, Portuguese, and Spanish.

He was always willing to teach others and would do anything to help if they showed a desire to learn. For instance, on his fifth voyage he taught all twelve crewmembers, including the ship's cook, navigational principles, and by voyage end all were able to make lunar observations and calculate positions. Captain Prince, who had been captain on each of the five voyages, mused that "all was harmony on board; all had a zeal for study; all were ambitious to learn." These twelve men Nathaniel had trained eventually rose to the rank of first or second officer of a ship.

During his time at sea, Nathaniel began applying his abilities in mathematics to correct errors in the *Navigator*, the current manual used for celestial navigation. To have exact tables to work from, Bowditch recomputed all of the tables and rearranged and expanded the work. The task was so extensive that he decided to write his own book. In 1802 he published *The New American Practical Navigator*. This new publication quickly became used by shipmasters throughout the world, and subsequent revisions are still in use today. It led to Bowditch being deemed the "Founder of modern maritime navigation."

In the *Memoir of Nathaniel Bowditch*, written by Nathaniel's son Nathaniel Ingersoll Bowditch, he records the following incident:

> On his last voyage, Nathaniel Bowditch arrived off the coast of Salem in mid-winter, and in

the height of a violent northeast snowstorm. He had been unable to get an observation for a day or two, and felt anxious and uneasy at the dangerous situation of the vessel. At the close of afternoon of Christmas day he came on deck, and took the whole management of the ship into his hands. Feeling very confident where the vessel was, he kept his eyes directly towards the light on Baker's Island, at the entrance of Salem harbor. Fortunately, in the interval between two gusts of wind, the fall of snow became less dense than before, and he thus obtained a glimpse of the light of which he was in search. Confirmed, however, in his previous convictions, he now kept on the same course, entered the harbor, and finally anchored in safety. He had given his orders with the same decision and preciseness as if he saw all the objects around him, and thus inspired the sailors with confidence, which he felt himself. (Bowditch, 1840)

Nathanial Bowditch left a legacy of strong leadership through his perseverance, humility, and conviction. A copy of *The New American Practical Navigator*, first published in 1802 and now in its fifty-second edition, is still carried on board every commissioned US Naval vessel. Nathaniel Bowditch has provided direction and guidance through *The New American Practical Navigator* for over two hundred years. The principles of navigation and tables he developed have helped ships navigate the oceans safely for generations. He started from very humble beginnings, but his thirst for knowledge and willingness to learn and help others learn endeared him to all who came in contact with him. He changed the world and demonstrated many of the characteristics of a good leader.

The world is looking for leaders who can navigate organizations, businesses, and governments through the turbulent times we are in as a society as well as in business. The waters are deep and the hazards are real. Just as ship captains have always needed accurate charts and sound navigational practices, so organizations need tools for selecting leaders and improving leadership practices. This book presents a tool, a sort of chart, for understanding the dynamics of strong leadership and assessing where individuals are at in their leadership skills.

The Quest

The challenge of finding and developing effective leaders is a quest being carried out within industry, education, government, and the military as well as the non-profit sector. Like knights of old on a holy quest, executives and human resource departments have pursued hiring and developing leaders. Bookshelves have been filled with books written on the subject, yet the journey continues for finding, developing, and understanding leadership. Consultants have been hired to help organizations understand the attributes and identify candidates.

There now is a basic understanding that leadership and management share several similarities. However, the aspects of effective leadership transcend being a good manager. A person can be both, but the ability to actually lead people has different dimensions than the capacity to effectively manage a business process and the people running that process. Both leadership and management are essential for the success of an organization, but times and situations require different strengths and attributes for each position.

Historically at Eli Lilly, there has been a long history of strong management abilities. I was in management for twenty-eight of my thirty-four years at Lilly. I managed a variety of groups, including manufacturing, engineering, maintenance, environmental and safety groups, as well as finally a corporate engineering team responsible for commissioning and the qualification of new facilities around the world. Lilly has demonstrated the ability to operate in a disciplined manner and produce repetitive results year after year. However, as the winds of change impact corporations, so also Lilly has been dramatically impacted. Patent losses, product competition, changing healthcare, and globalization have all contributed to a dynamic business culture that has required Lilly to adapt and become more flexible. This dynamic business environment does not lend itself well to a management-dominated culture. It instead requires strong leadership to challenge, navigate, and create vision for a new future that will bring the company to a new place, a new state of being.

As important as leadership is, there is no widely accepted definition for what a leader is. Rather than explore the strengths and weaknesses of the various conceptions of leadership, I will use the following definition for *leaders*:

> Leaders are people who know how to set vision, achieve goals, and inspire people to follow and take specific actions.

During the last fifteen years, I became very interested in understanding and creating a model for leadership in my own organization. There had been increasing discussion within Lilly about the need for a new kind of leadership, and as I looked at my specific team, it became clear that I should focus attention on helping my staff become strong and effective leaders. I needed to help our team understand the key attributes of an effective leader. I also needed them to have a clear understanding of their own leadership skills. My goal was not just to tell them what good leadership looked like but to also equip them to identify personal strengths and weaknesses and be able to take deliberate action to improve themselves as leaders.

As we explored leadership, I, with the help of many company managers, developed the Leadership Model to describe the relationship between key dimensions and the importance of values, traits, and behaviors in the leadership process. The following diagram is a representation of these relationships and has been used as a means for assessing leadership strengths and developing leaders. As we move forward in this book, I will discuss each aspect of this model and refer to this diagram as a reference for describing the Leadership Model.

It is important to recognize that this leadership model is a dynamic reinforcing system—namely, the many elements of the model interact with each other, like a chain reaction, to reinforce positively or negatively, depending on the actions of individuals. People who have been asked to lead or who desire to take on a leadership role are entering into this reinforcing system. To be successful in it, you need to understand system dynamics.

One important aspect of this model is that the leader is creating experiences for those he or she is leading. These experiences will impact a leader's credibility and the trust and respect the organization has for that person's leadership. These experiences will also impact the view people have in the leader's ability to achieve results or have impact. Finally, these experiences will influence the way others view the leader's ability as a change agent or guide to lead others into the future.

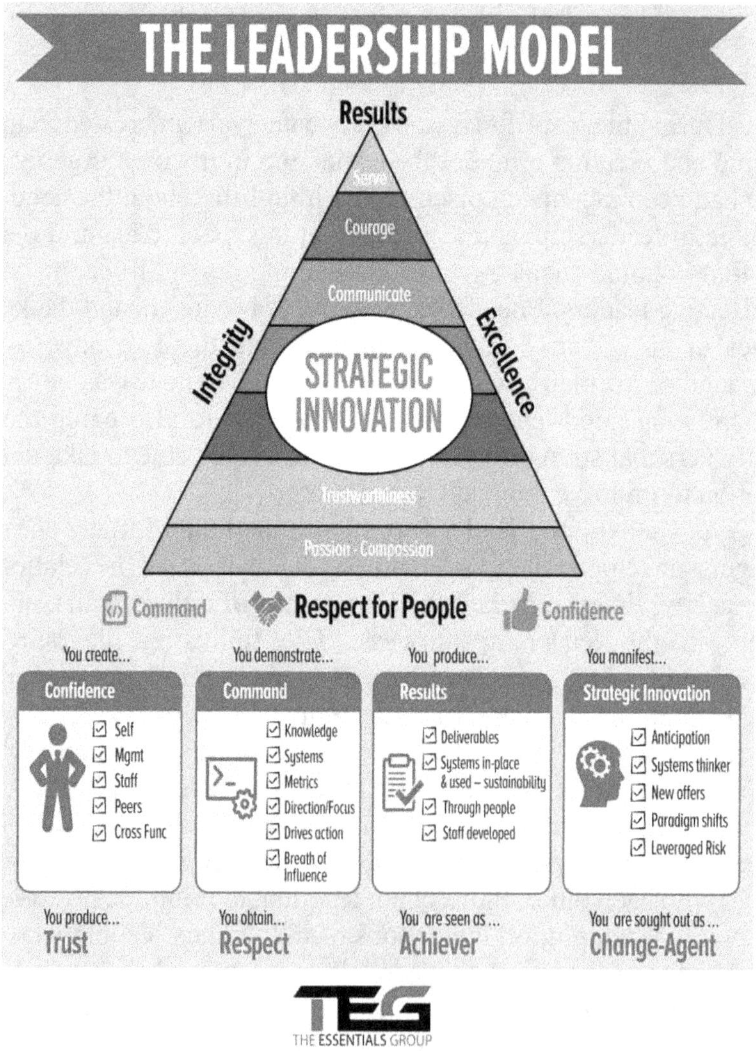

THE LEADERSHIP MODEL

Results

Serve

Courage

Communicate

Integrity — **STRATEGIC INNOVATION** — *Excellence*

Trustworthiness

Passion - Compassion

Command   **Respect for People**   Confidence

You create...	You demonstrate...	You produce...	You manifest...
Confidence	**Command**	**Results**	**Strategic Innovation**
☑ Self	☑ Knowledge	☑ Deliverables	☑ Anticipation
☑ Mgmt	☑ Systems	☑ Systems in-place & used – sustainability	☑ Systems thinker
☑ Staff	☑ Metrics		☑ New offers
☑ Peers	☑ Direction/Focus	☑ Through people	☑ Paradigm shifts
☑ Cross Func	☑ Drives action	☑ Staff developed	☑ Leveraged Risk
	☑ Breath of Influence		

You produce...	You obtain...	You are seen as ...	You are sought out as ...
Trust	**Respect**	**Achiever**	**Change-Agent**

THE ESSENTIALS GROUP

40

Leadership Takeaways

- There are similarities between leadership and management. However, the aspects of effective leadership transcend being a good manager.

- Leaders are people who know how to set vision, achieve goals, and inspire people to follow and take specific actions.

- The Leadership Model was developed to describe the relationship between key dimensions and the importance of values, traits, and behaviors in leading people.

- Leaders create experiences for those they are leading, and these experiences will ultimately impact their effectiveness as leaders.

Part 2

The Essential Core Values

5

Not Just Words on a Wall

Values are like fingerprints. Nobody's are the same, but you leave 'em all over everything you do.

—Elvis Presley

Values provide a foundation and compass for our lives by influencing decision making as well as behaviors. Individuals may not always be capable of clearly articulating their values, but their values have been influenced by upbringing, mentors, community, and life experiences. Values define what is ultimately important. They influence behavior, attitudes, priorities, and interactions. Values can be defined as "broad preferences concerning appropriate courses of action or outcomes." They reflect a person's sense of right and wrong or what ought to be. "Equal rights for all," "Excellence deserves admiration," and "People should be treated with respect and dignity" are statements representative of values. Values work within us consciously and unconsciously. They are our internal measuring stick for evaluating what is really important to us. Moreover, our true values are reflected in our character. The manner in which we conduct our lives, react to situations, and deal with others reflect our character, which is shaped by our values.

Successful organizations should have written established values that define what is important to their business culture and how they want to conduct business. Sometimes, though, values in the business world have been grossly neglected or even violated with horrendous consequences. For instance, in the 1990s, the Enron Corporation was the paragon of corruption as its leaders were brought to trial for misusing billions of dollars of investors' money. Ironically, in its 2009 annual report to shareholders, Enron listed its core values (Grant, 2014):

> *Communication* – We have an obligation to communicate.
> *Respect* – We treat others, as we would like to be treated.
> *Integrity* – We work with customers and prospects openly, honestly, and sincerely.
> *Excellence* – We are satisfied with nothing less than the very best in everything we do. (Enron, Annual Report, 2000, 29)

Today as we look at these statements of Enron's core values, it's difficult not to laugh at their audacity in light of the facts regarding this corporation's absolute meltdown and corruption at the highest levels. Enron's leaders essentially violated each of their company's core values for financial gain. They lied to the Federal Trade Commission, their shareholders, and employees. They showed no respect to their employees and investors by destroying pensions and personal finances. Openness and honesty were long forgotten as they manipulated financial reports, lied to auditors, and shredded documents. Shell companies were created to hide debt and misrepresent company performance. This was all being done while senior executives such as Chairman Kenneth Lay and CEO Jeffrey Skillings were reaping millions of dollars in personal gain through salaries, stock deals, and Enron personal lines of credit. Lay and Skillings and other senior executives were "Takers," as Adam Grant writes in his book *Give and Take* (Grant, 2014). It was clear that the leadership of the company valued personal gain over any of the stated corporate values. Their personal values and resulting character simply did not line up with Enron's values. As a result, the corporate values became nothing more than a slogan—a slogan that executives began company meetings with and espoused for stockholder and public consumption.

A leadership style without ethical clarity produces moral and economic bankruptcy.

—*Bill Donahue*

Whether written or not, an organization's values will ultimately be reflected in its culture. I have seen situations where the organization's culture is so poisonous that there are no real corporate values at work. Instead, the reigning mentality is every man for himself. This results in an extremely ugly culture of backbiting, deception, and betrayal. When corporate values are left unestablished or not lived out, the organization's culture erodes and often in horrible directions.

What's true for corporations is true for nations. In war-torn countries where societal norms break down, incredible atrocities take place. Values matter—for nations, cultures, businesses, groups, and individuals.

Every organization has a culture that reflects what is acceptable, what becomes normative for that organization. If the norm is not explicitly defined, this culture becomes a reflection of the individuals making up the organization, for good or for ill. A leader can establish with their organization what the values will be that will come to define the acceptable standard of the organizational culture.

Once those corporate values are established, leaders must live them and never treat those values as inapplicable to them while demanding that others embrace them. If leaders cannot align with a corporate value because it conflicts with personal values or they simply want to go a different direction, they should either try to change the corporate values through articulate discussion and debate or align with the corporate values as long as they do not violate a moral position. In some cases, it may be necessary for a leader to move on to another organization whose values more closely align with his or hers.

Defining and understanding values is paramount to successful leadership. Values must be clear for the individual as well as the organization. Values become the cornerstone for the endeavor. This principle is universal and applies to companies, churches, the military, universities, and all other types of organizations. On an individual basis, understanding one's personal values provides clarity, focus, and a means for evaluating and making decisions. The absence of values turns individuals and organizations into rudderless ships; they can stay afloat for a time, but they cannot steer, and they will surely suffer shipwreck given enough time and situations.

It is important that leaders not only understand organizational values but translate those values into action. Decisions and behaviors must be consistent and supportive of these values. Leaders must also engage their organization in meaningful discussion about values and be willing to be challenged if their behavior does not align with the established values. This takes courage, but it also compels clarity and enhances focus on what is important company-wide, who we are as an organization, and how we conduct business.

While at Lilly, I can remember engaging several times in an animated debate with colleagues around personnel and organizational structure as we were confronted with tough decisions. On more than one occasion, one of our group would step in and ask a powerful question: "But is that respectful to people?" It would immediately stop everyone and elevate the discussion back to a fundamental Lilly value, which was respect for people. The challenge caused us to stop and re-center our discussion to make sure our decisions did not violate this value. It did not mean we avoided tough decisions or action, but we made them in the best way possible to maintain a value of respect for people.

When organizational values are well defined and understood and a leader's actions are consistent with and reinforce these values, a value-enriched culture is created and more easily sustained. All organizations have some form of culture. Be it positive or negative, a culture exists. Leadership either reinforces this culture or changes it based on their decisions and actions. These choices are driven by leaders' values. Leaders ultimately impact the culture of their organization, so they must pay attention to that culture, including on the team level. They must consistently evaluate if the culture reflects the values they want to instill or reinforce. Near-term apparent success could ultimately lead to long-term failure if the culture is in conflict with corporate values.

Foundational to the Leadership Model presented here are the Lilly Core Values of *Integrity, Excellence,* and *Respect for People.* In the Lilly culture, it was imperative that leaders understand, embrace, and endeavor to represent these values. These three values were to provide context for who we were and how we performed our jobs. They gave us anchors for our behaviors and decisions.

Such values must be the result of deep personal beliefs that a leader holds as paramount to his or her essence, not only as a leader but as a person. When people believe that a leader is grounded in integrity, passionately pursuing excellence, and truly respecting and appreciating them as persons, they will listen and they will follow. These values must be the bedrock for any effective leader because they speak to character, perspective, and intent.

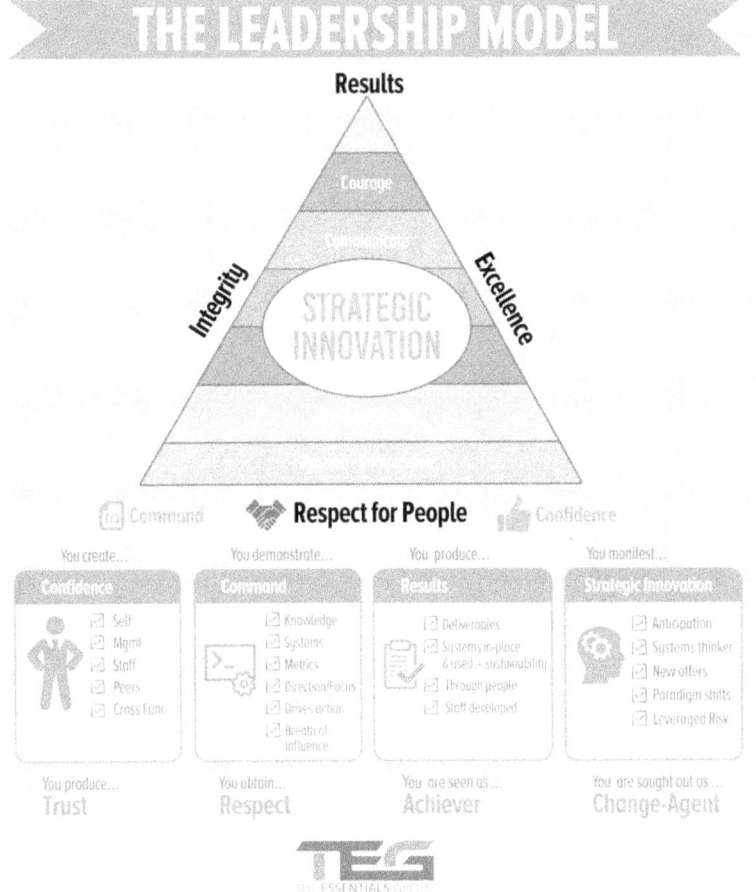

Three Core Values

Let's consider the three essential values of *Integrity, Excellence,* and *Respect for People.* I will provide a description of each one and then relate each to the Leadership Model.

Integrity

> Integrity is doing the right thing when you don't have to—when no one else is looking or will ever know—when there will be no congratulations or recognition for having done so.
> —*Charles Marshall*

Integrity embraces the very highest standards of honesty, ethical behavior, and exemplary moral character. Integrity can also be defined as the quality of being honest and having strong moral principles or moral uprightness. It is a personal choice to uphold oneself to consistently moral and ethical standards. Integrity is a fundamentally important value for human beings no matter what endeavor they embark upon. Unfortunately, not everyone lives to such a code or interprets behaviors similarly.

As we discuss leadership, you may think of people you have worked with who have lived and acted with great integrity. These indi-

> It is true that integrity alone won't make you a leader, but without integrity you will never be one.
> —*Zig Ziglar*

viduals were probably honest and truthful in their communications, and they acted in a manner consistent with their word. They may have even taken steps to right wrongs that they may have committed unintentionally. They probably valued their commitments to others and made great effort to live and act in an ethical manner. Such individuals highly value their integrity and take strides to protect it. Their integrity defines their character to their family, friends, co-workers, and community. Integrity runs deep in them, and for them it is non-negotiable.

Unfortunately, integrity can too often be sacrificed on the altar of greed, ambition, and fear. When leaders act with poor integrity, they rip at the very foundation of their leadership. They may feel they can get by with it for a season. They may even achieve some desired result. But inevitably their lack of integrity tears down trust, confidence, and credibility. These individuals pay a high price for sacrificing their integrity, but their choice not only hurts them. It's detrimental to their team and destroys team dynamics. I have seen people get by with this for periods of time, playing backroom politics and maybe even advancing their careers. Eventually, however, this type of behavior comes home to roost. When a leader acts with poor integrity, their team can take this as a cue for what really constitutes "acceptable" behavior. Before long an entire team can be acting with poor integrity, violating rules and regulations, making commitments with no intent to follow through, making questionable deals or backstabbing co-workers to get ahead. A leader who demonstrates poor integrity can become a cancer in an organization.

Excellence

Excellence reflects individuals' and their organization's continuous search for new ways to improve the performance of their business to become the best at what they do.

Excellence embodies an intent and commitment to perform and pursue at the very best level possible. To always look for the new frontier, the new possibility, not to become complacent and satisfied but have a continuous restless spirit and wonder what could be next. The pursuit of excellence calls others to join and function at their optimum. The leader who values excellence challenges his team to continually improve, to always strive for better efficiency and improved effectiveness. Leaders want their organization or team to be a leader in the industry and be valued for their creativity, quality, and ability to produce and innovate. Companies like Google and Apple have captured this image.

When a leader or organization does not value excellence, they can become complacent and satisfied. They view the world as evolving around them, and they can slip behind in performance compared to their competitors. Their product or service can become obsolete or drop in value as others make new offers or demonstrate better capabilities. When organizations do not value excellence, they can become tolerant of errors and sloppy in performance. Coaches in sports deal with this issue often. Teams become complacent and chaotic; teams competing against them get better, and suddenly they are losing games that they used to win. Errors and sloppy performances often happen when groups have had some measure of success. Keeping a level of excellence in performance and fighting complacency are constant pursuits for any coach—and for any organization.

The pursuit of excellence must be a constant drum beat in the ears of a leader and his team, always pushing them along to discover

> Perfection is not attainable, but if we chase perfection we can catch excellence.
> —*Vince Lombardi*

new products, new capabilities, and improve performance to new heights. However, when the pursuit of excellence is embraced and valued, it does not need to become a millstone of pressure on the leader or team. Instead it can create excitement and anticipation for the next discovery. An atmosphere of purpose, excitement, and accomplishment can accompany excellence. The leader is fundamentally responsible for assuring that the pursuit of excellence is not only embraced but also energizing and even enjoyed by those in the organization.

Respect for People

Respect for People shows our concern for the interests of all people worldwide who touch or are touched by our company: customers, employees, shareholders, partners, and communities.

Valuing people was at the core of Lilly family values from the company's start. The Lillys were well ahead of their time in developing a documented personnel philosophy and employee manual. These were developed many years ahead of other corporations. The Lilly family took a view that buildings could be rebuilt, but people were at the heart of their endeavor, and people were the true lifeblood of the corporation's success. Many other companies soon followed suit. Today there are many businesses that spend enormous effort creating the proper work environment and work-life balance. This value can act as an essential balance for the other two core values. Respect for people helps ensure integrity is sought and recognized in people. It can also make sure that the pursuit of excellence does not cross a line of disrespecting people.

The *Respect for People* value also implies respect for customers, shareholders, partners, and communities. This value requires that a conscious effort be made to consider and understand the impact of decisions and actions on these various groups. For instance, if the customer is truly respected, then effort will always be made to maintain the quality of the product or service provided. Leaders make decisions that demonstrate value to their customers when leaders lend a listening ear to their concerns and needs. The same applies to their stakeholders and partners.

When respect for people is violated, trust is destroyed. People become suspicious and skeptical of leadership motives and intentions. It is incredibly important that leadership and management respect and carefully consider how their decisions impact peoples' careers, families, and working conditions. Difficult decisions often need to be made by a leadership team, but in making these decisions, they must thoughtfully evaluate the impact and work with people to create understanding. This effort will help people move through the transition. When leadership drives ahead with little thought or effort to how to help people transition through tough decisions and dramatic change, they run the risk of deeply violating trust. When this happens, it can be an arduous and long journey to rebuild the trust lost. Without trust, the organization will struggle, and its leadership will have an extremely difficult time gaining success.

The three core values of *Integrity, Excellence,* and *Respect for People* are absolute ground zero for a leader. The individual's personal position concerning these three values should be a significant part of any leadership selection evaluation. These values should be what the leader brings with her as internal, personal qualities. Quite honestly, the path for embracing these values runs deep and long and is linked to the individual's journey long before she comes to your company. As a result, my advice to you is this: *If a leader or leadership candidate does not have these core values well ingrained into their character, I recommend moving quickly to considering other candidates. The risk of failure is simply too great, and the potential repercussions are potentially devastating to an organization.*

Finally, it is ironic to note that the three Lilly Core Values matched three of the four Enron Core Values. The only additional value by Enron was "Communication – We have an obligation to communicate." Furthermore, Kenneth Lay, former Enron chairman, was a member of the Lilly board of directors in the 1990s before the Enron meltdown. The irony of similar values by each company along with Kenneth Lay's association with Lilly should not be lost. It highlights the point that values are only slogans or words on a plaque unless leadership embraces and brings life to the values through their actions and decisions. Words are just words without actions backing them up. Actionless slogans are nothing more than slogans, and we do not need anymore of those. We need more organizations and their people, especially their leaders, living out those slogans in all they say and do. That's what turns a slogan into a real-life value.

Leadership Takeaways

- Values provide a foundation and compass for our lives by influencing decision making as well as behaviors.

- Our true values are reflected in our character.

- Successful organizations should have values that define what is important to their business culture and how they want to conduct business.

- All organizations have some form of culture; positive or negative, a culture exists.

- Leadership either reinforces culture or changes it based on their decisions and actions.

- *Integrity* can be defined as the quality of being honest and having strong moral principles or moral uprightness.

- *Excellence* embodies an intent and commitment to perform and pursue at the very best level possible.

- The *Respect for People* value means that a conscious effort must be made to consider and understand the impact of decisions and actions on various groups.

Part 3

The Essential Leadership Dimensions

6

The Confidence Dimension

The most essential quality of leadership is not perfection but credibility. People must be able to trust you.

—Rick Warren

The Leadership Model consists of four major dimensions: *Confidence, Command, Results,* and *Strategic Innovation.* The model reflects the need for focus and success in all four dimensions. The key to this model is that all dimensions are important, and there is a logical progression through each dimension and its essential elements. Understanding the relationship between each dimension is critical to successful leadership. As an example, confidence is reinforced by demonstrating command as well as by the ability to deliver results. All dimensions are connected and reinforce one another. This is genuinely a leadership *system.*

The intent of the model is not to provide a roadmap for upward progression through promotion. Rather, it is designed to facilitate defining critical values, dimensions, behaviors, and traits of effective, successful leadership. By using this model, people can recognize, understand, and work on their personal leadership development and interaction with others. The model is also useful to management for identifying and recognizing effective leadership. Too often too little thought or effort has been put into the selection or recognition of leadership. This model will provide a context for evaluating and recognizing strengths and weaknesses of those we place in such positions.

In the following pages, I will discuss each of the four dimensions, providing you with an essential understanding of each one and the corresponding elements of each. Later we will dive deeper and discuss specific essential leadership behaviors and traits. However, for now I want to establish a foundational understanding of the basic model.

Captain, O' My Captain

In 2001, an apparent routine FDA inspection occurred at one of Lilly's primary parenteral manufacturing facilities in Indianapolis, a building called K105. The FDA inspector came for a regular inspection, which typically would last no longer than a couple of weeks. This time, however, he stayed for nearly six months and brought friends! This inspection and the subsequent 483 Citation issued by the FDA rocked the Lilly manufacturing and quality world. Lilly would never be the same.

As a result of the 483 findings, Lilly agreed to a number of significant actions to upgrade existing facilities and operations. The most extreme action called for Lilly to completely rebuild the K105 building to meet regulatory expectations. The commitment to the FDA began an unprecedented renovation project that required $240 million being spent in about six weeks to rebuild the K105 building. The building needed to be stripped down to its concrete and steel structure, and all of its equipment and walls had to be removed and rebuilt. This extreme plant makeover had to occur over a six-week shutdown. The effort called for intense coordination of multiple groups of Lilly staff and contractors. At the peak of the work, more than twelve hundred contractors worked daily on the site, tearing out, rebuilding, and commissioning and qualifying the facility.

This herculean task required incredibly effective leadership to have any chance of success. The significant regulatory requirements and commitments had to be met while not interrupting the supply chain of Lilly's product to the market. The company needed someone whom they had very high confidence in their leadership abilities. This individual had to have a proven track record of success and delivering results. When the list of potential candidates was drawn up, it was very short.

The leader chosen for the job was Bob Cole, an executive director in manufacturing. He was called upon to lead the overall effort. Bob Cole had built a powerful reputation as a leader. He had come up through manufacturing and managed Ceclor production at Lilly's Clinton facility in the 1980s and 90s. His leadership at Clinton was during a time when Ceclor was the most important and profitable product for Lilly. Bob had developed a strong reputation for being disciplined in his approach to managing and problem-solving. He had high expectations of himself and others and was effective in communicating these expectations clearly and succinctly. People were rarely confused with where Bob stood on an issue or with his expectations.

In the late 90s, Bob moved to Indianapolis and took control of the Bulk Insulin Manufacturing operations at Lilly's Technology Center. He brought the same well-honed skills of a disciplined logical approach to managing the business and was equally as successful in leading Lilly's Insulin Production areas. It was clear that he had a well-established track record for successful leadership.

The 483 citations Lilly received for the K105 operations area required dramatic action. Many people doubted that Lilly could accomplish such a monumental task in such a short time.

To get the job done, Bob applied the full breadth of his experience and skills as a leader by first identifying key resources that were also leaders and who could provide critical leadership for pieces of the overall plan. One of these individuals was John Beyrau who became the project manager. Bob empowered John and the other leaders to make decisions and expedite as needed. He also set a tone of communication upward, sideways, and downward into the organization. He knew that clear communication and understanding of status and intent was going to be critical to the success of the project. Each group had needs. Senior management wanted assurance of status and progress. Peers needed to understand expectations regarding production schedules, shutdowns, and requirements, and how their decisions could impact the massive project. Moreover, the huge group of people executing in the field doing design, demolition, construction, and commissioning and qualification needed a clear and consistent understanding of expectations. Bob also needed an effective mechanism to receive accurate, timely information from all of these levels but especially from the field. The leaders he put in place were superb at reinforcing active communication and providing him with an accurate picture of status, issues, and progress.

Throughout his career, Bob had demonstrated a significant command of any operation he was responsible for leading. He understood the business processes and knew how they functioned and how to impact results. This capability to grasp complex systems served him well in leading the K105 rebuilding project. He could assimilate the information he received from the field, direction he was getting from senior management, and develop with his team strategies to meet business and regulatory requirements. Finally, he had a long history of producing results in every area he led, so management trusted his leadership to get the job done in the K105 rebuild. Not only management, but those at all levels on the project respected Bob for his track record of producing positive, sustainable results.

The nearly inconceivable occurred with complete demolition, reconstruction, and requalification of K105 in the period needed. Regulatory commitments were met and the supply chain was sustained for the patient and the company.

Fundamental to the K105 rebuilding success was the leadership provided by Bob Cole and the leaders he assembled. Lilly's management team selected him because they had confidence in his abilities to take on such an enormous responsibility. Bob then chose leaders in whom he had confidence so together they could deliver the needed results.

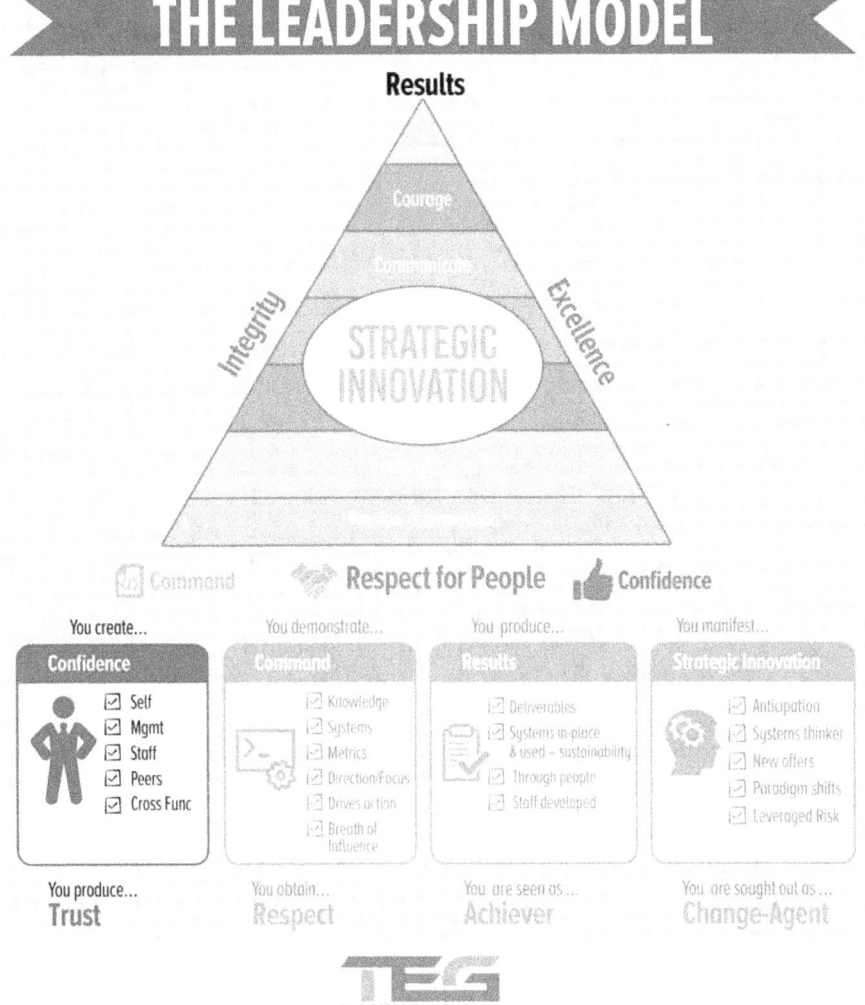

Aspects of the Confidence Dimension

Confidence is defined as the feeling or belief that one can rely on someone or something, can place firm trust in abilities, words, and actions. Confidence, then, requires credibility, and without credibility a leader will struggle to be effective. A strong leader must instill confidence in his abilities and create credibility with a number of groups of people. Ultimately, confidence and credibility produce trust by others. People listen better and act accordingly when they have trust. The leader must understand and manage this dimension and recognize its importance. Some leaders have created excellent results but not created confidence in their ability to attain the results consistently.

The following elements describe various aspects of the Confidence dimension that leaders need to thoughtfully manage.

Self-Confidence

As a leader, it is hard to lead without *self-confidence*. Confidence in oneself should not be mistaken for arrogance. Arrogance will ultimately destroy a leader's credibility because arrogant people are never as good as they think they are, and they are always the last ones to find that out. The strong, effective leader, however, has high self-awareness, knows her limitations, and does not try to hide them but rather supplements them through collaboration with others. Self-awareness and public recognition of an individual's strengths and weaknesses can be liberating to the leader and empowering to those around her. It is incredibly frustrating to a team to have their leader refuse to acknowledge her personal limitations while leading the team into a malaise.

A number of years ago, I worked on a church board. Shortly after the new pastor arrived, he looked at us one day in a meeting and said, "Guys, I really need your help on all this financial stuff because I am not very good at it!" Immediately, there was a sense of relief in the room as the leader-pastor merely stated what his personal weakness was and asked for help. In the room were businessmen who were more than capable and dealt with these types of financial numbers and decisions every day. Instead of dancing around an issue for months, with the team being frustrated and the pastor trying to bluff his way through it, he simply and straightforwardly asked for help. He was refreshing, and he cleared the way for more open discussion. Besides, we hired him to be a pastor, not a financial expert.

As management assesses leaders, they evaluate the leaders' self-confidence. If the confidence displayed is genuine, those leaders will be humble, and they will act calmly and encourage calm and courage in the face of adversity. But if arrogance has replaced confidence, arrogant leaders will ultimately destroy the confidence others have in themselves, and they will produce more chaos and fear, even as they often exhibit arrogance to mask their own personal fears.

Of course, leaders who lack self-confidence are not always arrogant. Sometimes they are simply insecure. And an insecure leader is very dangerous to any organization. John Maxwell said it well in his book, *The 21 Indispensible Qualities of a Leader* (Maxwell, 1999).

Unsure leaders have several common traits:

1. They don't provide security for others – To become an effective leader; you need to make your followers feel good about themselves.
2. They take more from their people than they give – Insecure people are on a continual quest for validation, acknowledgment, and love. Because of that, their focus is on finding security, not instilling it in others.
3. They continually limit their best people – Show me an insecure leader and I'll show you someone who genuinely cannot celebrate victories. The leader might even take credit personally for the best work of the team.
4. They continually limit their organization – When followers are undermined and receive no recognition they become discouraged and eventually stop performing at their potential. And when that happens the entire organization suffers.

Management Confidence

Management confidence is the second attribute of the *Confidence* dimension. A leader must generate confidence in her abilities with the management team. This is critical to success and is firmly linked to the other dimensions of *Command*, *Results*, and *Strategic Innovation*. Indeed, delivering results and having command of an area of expertise or responsibility, as well as the ability to see new opportunities, all positively impact management's confidence in an individual.

However, besides the obvious effects of success in these other dimensions, it is important that the leader build confidence by demonstrating clear and concise communication skills. Leaders need to be able to share critical information in an appropriate manner. This includes sharing the right level of details to the right audience in a timely manner. Leaders must also be adept at listening carefully to management and understanding their needs and views.

Finally, leaders can build the confidence of their management by the manner in which they work with others, including with their team, peers, and customers. No leader should be an island. The effective leader interacts and collaborates very well with others. Senior leadership and management understand the importance of this ability. When they see a leader reaching out to others and collaborating, sharing, growing, and learning together, their confidence in that leader grows. They also take notice when others reach out to the leader for input or participation and view the leader as a valuable resource. Building the confidence of the management team is of paramount importance and pays huge dividends with the subsequent trust achieved. The result of all of this is that doors become open for deeper engagement with senior management and leadership.

Bob Cole represented all these characteristics in his leadership. He was credible and instilled confidence with senior management. When he spoke to them, they listened and accepted his input and perspectives. They responded with decisions, support, and resources. They trusted him.

Staff Confidence

Staff confidence, the third element of this dimension, involves leaders creating confidence in the people reporting to them or working with them. This group can be the hardest to convince because they are often in the trenches doing the day-to-day work and are the closest to the reality and truth of what is really going on. A leader trying to gain a team's confidence should avoid "blowing smoke" because this group can usually detect smoke faster than any other group. Open, honest communication serves the leader far better than arrogance or deception. Asking for people's input and thoughts and then actually listening to them goes a long way toward establishing trust and confidence.

A number of years ago, a new leader was hired into an organization where I was a board member, and in our first meeting we were attempting to review past performance and methods we used in running the organization. As people explained different aspects, he kept cutting them off, saying, "I know that, I know that." He was dismissive of people and their knowledge and expertise. The reality was that he did not know all he claimed, and it soon became evident to everyone how uninformed and ill-prepared he was to lead this group. As a result, he only lasted a few painful months before he was removed from leadership.

Building confidence with a team takes time for a new leader and should begin with him demonstrating the following.

- Listen: seek to understand the business as well as the concerns, issues, and perspective of staff.

- Communicate: provide clear direction for expectations, and speak with candor.

- Coach: take deliberate actions with staff to achieve objectives and execute plans.

- Value the people: show people that you care about their needs and development.

- Celebrate: recognize success and contributions by others.

Helping the team as a whole as well as individuals to achieve company and personal goals and objectives will go a long way to building confidence.

Peers Confidence

The fourth element, *Peers' Confidence*, involves creating confidence among peers. A strong leader must establish confidence with other leaders. *Confidence* comes from networking and collaboration as well as being successful in all of the other dimensions: *Command, Results*, and *Strategic Innovation*. In the spirit of learning, a good leader shares not only her successes but also her failures. Transparent leadership with peers can be incredibly powerful and create an open dialog. Communication is vital to successful leadership. Seeking out peers and creating an open, transparent dialog on issues and topics builds not only credibility but also confidence with peers. In addition, fulfilling commitments to peers builds confidence. This behavior demonstrates a leader's respect and value of her peers and her desire to collaborate and work together with them.

Cross-Functional Confidence

The fifth element in the dimension of *Confidence* is *cross-functional confidence*—creating confidence across organizational boundaries. This requires demonstrating success in the other three dimensions and broad networking. Breadth of influence across the organization has a significant impact on management's perception.

A successful leader should pursue what others are doing and learning. He should reach out proactively beyond his business unit to communicate, collaborate, and share learning. Other leaders and staff outside the organization should see a leader who is in command of his area of responsibility, achieves results, and is driving effective change. When others see this, and experience a leader who is reaching out, collaborating, listening, and pursuing excellence, they are confident in that leader. This also makes the leader highly credible in their sight, and this leads to a high trust level.

Leadership Takeaways

- Confidence translates into trust, and without trust a leader will struggle to be effective.

- Leaders must have enough self-confidence to be transparent.

- Strong, effective leaders have high self-awareness, know their limitations, and do not try to hide them but rather supplement them through collaboration with others.

- Insecure leaders don't provide security while they take more than they give, limit their best people, and ultimately limit their organization.

- Leaders must generate confidence in their abilities with the management team.

- Leaders must create confidence with their staff or team.

- In the spirit of learning, good leaders share their successes and their failures.

- Effective leaders create confidence across organizational boundaries.

7

The Command Dimension

It is not the critic who counts. ... The credit belongs to the man who is actually in the arena; whose face is marred by the dust and sweat and blood; who strives valiantly ... who, at worst, if he fails, at least fails while daring greatly; so that his place shall never be with those cold and timid souls who know neither victory nor defeat.

—Theodore Roosevelt

D avid McCullough tells the story of Colonel Henry Knox in his best-selling book *1776* (McCullough, 2005). "Town-born" in Boston, in a narrow house on Sea Street facing the harbor, Henry Knox was seventh of the ten sons of Mary Campbell and William Knox, both of whom were Scotch-Presbyterians. After his father, a shipmaster, disappeared in the West Indies, nine-year-old Henry went to work to help support his mother. Almost entirely self-educated, he became a bookseller in Boston. As a bookseller he developed an interest in "the military art" and self-educated himself on gunnery and military tactics. He signed up with the Boston Grenadier Corps, and, as McCullough describes, "enjoyed everything about it, including the eating and drinking that went on."

Sometime later Knox became a patriot and, following the bloodshed at Lexington and Concord, joined the forces of General Atreus Ward in fighting for the patriot cause.

Henry Knox was a junior officer at the time and had met General Washington on several occasions, but in the fall of 1776 he suggested to Washington that the cannons at Fort Ticonderoga on Lake Champlain could be retrieved and transported to Boston for its defense against the British. McCullough describes the proposal as "an undertaking so enormous, so fraught with certain difficulties, that many thought it impossible." Fort Ticonderoga had been captured in May, but then the fort and the captured artillery had been abandoned as militarily insignificant. Knox proposed to retrieve the artillery and transport it in the dead of winter nearly three hundred miles to Boston. Washington approved the plan.

Knox arrived at Fort Ticonderoga on December 5th to begin the process of extracting the artillery and starting the long haul to Boston with approximately one hundred and twenty thousand pounds of artillery pieces, including fifty-eight mortars and cannon. The plan was to transport the guns by boat down Lake Champlain before it froze and then begin the long-haul overland using sleds and wagons.

The expedition immediately encountered challenge after challenge. Unfavorable winds on the lake slowed progress to a near crawl. Boats sank, and canons had to be retrieved. Delayed snows turned roads and paths into nothing but mud bogs. Then when the snow finally came, it was a blizzard. Finally, after two months of peril, the expedition arrived in Framingham where the guns were unloaded. McCullough goes on to say, "to those who rode out from Cambridge to Framingham to look over the guns, it was clear that the stalemate at Boston was about to change dramatically."

As for Knox, not a gun had been lost. Hundreds of men had taken part in the expedition. However, as McCullough so eloquently states: "It was the daring and determination of Knox himself that had counted above all. The twenty-five-year-old Boston bookseller had proven himself a leader of remarkable ability, a man not only of enterprising ideas, but with the staying power to carry them out. Immediately, Washington put him in command of the artillery."

Aspects of the Command Dimension

In the Leadership Model, the major dimension after *Confidence* is a leader's *Command* capability. By speaking of a leader who can command, I am not referring to a person who is a tyrant or an autocrat. Rather I mean that the leader understands, appreciates, grasps, or has a thorough understanding of the area she is leading. This does not require that she be the resident expert in all things, though she could be an expert in her chosen field. What I'm saying is that the leader is invested enough in her area of responsibility that she has studied it and made it her personal intellectual investment to engage it, understand it, and participate in it.

Once again, all four dimensions work in unison for a leader to be successful. A leader may develop each dimension at different rates, but ultimately, to be successful in each of the dimensions, she must be working simultaneously on the other dimensions.

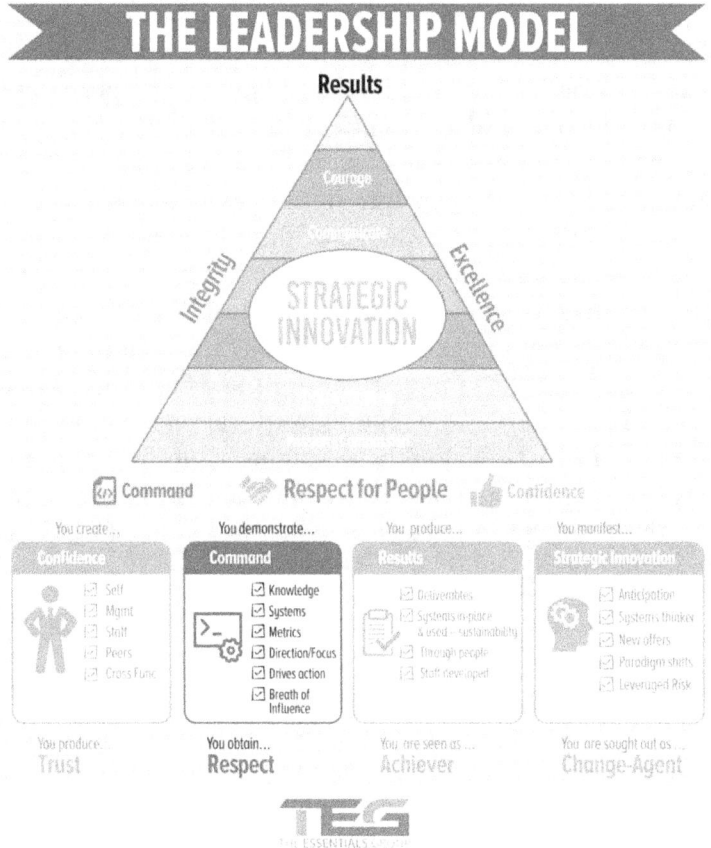

The following are key elements of the *Command* dimension.

Knowledge

The leader must have a sound, in-depth knowledge and understanding of the business he is trying to lead. It is a near fatal flaw to one's credibility and respect not to engage in the business enough to have a sound foundation of understanding. The leader does not have to be the most knowledgeable person but should endeavor to learn the business. Some leaders have failed to learn the business only to find out that their ignorance erodes the staff's confidence in them. Management and others also lose their confidence in leaders who fail to understand the business in which they work. This failure can also negatively impact results when leaders do not provide essential direction at critical times. A strong leader is a student who wants to learn and is inquisitive about how the business really works. He asks questions and continually sharpens his understanding and perspective.

The effective leader also invests time and energy to understand the skills and capabilities of his people. When a leader makes this investment, he builds a clear picture of the organization's strengths and weaknesses. Combining knowledge of the needs of the business, with a clear understanding of the team's strengths and weaknesses, allows the leader to match people's skills and capabilities to meet specific needs. There are few things for a leader that are as important as positioning the right people with the right skills and capabilities in the right jobs in an organization. If the required skills are not available, a leader must decide if he can develop the existing staff to meet those needs or must instead reach outside the organization and bring in new skills. Either way, the smart leader makes it a high priority to put the right people in the right positions.

Systems

Many years ago, Peter Senge wrote a book called the *5th Dimension: The Art and Practice of a Learning Organization* (Senge, 1990). In this work, Senge focused on applying *systems thinking* to problem-solving in business. As he so accurately pointed out, the successful leader should have a sound understanding of the business processes that her organization is responsible for executing. These processes should be documented with well-defined roles and responsibilities. Successful leaders ensure their team is following the established procedures and methods. When such leaders apply Senge's system-thinking approach, they and their staff will be able to examine and understand not only how the business systems function and interact but also identify opportunities for improvement. A leader in command endeavors to define, understand, and improve through well-defined systems and systems-thinking approaches.

Moneyball

The book *Moneyball*, written by Michael Lewis (Lewis, 2003), tells the story of Billy Beane, the General Manager of the Oakland Athletics Major League Baseball team during the 2003 season. Billy was faced with the enormous challenge of staffing a competitive team using one of the lowest budgets in all of baseball. The A's were a "small market team" and had an annual budget of $44 million, while the New York Yankees were spending over $125 million on their players.

Billy began to challenge the conventional approaches to evaluating major league talent. He knew he could not compete for players in the marketplace with teams like the Yankees. So Billy brought in people who were promoting a radical, different statistical manner for evaluating talent. This approach was controversial because it challenged the traditional evaluation methods and approaches.

Using the new controversial method known as sabermetrics, Billy and his staff began to re-evaluate the Major League Baseball system. Old paradigms were thrown out as data and statistics pointed to new ways to evaluate talent. Players who had been deemed as limited in their abilities or past their prime were now looked at differently, and it became clear that when combined with other players and their unique abilities, the potential for the success of the A's would significantly improve.

Billy began signing players that few other teams were interested in. Critics scoffed at his approach and predicted absolute failure. Nevertheless, Billy continued evaluating and signing these players.

The season began with little expected from the A's. Billy and his manager encouraged each player to "simply do what they do best."

Each player had been selected for specific skills and abilities they had demonstrated in their career, and the A's needed each player to execute to his particular skill set. After a slow start and continual reinforcement of the coaching staff's new mantra, the team began to win … and win … and win. That year the Oakland A's set a modern-day major league record of twenty straight wins. They won 103 games that year, including the American League West Championship. The A's lost in the playoffs, but the use of sabermetrics changed the manner in which baseball talent is evaluated. Major League Baseball would never be the same again because Billy Beane dedicated himself to really understanding and looking deeply at the systems, as well as knowing the skills and abilities of his players.

Organizations can often be resistant to change. This resistance can be driven by fear and uncertainty. I have seen organizations continue horribly inefficient and ineffective practices because they were too scared to navigate through the needed changes. Unfortunately, this occurs more frequently than many people realize.

Billy had reservations at first, but he became a student of understanding the principles of sabermetrics and its application to the systems of Major League Baseball. As his understanding grew, his confidence increased, and he was able to effectively lead his entire staff to evaluate talent in a different manner. Leaders who apply themselves to understanding the business systems they are leading gain insight, confidence, and an ability to effectively communicate needed changes. This depth of understanding creates respect among followers and watchers. They see such leaders as possessing a genuine grasp of the situation they face. When people have this level of respect, they are more willing to listen, act, and follow.

Metrics

In addition, the leader must understand the key metrics to track and measure for evaluating the performance of her organization's business processes. These metrics should be well established with a reporting and review process in place. The metrics should provide an understanding of the enterprise and a systematic approach to assessing performance. Failure to have a means to measure performance degrades the perception of command. It raises the fundamental questions:

"How do you know if we are in control?" "How do we know if we are capable?" Metrics are a form of communication, and a leader who establishes and uses metrics effectively can clearly articulate the state of command of the business. Metrics provide data, and this establishes credibility and demonstrates a healthy level of oversight and understanding of the enterprise. Successful leaders measure performance and speak with data.

Direction/Focus

An effective leader must establish and set specific vision, direction, and focus for the team. The leader must be able to articulate the goals and objectives and translate these into concrete actions. People must not only understand *where* they are going and *what* they are looking for when they get there but also *why* they are going in a given direction. When people understand the goals and objectives, there is a higher probability that they will personally engage in ownership for the results and success of the organization. When a leader provides clear direction, this creates confidence, and when she combines this with a strong understanding of the business, she creates respect. Once again, communication is vital for the success of a leader.

An effective leader should engage her people for input and perspective when formulating strategies and direction. When she includes staff and others in strategy development and vision casting, she uses a very useful tool for the buy-in and acceptance of change.

Over the last twelve years, my organization has held a two-day workshop every January. Staff members come from around the world and share learning with others, review improvement efforts they had been working on, and brainstorm potential improvements for the future. In the early days, I led this effort along with the managers working for me. We spent hours in planning. This event required active facilitation and coaching through the two days to help the group work through the variety of topics. However, after several years of doing this, a transition began to occur. The team members became increasingly engaged in the planning, and the sessions became more driven by the team. They challenged one another, and I found my role becoming more about facilitating and listening; I provided insight and perspective to clarify concerns and direction of the company. What resulted was robust planning with a high level of ownership by the team. The team's discussions were broad, and everyone took their subsequent plans and commitments seriously. It was incredibly gratifying to see the team evolve in the planning process and adopt a high level of ownership. Each member of the team had grown in their confidence and command of their roles and responsibilities.

Drives Action

The successful leader must be able to motivate himself, his direct reports, his peers, or even an entire organization to action. He must demonstrate an ability to make progress toward goals and objectives continually through his own effort and actions. The leader must be a self-starter and be able to see a situation and take appropriate measures. This includes helping remove barriers, which impede his team from taking action.

A common failure is "ever planning, never doing." Many people and organizations have simply failed, though they operated with good intentions. The ability to drive action may require some risk-taking by leaders. However, these risks can be managed effectively by using data analysis, good judgment, and effective communication skills. Effective leaders appropriately drive progress toward well-defined goals and objectives. Leaders must understand that it is important to bring others along and motivate them to action. Otherwise, leaders could find themselves far ahead with no one following their lead. Effective leaders motivate and often check for understanding and alignment from their team and organization. They make adjustments and remove barriers for people all along the path.

Influence/Breadth

This element is directly related to the cross-functional element under *Confidence*. The breadth of influence of a leader demonstrates a higher level of command. The leader should ask, *Am I sought out by others for knowledge, experience, and coaching? Am I able to influence organizations and groups outside of my organization?* High confidence by peers and cross-functional organizations, combined with strong results and excellent command, leads to breadth of influence across the organization. Leaders who have a wide breadth of influence usually have a strong network of colleagues they routinely work with on a variety of topics and issues.

Henry Knox took command of the expedition to recover the Fort Ticonderoga cannons. He was able to convince Washington that it was a feasible idea, and he then thought through what resources he needed to be successful. Not everything went as expected, but he improvised and kept driving his forces forward. Ultimately, his expedition succeeded in recovering and transporting the cannons to Boston. It was a task thought impossible by many.

Strong command presence based on knowledge, installed systems, metrics, focus, and breadth of influence can result in broad respect across the organization. In Knox's case, it led to a promotion.

Leadership Takeaways

- Leaders must have a sound, in-depth knowledge and understanding of the business they are trying to lead.

- A leader in command endeavors to define, understand, and improve through well-defined systems and systems-thinking approaches.

- Metrics are a form of communication, and a leader who establishes and uses metrics effectively can clearly articulate the state of command of the business.

- The leader must be able to articulate the goals and objectives and translate these into concrete actions.

- An effective leader motivates and routinely checks for understanding and alignment.

- High confidence by peers and cross-functional organizations, combined with strong results and excellent command, lead to breadth of influence across the organization.

8

The Results Dimension

If the highest aim of a captain were to preserve his ship, he would keep it in port forever.

—*St. Thomas Aquinas*

Ultimately, the leader is responsible for obtaining results, and this dimension can have a significant impact in assessing a leader's success. An organization or team assigned a task or responsibility will ultimately be evaluated on their deliverable and how well they meet expectations. The leader of a group or team will ultimately be evaluated on his ability to motivate, align, and direct the activities of others to meet the designated objectives.

If you are in a leadership role that has less defined deliverables and results, it may help to consider this dimension as Impact. Successful leaders create a positive impact on their team, the overall organization, the community, and even the world. They make a difference. The leader's presence, decisions, and actions impact culture, direction, and focus. When this happens, people see the leader as a difference maker.

Dr. Martin Luther King Jr. was an example of a leader who made a tremendous impact on his culture. His leadership was not about deliverables, such as profits or production quotas, but about leading real cultural change. Dr. King's leadership in the Civil Rights

Movement of the 1960s changed America and is still being felt half a century after his tragic death. He was a difference maker.

If your leadership role is less about tangible deliverables and more about leading change, establishing direction, and providing focus, then your results are measured by the impact you have in accomplishing these objectives. When you do this effectively. you will be seen as a difference maker.

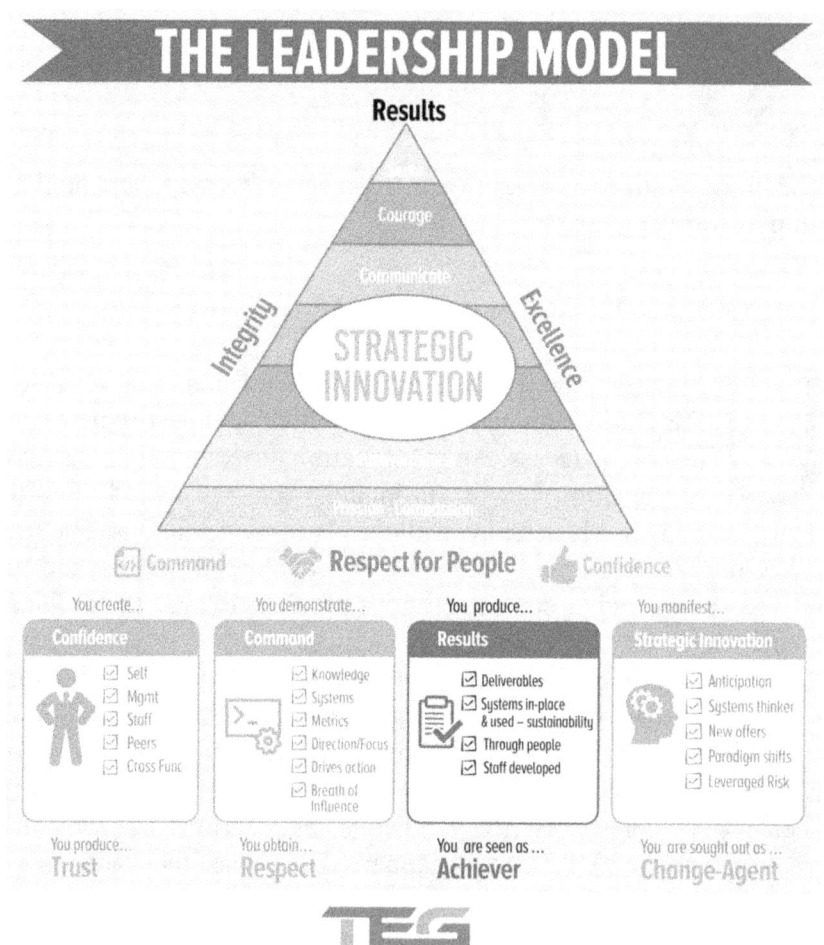

Aspects of the Results Dimension

Deliverables

Whether leading a capital project or an operations area, achieving the goals is the expectation for ultimate success. In capital projects, at the highest level, this requires achieving the established cost, scope, and schedule objectives. For manufacturing departments, this includes adhering to the budget and achieving a number of defined objectives, including quality, capability, service, and output. Other types of organizational objectives may include sales, deliveries, office visits, and the like. Regardless of the type of group, the leader must keep her team focused on the key goals and assure that plans are in place as well as actions taken to achieve the intended results. To actually achieve results, she must also have the appropriate command of the business processes and systems as well as the confidence of the team to make decisions relative to the objectives and organization's well-being.

Systems in Place

The most efficient manner to achieve results is by having healthy effective processes and systems in place that the organization actually uses. Sometimes results can be reached without such systems, but when they are in place, their use assures sustainability. Leaders make sure their organizations not only achieve success today but also continue to do so into the future. Using defined processes and systems provides confidence that the results will be sustainable due to skill and discipline and not just luck. Results obtained from reliable established processes and systems establish a state of control, command, and confidence that reinforces the perception of the leader as someone who can produce sustainable results with his team.

Through People

A leader multiplies his effectiveness as he engages and enables people around him to achieve results. An effective leader realizes that his personal strengths and capabilities are limited in impact unless he can replicate and engage others to achieve results as well. The leader must be able to motivate, challenge, teach, coach, mentor, and engage his people in a manner that creates a dynamic learning environment. This environment must be a place where people can grow through experiences, learn from successes as well as failures, and ultimately be results focused. The leader and his team must embrace accountability for achieving sustainable results. Effective leaders get results by working with and through people. They elevate those around them to reach higher, perform better, and achieve new levels of competence and capability.

Staff Developed

Leaders achieve not only business results but also have a responsibility for developing people. The strong leader must also coach and provide timely feedback to his staff, so they are continually improving and growing. Leaders must identify and develop the next generation of leaders through performance, coaching, and training. The strongest leaders make it a priority to have well-developed succession plans and development plans for their people and then link these to achieving tangible business success. In fact, a key result for any leader is not just improved processes, quality product, and higher profits but also a well developed, capable staff. An effective leader considers staff development a fundamental deliverable of his or her leadership. Such leaders recognize and embrace the value of empowering people to perform at greater levels of capability and effectiveness.

Nathanial Bowditch demonstrated the power of developing people by teaching sailors and ships' cooks how to navigate. In the late 1700s, education was limited in quality and availability, so his taking the time and effort to teach sailors skills they did not possess or could not easily obtain was significant. All twelve sailors and the cook he trained in navigation skills on his last voyage were ultimately promoted to first or second officers on other ships. It is clear from his memoirs that he created an atmosphere of learning and had a willingness to teach anyone who showed an interest to learn.

An individual who achieves results in a consistent manner and establishes sustainable results through people is perceived as an *enabling achiever*—someone who achieves results by enabling others and working through people around them.

In his book *The Fifth Discipline* (Senge, 1990, p. 3), Senge explained that learning organizations are "organizations where people continually expand their capacity to create the results they truly desire, where new and expansive patterns of thinking are nurtured, where collective aspiration is set free, and where people are continually learning to see the whole together."

The Power of Celebration

Finally, good leaders make sure they celebrate team success in very public ways. They acknowledge the team's accomplishments and value to the organization. They thank people directly and sincerely for their contribution to that success. Never underestimate the power of saying thank you or job well done. I have seen many a manager and leader who simply didn't appreciate or understand the power of celebration and acknowledgment. Celebration provides public acknowledgment, reinforcement, and value for people and their work. It can also create a band-of-brothers culture as people together celebrate achievements and acknowledge individual and team success. This says to people *We did it!* and *I appreciate and value you!* People will tell stories for years about some project they worked on together, and they will make sure the story includes the leaders' appreciation and acknowledgement of their success and effort.

***

When leaders take time to develop people's capabilities to achieve results together, they make the whole organization stronger. The individual feels empowered, which can lead to even deeper engagement and continued success. Through such efforts, a leader has essentially enabled skills and increased the entire team's capability for success.

Leadership Takeaways

- Ultimately, the leader is responsible for obtaining results.

- Leaders must keep their teams focused on the goals and assure plans are in place and actions are taken to achieve the intended results.

- Leaders must strive to obtain sustainable results—making sure teams not only achieve success today but that the organization can continue to achieve success in the future.

- The most efficient manner to achieve results is by having healthy effective processes and systems in place that are being used by the organization.

- Effective leaders realize that their personal strengths and capabilities are limited in impact unless they can replicate and engage others to achieve results also.

- Effective leaders elevate those around them to reach higher, perform better, and achieve new levels of competence and capability.

- Enabling achievers are individuals who achieve results by enabling others and working through people around them.

9

The Strategic
Innovation Dimension

But innovation comes from people meeting up in the hallways or calling each other at 10:30 at night with a new idea, or because they realized something that shoots holes in how we've been thinking about a problem.

—Steve Jobs

Demonstrative, loud, passionate, irreverent, determined, and brilliant are all terms used to describe Pete Vanevenhoven, former senior research fellow with Lilly Research Labs. Pete was the technical service leader for Product Recovery and Finishing at Lilly's Clinton manufacturing facility supporting Elanco Animal Health manufacturing in the 1970s through the early 1990s. He was a brilliant scientist, though unorthodox and often demonstrative in expressing his views and opinions. He exuded passion and determination and embodied the value of *Excellence*.

Pete had built a reputation as a leader in developing new and innovative solutions for Elanco products. He held numerous patents and regularly met with senior leaders to discuss new ideas and potential products. It was unusual to place Pete, a senior research fellow, at a manufacturing site in western Indiana. Normally, research scientists were located in Indianapolis or Greenfield labs, which were major development centers for Lilly. However, Pete's unique style and passion made running a "skunk works" research effort at Clinton ideal for Elanco. He and his team were able to directly support Elanco's most important products being manufactured at Clinton, while also performing developmental work for new products in cooperation with Greenfield. Pete and his group held multiple patents and developed processes and products, such as granular monensin and narasin and crystalline monensin. These products, known as ionophores, were and still are significant products for Elanco worldwide.

Pete exemplified several aspects of the Leadership Model. His *Strategic Innovation* abilities were outstanding. He made numerous offers to the company and then carried these ideas through to completion, ending up with not only multiple patents but actual products on the market. In addition, he understood the power of bringing people with him. He was a teacher, coach, promoter, and cheerleader, but most importantly he empowered his people to make decisions and offer their own ideas. Led by Pete, we always felt like we were a part of the team, and we succeeded together as a group.

His dynamic personality was often bigger than life. When he entered a room, he would never be shy about sharing his thoughts or beliefs. He took many stands on principle as well as in support of an idea or his people. Everyone who ever worked for Pete felt they had his complete support. Even when members of his team made mistakes, he encouraged them to think further and deeper. The confidence and credibility he created led senior vice presidents to call on him routinely. He was highly respected for his command of his field of expertise as well as the results he had produced.

In 1981, I started my career with Lilly after finishing my master's degree in chemical engineering at Ohio State University and went directly to work for Pete. For me, this experience was life-changing as this passionate, energetic scientist took me under his wings and taught me real-world exploration. Every day with him was an adventure filled with challenges and often much laughter. He would regularly gather his team around him in the office or lab to discuss issues in manufacturing, but often the discussion would lead to possible improvements to processes or products. Sometimes these discussions would erupt in a burst of energy from Pete. He would lead the team into the lab where chemicals and beakers would rapidly appear, and we would begin mixing and trying things to see if an idea had any merit. This felt like mad scientist moments. They were incredibly energizing and exciting, and they often led to deeper exploration and ultimately to new products or processes.

In the summer of 1985, Pete gathered the team together in his office to discuss an opportunity. He held up a jar of a bright yellow compound that we had never seen before and explained the challenge. The substance in the jar was a compound called nicarbazin, a coccidiostat used in the swine and poultry industry. This compound had been developed a number of years before but had not been well accepted in the marketplace. He shook the jar, which made the fundamental problem immediately evident. The bright yellow compound filled the entire jar and just hung in the air as a bright yellow cloud. When nicarbazin was originally developed, it was found that it only had efficacy if it was digested by the animal at a particle size of less than 200 mesh (or less than 74 micron). This particle size was extremely fine, and the material, if aerated, behaved more like a liquid or gas in containers. As a result, commercial feed yards found the material very difficult to handle, and they avoided using it because of the extreme material handling and exposure problems. Our challenge was to find a way to make this product more acceptable in the marketplace by addressing the material handling problems.

The team began brainstorming ideas, and Pete suggested using wax to adhere the particles to something as a carrier. Several months earlier, Pete had been studying waxes as a possible food additive for other product considerations. The group discussed this idea, and in no time the entire group was in the laboratory digging through shelves to find various samples of waxes. The team also began looking for different types of digestable materials for adhereing the nicarbazin with the wax. We pulled out glassware and warmed heating plates. That afternoon an idea took root and grew into a whole new product.

Over the next few weeks, multiple trials were run in the lab with various types of materials. Finally, a specific wax and ground corncobs were selected as the substances for the product. Pete asked me and another engineer in the group, Don Williams, to develop a commercial process for melting and blending together the wax, the ground corncobs, and nicarbazin. The result was a beautiful, dust free, granular product that we now called Carbigran. Adhering the nicarbazin particles to the corncobs with wax worked very well in eliminating all nicarbazin dust. It also flowed beautifully and made material handling very managable at the feed yard. Because the wax was digestible, it released the fine particles of nicarbazin into the animal's digestive tract. Moreover, we could make the drug available in the proper particle size for an animal. So, through Pete's leadership and our team's efforts, we managed to retain the drug's efficacy while making it much more "user friendly" for the customer. Eight months later, I found myself at Lilly's Alcobendas production facility outside Madrid, Spain, starting up the new Carbigran production facility for Lilly.

Though I was exposed to a number of outstanding leaders in my career, no one had a greater impact on me professionally than Pete Vanevenhoven. He taught me the passion, the joy, and the exhilaration of exploration and discovery for which I will be forever grateful.

Exploring the Strategic Innovation Dimension

The fourth significant dimension in the Leadership Model involves anticipation and innovation. *Strategic Innovation* is exploring and developing creative solutions and actions to achieve specific objectives and goals valuable to the business. In the model, it is deliberately placed in the middle to represent its dependence on the other three dimensions: *Confidence, Command,* and *Results.* It is very difficult to be successful in the *Strategic Innovation* dimension if a leader has not been successful in the other three dimensions. The credibility, the demonstrated command, and the ability to achieve measurable results are vital to anticipating future trends as well as to influencing others to move in a new direction.

Let's consider the key elements in the *Strategic Innovation* dimension.

Anticipation

This dimension can distinguish strong leaders from other leaders, for it involves a leader being able to anticipate future trends, needs, and opportunities. The headlights of the strongest leaders extend beyond those of others by anticipating the future. The effective leader is *forward-looking*. She continually asks, *What's next?*

Fundamentally critical to understanding trends, threats, and opportunities is having a sound command of the business one is in. Leaders must also have confidence in their assessment and have the trust of management, peers, and staff to lead in a new direction. If leaders enhance their understanding, they can further develop their ability to anticipate. By becoming a student not only of the business but also of the world, leaders can develop their ability to anticipate by understanding trends and connecting new ideas and concepts.

Systems Thinking

Earlier I discussed the importance of *System Thinking*. Leaders must be able to look at and think about their business and the world around them as numerous and often complex interactive systems. It is important that leaders be able to analyze and break down these systems to understand the cause-and-effect relationships within them and between them. Through this type of analysis, leaders can ultimately understand how to make improvements to critical business systems. Strategic innovation often evolves from a fundamental understanding of the enterprise systems and their unique interactions.

Peter Senge argues that one of the key problems with much that is written about and done in the name of management is that rather simplistic frameworks are applied to what are actually complex systems. We tend to focus on the parts rather than seeing the whole and then fail to see the organization as a dynamic process. Thus, the argument runs, a better appreciation of systems will lead to more appropriate action. Peter Senge (Senge, 1990, p. 92) concluded: "The systems viewpoint is generally oriented toward the long-term view. That's why delays and feedback loops are so important. In the short term, you can often ignore them; they're inconsequential. They only come back to haunt you in the long term."

Innovation

The ability to make *new offers* to the organization is a valuable capability for leaders. The strong leader is always looking for opportunities for improvement, including making the organization and people stronger, more capable, more productive, more efficient, more profitable, and even, at times, creating a new product for the customer. This is exactly what Pete Vanevehoven did when he created the granular product Carbigran. And by creating a new product for the client, Pete provided for Lilly an entire new opportunity in the marketplace.

New products or new processes may involve a *paradigm shift*, which may require influencing a broad section of the organization to adopt the new paradigm. The highly effective leader is inquisitive and always learning from a variety of sources. He or she can take various concepts or pieces of data and connect them to formulate new theories, business models, or a deeper understanding of the issues and needs at hand. Through this analysis, the effective leader is then able to propose new concepts, direction, and approaches. Pete had been exploring industrial waxes and their use when the application to nicarbazin appeared. His exploration and trying to understand the physical world around him allowed him to make the connection to applying waxes to nicarbazin and thus bring about a new product.

Credibility and influence are gained when the leader invites colleagues to become codevelopers and creates a stage for dialogue on new ideas and approaches. The new offers do not have to come directly from the leader, but he can facilitate and empower others to explore, understand, and formulate proposals. This requires that he create a safe place to do this type of work. Many new ideas are often stomped out by critical closed thinking from management. They can feel threatened by diverse thinking, considering it uncontrolled and a potential source of variability to the status quo.

The leader who creates confidence with his team that he is willing to listen can establish a rich culture for exchanging ideas. In this type of culture, people can express new ideas and challenge existing thinking. This culture can also be enhanced when a leader has strong command knowledge of the business. He can engage in meaningful indepth conversation about business processes and issues. I have seen too many leaders avoid these conversations because they are simply not as knowledgable of the business as they should be and feel threatened by challenges to the status quo.

Finally, leaders who have a track record of getting results should appreciate the importance of exploring opportunities for improvement in productivity, efficiency, and cost savings.

Leveraged Risk

The effective leader must understand risk and not run away from it. Driving change in an organization always has risk associated with it, but the leader must understand this risk and work closely with others to minimize it or effectively manage it throughout change. Often the leader must carefully navigate new ideas through naysayers and viable challenges. Understanding such risks, the gaps, and developing appropriate implementation paths are critical for a leader to become successful. The support of a leader in the communication and implementation of paradigm shifts is essential for overall success. An active strategic innovator understands how to leverage risk within the organization to introduce new ideas and concepts.

The leader who demonstrates the ability to anticipate future trends, issues, and opportunities and move the organization in a new direction through new offers and innovative approaches is seen as a real *change agent*.

Leaders who are change agents can see a new future state or direction for the organization. This is called setting a vision. But seeing the future for an organization is not enough. The leader must bring others with him who will see and also own the vision with him. The vision must become a shared vision.

Peter Senge starts from the position that if any one idea about leadership has inspired organizations for thousands of years, "it's the capacity to hold a shared picture of the future we seek to create" (Senge, 1990, p. 9). Such a vision has the power to uplift and to encourage experimentation and innovation. It can also foster a sense of the long-term, something that is fundamental to the fifth discipline. As Senge stated:

> When there is a genuine vision (as opposed to the all-to-familiar 'vision statement'), people excel and learn, not because they are told to, but because they want to. But many leaders have personal visions that never get translated into shared visions that galvanize an organization. ... What has been lacking is a discipline for translating vision into shared vision—not a 'cookbook' but a

set of principles and guiding practices. The practice of shared vision involves the skills of unearthing shared 'pictures of the future' that foster genuine commitment and enrollment rather than compliance. In mastering this discipline, leaders learn the counter-productiveness of trying to dictate a vision, no matter how heartfelt. (Senge, 1990, p. 9)

Visions spread because of a reinforcing process. Increased clarity, enthusiasm and commitment rub off on others in the organization. 'As people talk, the vision grows clearer. As it gets clearer, enthusiasm for its benefits grow.' (Ibid., 227)

The Model: Concluding Thoughts

In this section, we have introduced the Essential Leadership Dimensions of the Leadership Model. These dimensions are part of a systemic approach to looking at leadership.

The Leadership Model is intended to be a self-assessment tool for analyzing personal strengths and weaknesses. From this analysis, an individual can put together a leadership development plan, which focuses on improving specific dimensions and elements of his or her own leadership effectiveness. This model is not intended to reflect a particular leadership style and recognizes that a variety of styles can be effective. However, it does propose that leaders must be capable in each of these critical dimensions to maximize their leadership potential.

This model also distinguishes between leadership and management, though there are significant overlaps in keys to success for both. Not all managers are great leaders nor are all leaders great managers. An individual can be both, but in this model the focus has been primarily on leadership success.

Being a successful leader as described by these dimensions does not guarantee a promotion, but there is a high probability of being recognized as a successful, effective leader. A leader who has the broad confidence of the organization is well respected for his or her command of the business and gets results and has impact while always learning and developing new approaches.

In leadership, there is a reality that perceptions are crucial. However, these perceptions must be supported by experiences the leader creates. This is why in the Leadership Model I have talked about leaders building confidence that builds trust. Trust is an outcome of confidence. A leader must foster trust by creating experiences that build confidence. When people are confident in a person, they behave in a manner toward the leader that says, *I trust you and see you as very credible in your leadership.* The same applies for each of the other dimensions. Demonstrating a level of command of the business creates respect by people as they recognize expertise, knowledge, and capability. Likewise, achieving sustainable results by building an effective team demonstrates to others that the leader is someone who is actually capable of accomplishing challenging, difficult tasks by leading groups of people. The result of this perception is that the leader is given more challenging opportunities. Finally, when a leader manifests strategic innovation, he demonstrates an ability to look ahead and anticipate future needs and trends. As a response, people want this kind of leader to be a part of a broader discussion on the direction and future of the enterprise. Such leaders are highly valued for their insight and seen as individuals who can shape future direction. Perceptions by others are critical, especially when supported by direct experiences.

So the Leadership Model ultimately establishes that an individual who creates *confidence,* demonstates *command,* produces *results*, and manifests *strategic innovation* will be trusted, respected as an achiever, and seen as a real change agent. These attributes are highly valued in leaders anywhere!

Leadership Takeaways

- Strategic Innovation is exploring and developing creative solutions and actions to achieve specific objectives and goals valuable to the business.

- The effective leader can develop her ability to anticipate by understanding trends and connecting new ideas and concepts.

- The leader must be able to look at and think about the business and world around him as numerous and often complex interactive systems.

- A better appreciation of systems will lead to more appropriate action.

- The ability to make new offers to the organization is a valuable capability for leaders.

- Leaders must create a safe place to explore, consider, and develop new proposals.

- Understanding the risk, the gaps, and developing appropriate implementation paths are critical for a successful leader.

- The leader who demonstrates the ability to anticipate future trends, issues, and opportunities and move the organization in a new direction through new offers and innovative approaches is seen as a real *change agent*.

Part 4

The Essential Behaviors

10

Create Confidence

Leadership is not a title. It's a behavior. Live it!

—*Robin Sharma*

I had been mentoring an associate for a couple of years. One day we got into a discussion on leadership, and I had the opportunity to share the Leadership Model with him. After an excellent discussion and giving him the model to take away to digest, I thought I had been successful in sharing the model and was feeling good about our exchange.

A couple of weeks later, he came back to continue our talk and brought up the model. He thanked me for sharing it with him but then asked a fundamental question that stopped me in my tracks. He asked, "But what do I do?"

His question challenged me to think about the practical application of the Leadership Model. *What should we do as individuals to actually put the model into practice?* The model's principles are sound, but my associate's question led me to ask a number of additional questions, such as: *What does an individual need to do to improve confidence, which leads to trust? How do leaders demonstrate command and generate respect for their understanding and control of the business?*

In the late 1980s, Lilly brought Roger Connor and Tom Smith, authors of the book *The OZ Principle: Getting Results through*

Organizational and Individual Accountability, to Lilly and consulted with them on improving accountability. Their work corresponded well with the business improvement work underway across Lilly. It was also a great fit with a communication tool that Dale Martlage and I had developed at Lilly's Clinton manufacturing facility. In the course of working with Tom and Roger, they introduced us to a model that explained fundamental human behaviors. This model, the Behavior Model (Connors, Smith, & Hickman, 1990), became quite useful in answering the question, *but what do I do?*

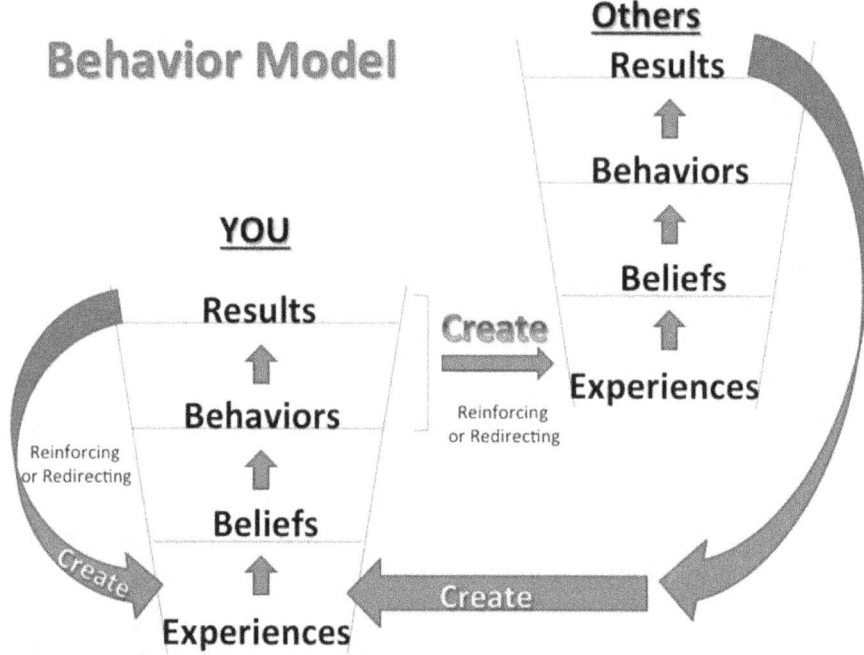

The Behavior Model establishes that people's behaviors are driven from a set of beliefs they hold. These beliefs consciously or subconsciously impact their behaviors when they respond to situations or deal with other people. For instance, I may treat a police officer with politeness and respect because somewhere in my internal beliefs I fundamentally believe this is the appropriate manner to address authority and specifically a police officer. Another individual, however, may treat the same police officer in an entirely different manner. This person (let's say she's a woman) may be suspicious and cautious and even un-cooperative with the officer. Her behavior is driven by an internal belief system that has taught her to believe cops are a threat or simply untrust-worthy. Her beliefs and mine are the result of experiences that each of us have had. Experiences drive beliefs.

These experiences can come from a number of sources, ranging from direct personal involvement to knowledge received from such sources as the media, social interaction, religion, education, and family upbringing. These experiences, whether strong or weak, influence and drive beliefs we develop regarding a broad range of topics. Ultimately, our behaviors lead to some result, the final step in our Behavior Model. In other words, our behaviors have consequences that may create ex-periences for us as well as for others.

So how does this help in telling us what we need to do as lead-ers? The Behavior Model establishes that people's behaviors are driven by their beliefs and their behaviors always create some result. This ap-plies to leaders too, for they will create an experience for others through their behaviors. The experience is unavoidable and a part of human dy-namics. So, focusing on a leader's behavior relative to each dimension of the Leadership Model can help us understand what behaviors are helpful in becoming an effective leader. Simply put, since leaders cre-ate experiences for other people, they must be conscious and deliberate regarding the experiences they are creating. Granting this, let's turn our attention to the specifics of the Leadership Model to see how this helps us put it into practice.

Ways to Create Confidence

Leaders need to create confidence, and their behaviors need to create experiences for others that influence them to place their confi-dence in those who lead them. The most important thing is to consciously recognize that behaviors and the consequences of behav-iors create experiences for others. These experiences will then influence the beliefs of those who are led. So, what are the behaviors that create the right experiences for others? Many potential behaviors can create confidence. Here are a few key ones.

Fulfill Commitments

It sounds simple, but it is incredibly important that leaders fulfill their commitments. Possibly nothing will degrade confidence quicker than the inability or lack of attention or persistence to meet one's obligations. Failure to fulfill promises creates a very negative experience for others and especially to those to whom the commitment was made. If you cannot fulfill a commitment, it is imperative that you help people understand why and what you are going to do about it. If you avoid the issue, this will only reinforce to others that you do not keep your commitments and fail to recognize or care about the impact that has on others. From a leadership perspective, the impact is that people's confidence in you and their view that you are credible are seriously degraded.

One of the keys to keeping commitments is to understand clearly what exactly an individual is committing to do or provide. This requires conversation and clarity around deliverables and expectations. Sometimes documenting the commitment helps bring clarity and agreement about what is precisely expected by all parties. Being deliberate in commitments demonstrates the importance the leader places on his or her commitments. It is also important that the leader not overcommit. Many leaders become overcommitted, making it impossible for them to keep all their commitments. For a leader to be effective, she must manage her commitments, and if needed, engage the help of others to help her keep her promises.

Finally, keeping commitments has a profound impact on others whether the commitment was significant or small. It leads people to recognize and believe that you will do what you say you will do. Creating this belief in others is powerful for any leader because it creates a behavior of trust in others. So, by fulfilling commitments, we create experiences for others that create a belief that we will keep our promises and, as a result, others' behavior will be to trust us. The ultimate result is others will see us as genuinely credible.

In contrast, if a leader creates experiences that lead to a negative set of beliefs by others, the result can be that people will not trust him and their behaviors will reflect this belief. If a leader has created this set of beliefs for people, he has a severe problem that can impact his entire leadership role. Trust must be guarded and valued highly within all levels of the organization. Violating trust will ultimately destroy effectiveness.

Follow-up

An effective leader follows up with people to check on their status and inform people of progress. The leader should not only ask questions showing interest and importance, but also provide updates regarding the status on commitments that he or his team have made to others. Follow-up reinforces importance, interest, and engagement. A leader who does not follow-up with his people can create a negative experience that interprets the leader as uncaring or disengaged. It can also leave people wondering or confused over whether he is really leading.

Active follow-up should involve the people reporting to the leader, to his peers, and to upward levels in the organization. Follow-up on status allows the team and leader to provide clarification and even re-direction if necessary. It keeps status and issues in the forefront and reinforces importance. It also gives the leader opportunities to understand how he can help the team, what obstacles he can remove, and what resources he can provide.

A leader's successful follow-up creates the experience for others that he is engaged and cares about the status and success of the team. It reinforces upward in the organization that the leader understands status and issues. This experience creates the belief in all levels of the organization that the head is engaged, committed, and understands the situation. When people have this belief, they not only trust the leader but will also listen to him. When people listen to him, they do it because they believe he is credible.

Be Factual

Effective leaders deal with facts and data as a basis for their views and opinions. Leaders must differentiate opinions and bias from truth and fact. The world is filled with much passion and ideas, but when leading a team, the leader must endeavor to be as factual as possible. She does this by asking questions, asking for data, and requesting the demonstrated rationale for the opinions and views of others. Facts can be unpopular because they do not always support personal opinions or bias, but when presented well, they can disarm even the most ardent opinionated viewpoints.

Strong opinions and bias can sway a leader who does not master this area. She can be swept away in group-think, which ultimately results in poor decisions. When poor decisions are made without factual basis, it erodes the confidence of others at all levels of the organization.

In everyday life, we are inundated with information. It comes from conversations, television, the Internet, texting, and a host of other sources. Never before in the history of humanity has so much information been so readily available. However, with this avalanche of information can come confusion, inaccuracies, and even deception. The adage "Don't believe everything you hear (or read)" has never applied more. I encourage you to use a simple test as you go through your day. Whether you receive written, verbal, face-to-face, or electronic information, ask of it this straightforward question: Is it supported by solid data? If so, it has a justifiable factual basis. If not, it is mere opinion or conjecture.

A grounded or adequately supported statement is a declaration of a fact. Facts are things in the world which are worthy of declarations. For instance, I can state that New York City is east of Chicago or that Mount Everest is the tallest mountain in the world. There are other facts and data that support such statements.

Declarative statements are either true or false. Either it is true that New York City is east of Chicago or it is false. If it is true, evidence and reasons can be marshaled to confirm that it is. If it is false, evidence and reasons can also be provided to show that this is the case. In both instances, evidence and reasons either support or falsify a statement that claims to be true.

Now an assessment is the evaluation or estimation of the nature, quality, or ability of someone or something. Assessments are more opinion based because they evaluate the meaning of data and information. Furthermore, assessments are either grounded with adequate supporting data and accurate information or ungrounded with no or inadequate supporting data and information. I could say Peyton Manning is the best quarterback ever to play professional football. This is an assessment, which is either grounded or ungrounded. There are other individuals who would argue this point adamantly and present other quarterbacks, such as Tom Brady or Joe Montana, with their supporting evidence. Regardless of who each of us claimed was professional football's greatest quarterback, our assertion would be groundless if we failed to present adequate support for our claim.

As a leader, you must be able to discern between declarative statements and assessments. In both cases, claims to truth are made. And in both types of statements, evidence, reasons, data, and accurate information are needed to ground and confirm them as true. Without that support, neither should be acted upon as true.

As you go through your day reading various documents, meeting with people, and taking phone calls, ask of what you're hearing, *Is it a declarative statement or an assessment? Is it supported by solid supporting data?* I think you will discover that many people in the world often make assertions that amount to their assessments or opinion. In other words, they talk about something as if it were fact when in reality it is their interpretation or opinion of the matter. In some

> Data is the currency of credibility.
> —*Bruce Beck*

cases, their claims will be ungrounded or inadequately supported. Leaders need to be sensitive to this difference between fact, interpretation, and opinion and ask questions to clarify if what they are being told is actually true and can be supported by adequate evidence, reasons, data, and other forms of accurate information. If that is not the case, then leaders are hearing ungrounded opinion.

Leaders, of course, should base their decision making on facts and data. When they do this, it should ultimately result in sound decisions. These successful decisions then create experiences for others, confirming to them that those individuals leading them will deal with facts and data when making decisions. Others then believe their leaders want facts and data and are less interested in the strongest opinion or loudest voice. When people believe that a leader can be trusted, will listen, and deals in facts and data, they will seek her out as highly credible.

Be Prompt

The effective leader understands the importance of promptness in responding to people, requests, and assignments. Promptness should not sacrifice completeness, accuracy, or quality, but the leader should understand the importance of promptness in decisions and deliverables. Promptness is linked closely to the previous attributes of fulfilling commitments, follow-up, and being factual. Every leader must understand the delicate balance and also the urgency needed for a response to needs or requests for direction.

Sometimes failure to make a decision in a timely manner can result in the decision being made by others or through circumstances. Delays in decisions can lead to others believing the leader does not care, or worse, is unable to make a decision or provide direction. When others draw this conclusion about their leader, they will go around him when an urgent decision is needed. Empowering people to make decisions is good, but if it is their default position because they believe their leader is incapable of making a timely decision, then this undermines their confidence in him. Leaders must understand the situation and be capable of making a decision or guiding the team to a decision in a timely manner.

When leaders are appropriately prompt, they create experiences for others that they are on time in responding to requests, are capable of making tough decisions, and show up when expected. These experiences then form a belief that leaders are capable of making decisions, respect others' time, and care about success. This belief reinforces the leaders' credibility and leads to trust.

Fulfilling, Follow-up, and Being

We have focused on four behaviors that can impact confidence and build trust: *fulfilling commitments, follow-up, being factual,* and *being prompt.* Leaders should recognize that all these are related and work together to create confidence by others in their leadership. I have shown that the Behavior Model supports the Leadership Model. I have emphasized that experiences create beliefs and beliefs create behaviors that lead to results. Leaders can apply this model to identify specific behaviors they need to exhibit to build confidence in their leadership.

In the subsequent sections, we will follow a similar approach as we explore behaviors that impact *Command, Results,* and *Strategic Innovation.*

Leadership Takeaways

- The Behavior Model establishes that people's behaviors are driven from a set of beliefs they hold.

- Experiences drive beliefs.

- Since leaders create experiences for people, they must be conscious and deliberate regarding the experiences they create.

- Confidence can be created by ...

   o Fulfilling commitments

   o Effective and timely follow-up

   o Being factual

   o Being prompt

- Credibility builds confidence, which leads to trust.

- Experiences create beliefs and beliefs create behaviors that lead to results.

11

Demonstrate Command

Wise leaders understand that the single greatest determinant of whether followers will ever own a vision deeply is the extent to which those followers believe the leader will own it.

—*Bill Hybels*

L eadership is always about leading something. The "something" is the mission and is often about delivering some quantity or capability in product, assets, or service. Clearly, understanding not only "the mission" but also how that mission is to be accomplished are crucial for the dimension of *Demonstrating Command*. Leaders must have a sound understanding of the people, their capabilities, and the processes and systems they have a responsibility for leading. I am not implying that leaders must be "the expert" in all things, but they must have sufficient understanding to make sound decisions and ask useful questions if they are to lead effectively. I call this *Demonstrated Command*, and here are the behaviors that demonstrate command.

Pursue Understanding—Be a Student

An effective leader pursues understanding of the people, the business patterns, and systems over which she has a responsibility. She applies energy and focus on understanding relationships and dynamics. She also challenges her organization to learn and understand the systems and patterns that make up the work. When the leader creates this type of organization, it becomes what Peter Senge (Senge, 1990, p. 3) referred to as a learning organization and described as

> organizations where people continually expand their capacity to create the results they truly desire, where new and expansive patterns of thinking are nurtured, where collective aspiration is set free, and where people are continually learning to see the whole together.

Senge also introduced as his cornerstone to the *Fifth Dimension* the concept of systems thinking. He argues that

> one of the key problems with much that is written about, and done in the name of management, is that rather simplistic frameworks are applied to what are complex systems. We tend to focus on the parts rather than seeing the whole, and to fail to see organization as a dynamic process. Thus, the argument runs, a better appreciation of systems will lead to more appropriate action.

Therefore, for Senge, to pursue understanding is to understand the systems and apply systems thinking so that the complex nature and relationships are understood by the leader and their organization.

Leaders who do not endeavor to understand or encourage their team to understand the systems and business relationships often fall into the pattern of making short-term decisions without understanding long-term consequences. Senge went on to address this concern: "We learn best from our experience, but we never directly experience the consequences of many of our most important decisions." Considering this problem in regard to organizations, he observed:

> We tend to think that cause and effect will be relatively near to one another. Thus when faced with a problem, it is the 'solutions' that are close by that we focus upon. Classically we look to

actions that produce improvements in a relatively short time span. However, when viewed in systems terms, short-term improvements often involve very significant long-term costs. For example, cutting back on research and design can bring very quick cost savings, but can severely damage the long-term viability of an organization. (Senge, 1990, p. 23)

Leaders who fail to understand the systems with the cause-and-effect relationships can create negative experiences for people and their organization. If members of an organization understand the systems relationships much better than the leader and see decisions with negative consequences, they will believe the leader really does not know the business. Worse yet, staff may conclude that the leader has no interest in really learning the business. This perception and belief can lead to a lack of respect, trust, and even cooperation.

However, when a leader pursues understanding of the systems and patterns, he creates an experience for others that establishes a mutual desire to learn the business and master his craft. This experience leads to the belief by his team that he has genuine expertise and understanding. When people believe the leader has these characteristics, they treat him as an expert and that results in respect for him and his leadership.

Be Proactive—Take Initiative

Demonstrating Command requires being proactive and taking initiative. A proactive leader seizes the opportunity to address issues and improve his business unit's performance. He has understood the systems and patterns as described above and then takes the initiative to make improvements or correct deficiencies. He also effectively represents improvement opportunities to gain the support of senior management. The leader who does this is able to manage risk appropriately for his organization.

If a leader does not take initiative but instead has others always telling him what to do, he raises questions over his understanding and command of the business. This type of behavior creates doubt with his team as well as with upper management. It also erodes confidence in him and his leadership. If this belief is created, then people avoid their leader or work around him to address issues. Ultimately, they do not expect him to take action. As a result, they do not respect him.

However, a leader who can proactively take action to correct deficiencies and improve performance in a systematic manner demonstrates command of the business. Such leaders create an experience for others that expresses an understanding of the business. When this happens, leaders are seen as masters of their craft and are truly engaged to help the team improve. As a result, people treat these leaders as experts, seek them out for direction, and listen carefully to their insight. They are respected.

Own It!

Effective leaders demonstrate ownership of their business and thus demonstrate command. "Owning it" means they are accountable for the performance and results of their team. They do not shy away from this but stand up and accept criticism and accolades as a team. By stepping up to address issues, they demonstrate that they are accountable. They also support people in their decisions and actions, and when necessary act as advocates for the team. As needed, such leaders also provide clear direction and focus. Demonstrated ownership means the leader is accountable and thus displays command in the Leadership Model. The successful leader can also challenge and motivate others to "own it" and accept accountability. She creates an environment of accountability and responsibility, an environment where others embrace the importance of ownership and personally step up to be accountable and responsible.

If a leader fails to take ownership, she will create negative experiences for others. These negative experiences will create beliefs that she is unaccountable or unsupportive and that she fails to provide clear direction. This can lead to a lack of trust and even avoidance of the leader. It may result in people working around the leader instead of with her.

On the other hand, if a leader takes ownership, she reinforces positive experiences for others and fosters a belief that she has high ownership, is supportive, and will provide clear direction. People who believe this about their leader will treat her as an expert, seek out her guidance and support, and listen to her input and counsel. They will ultimately respect her.

Striving, Addressing, and Accepting

In summary, leaders *Demonstrate Command* by striving to understand the business through systems thinking and ascertaining patterns. They become students of the business enterprise and work closely with others to grow in their understanding and identification of issues and opportunities. As a result, they and their team gain an intimate understanding of the systems that make up the business. Leaders are proactive in addressing issues and taking the initiative to drive improvements and change. They demonstrate ownership by accepting accountability for performance, direction, focus, and support of the team. A leader who acts in this manner will *Demonstrate Command* and be highly respected.

Leadership Takeaways

- Leaders must have a sound understanding of their people, their capabilities, and the processes and systems that they have a responsibility for leading.

- A leader can *Demonstrate Command* by

   o Pursuing understanding—being a student

   o Being proactive—taking initiative

   o Owning it!

- Leaders create an environment of accountability and responsibility where people understand the importance of ownership and personally step up to be accountable and responsible.

- When leaders *Demonstrate Command*, they will be highly respected as knowledgeable, accountable, and responsible.

12

Produce Results

Finish well; anyone can start well.

—*Miles Anthony Smith*

Ultimately, producing results is imperative. Much can be said about leadership skills, approaches, and methods, but the bottom-line is that the leader must be successful in leading a team or organization to produce meaningful and measurable results. The leader must provide clear direction and focus for the organization and define what success means. The *Producing Results* dimension also includes the leader's ability to work with her team and with others outside of the organization to produce the needed results. This dimension emphasizes that a leader must have positive impact and ultimately make a difference in the organization.

The following behaviors are necessary for creating the right experiences in others that will lead to the required results and impact.

Complete the Task—Finish Strong

Effective leaders know how to finish. They understand what *complete* means and ensure the team crosses all the t's and dots all the i's. Leaders must also make sure that the team understands and is aligned around the definition of what actually completes a task or a project. Leaders see to it that the details are taken care of and the whole job is completed to expectations. By doing this, they guarantee the story is complete, that the work is not left undone.

A poorly completed task can create a very negative ending to a project. If this happens, people may believe that the leader and team have a lack of attention to detail or that they are pushing the work to others and not owning closure. This belief can lead to behaviors of suspicion and accusation toward the leader and his team. In addition, the recipient of the work may require additional documentation or proof of completion prior to taking delivery.

The leader who can successfully assure completion of the task, job, or project creates experiences of "a job well done" or "closure" or "attention to detail." He creates the belief that he and his team "finish well." As a result, people see them as a team who "gets the job done right!" People seek out these leaders and include them in future discussions and see them as "go to people." They see such leaders as achievers and difference makers.

Resolve Issues

> Quiet down! Let's stay cool. Procedures, I need another computer up on RTCC. I want everybody to alert your support team. Wake up anybody you need. Get them in here. Let's work the problem people! Let's not make things worse by guessing. (Broyles & Reinert, 1995)

These were the words of Gene Kranz (played by Ed Harris) in the 1995 docudrama movie *Apollo 13*. Gene said these words after the ill-fated Apollo 13 lunar mission had experienced an oxygen tank explosion in the service module that severely crippled the spacecraft. Landing on the moon was lost—out of the question. The mission was now to save the crew and find some way to get them home safely.

The movie has been critically acclaimed for its representation of the actual events associated with the Apollo 13 mission. The film chronicled the technical challenges, the stress, and ultimately one of NASA's most significant success stories in its long history. The real Gene Kranz, who was the Apollo 13 flight director, was a veteran of the space program, having been involved in many launches. As flight director, he had to lead the group of Mission Control engineers and scientists in finding a way to bring the crew home.

Challenges are a part of every job. Often leaders find themselves and their teams in situations where problems must be resolved. The successful leader knows how to address issues, motivate his team, and utilize their abilities to solve the problems they face. Others expect the leader to recognize problems and take appropriate actions. Sometimes, however, other leaders surface when problems occur. In fact, some of the greatest leaders arise out of problems and crises. Individuals see the need, rise to the occasion, provide direction, and mobilize people to take action.

Leadership is ineffective when it does not recognize issues or avoids taking action to address them. That's when problems grow and more severe consequences often occur. These consequences can lead to a number of problems, including team dysfunction and failure to deliver. If a leader does not recognize and resolve issues in a timely manner, he will create a belief by others that he is ineffective or unwilling to address the issues. This results in a lack of trust and often leads to avoiding the leader.

However, when a leader successfully addresses issues and engages others to help identify solutions, he creates support, confidence, and trust. People see him as an individual to go to with questions and problems because they believe he will address the need.

In *Apollo 13*, Gene Kranz storms out of a briefing with the Mission Control team, stating emphatically, "Failure is not an option." Effective leaders adopt this attitude and motivate their team to identify problems and address them, not to run from them and use them as excuses for failure. They see problems and issues as opportunities to eliminate hindrances and improve performance.

In one of the final scenes of *Apollo 13*, two of the Mission Control engineers are talking about everything that could go wrong on the re-entry of the capsule carrying the Apollo 13 crew. One of the NASA engineers says, "This could be the worst disaster NASA has ever experienced." Gene Kranz interrupts and says, "With all due respect, sir, I do believe this is going to be our finest hour." The best leaders act with conviction when confronted with a problem and seize the opportunity to do what they can to create the team's *finest hour.*

Make People Better

Successful leaders make people better. Leaders understand the importance of developing people and helping them improve. They understand the "power of replication." If a leader is personally capable and skilled, she may have the tendency to rely on her skills and capabilities to perform a task or make decisions that should be within the purview of the entire team. If this occurs, then the team can only be as good as the capacity of the leader to perform certain tasks or make individual decisions. However, an effective leader looks for opportunities to stretch and grow her people. She evaluates capabilities and understands the strengths and weaknesses of her team and the individuals who comprise it. She realizes that one of her primary roles is to challenge her people and develop their skills. She does this by looking for opportunities to engage her people in decision making or give individuals opportunities to lead efforts. She sometimes asks questions instead of giving answers; she sometimes lets a team member take a lead position and supports him, coaches him, and provides him with the resources to be successful.

If a leader does not encourage personal improvement, she limits the overall team and each individual's effectiveness and ability. Sometimes strong leaders can make the mistake of being the go-to-person for everything. When this happens, people believe that the leader wants absolute authority and they behave accordingly: they refuse to make decisions and will not accept responsibility or accountability.

When a leader understands that making people better is one of her key roles and embraces this challenge, she can truly have a significant impact on people's lives as well as on the business. When a leader coaches, trains, and enables people to grow and embrace challenges, she replicates her abilities and that of others. The organization and team become stronger and more efficient. Instead of one person leading, she now has many, with each person possessing the capability of leading and taking on challenges. A leader who behaves in this manner will create beliefs in others that they are valued. Others will believe that the leader is interested in the greater good of the team and its success and not her personal agenda alone. They will believe the leader is someone who can be trusted. When these are the beliefs about a leader, people seek her out for coaching and value her input and seek her wisdom.

In 2002, I sat in a conference room with Bob Cole who was at the time the executive director of Production of Lilly's Indianapolis bulk pharmaceutical manufacturing operations. Also present was Mark Owens who was the executive director of Global Facilities Delivery (GFD). Though Mark was my boss, Bob looked at me and said he had a problem and needed my help. He went on to explain that he was going to be receiving over half a billion dollars in new assets into his business unit in the next two years, and he wanted me to figure out how to get all the "right information" to his engineers, maintenance, and operations staff. He did not know exactly what all of this "right information" was or entailed.

A tremendous amount of data and documentation was being generated as a part of the capital project delivery process. He was asking us to define, organize, and document this data so that it would be readily available for his staff. He also wanted maintenance records established for each new asset. I sat there a bit dumbfounded because the task seemed overwhelming. The new facilities involved installing over fifty thousand new pieces of equipment into three separate facilities. We had never been asked to do this before and really had no starting point.

I was given authority to put a team together to address this issue. I immediately assembled a small group of individuals with a variety of backgrounds, including operations, maintenance, and capital project delivery. My job was to lead this effort and develop an adequate solution to meet Bob's needs. As a team, we needed to understand the problem, so I began by asking the group to explore what were the current practices across projects and operation areas that were receiving new assets delivered by GFD. What we found was chaos. No systemic process was being used from one project to the next. Each project operated independently regarding data and documentation requirements, expectations, and handling. The only common feature was that none of the GFD projects did this collection and assembly well.

We next talked to the engineering firms as well as the vendors from whom we had procured the new assets to understand how they collected and managed data and documentation. Our discovery was a bit overwhelming as we discovered that the engineering firms and vendors did not have adequate processes or systems for assuring completeness and accuracy of data and documentation.

Our problem became clear. We needed to build a new system that addressed not only internal Lilly processes but also the engineering firms' and vendors' processes.

Over the next several years, our team developed methods to collect, organize, and evaluate asset data and documentation. As we progressed, we experimented and developed tools. We spent hours working with project teams, including engineering firms and vendors. Our journey was difficult and incredibly challenging. Establishing systems in Lilly and with engineering companies and suppliers required a great deal of diligence and patience. Eventually, however, our understanding increased, and new systems were developed. Slowly data and documentation started to flow from all GFD projects in an organized manner. As this occurred, other groups began to realize that this collection was a rich source of accurate information associated with the project.

While the data and documentation accuracy was being improved, processes were also being developed for analyzing this information as well as developing maintenance strategies for the facilities. Our team identified contractors to develop maintenance plans and provide strategies to operations for thousands of new assets.

> A leader is best when people barely know he exists, when his work is done, his aim fulfilled, they will say: we did it ourselves
>
> *—Lao Tzu*

The technical details of this journey can wait for another day and another book. However, the people development that occurred is a vital part of the overall story. The team I put together collectively had experiences in maintenance, operations, and project delivery, but had essentially no experience outside the Indianapolis area. They were not engineers or business management experts. They did have rich, deep experience in the practical needs of site operations and the maintenance of facilities. They understood what people needed to do their jobs efficiently and effectively.

I gave these people the opportunity to grow in their job. I also made sure they had the support they needed while encouraging them to grab hold of opportunities and learn together. They not only learned but built systems and processes for how this could be done on all Lilly capital projects. They learned how to deal with engineers and vendors. They were continually stretched outside of their comfort zone. They worked with contractors to define expectations and create estimates and budgets for projects. Almost all their experiences were new and so were the skills they developed. During this entire time, I was coaching, teaching, and monitoring the team's progress. I made sure team members understood the objectives and that they did not lose focus. I monitored their progress and made corrections as needed. All the while, I continually worked through the staff as they grew and learned to perform this work independently around the world.

Today these individuals manage data and documentation worldwide in every country Lilly operates. Together they manage the information flow and maintenance plans for projects totaling over a billion dollars a year. These individuals routinely fly to sites and vendors in China, Italy, France, Germany, and Ireland as well as the United States. They walk into offices and set up and lead teams of people from different companies, nationalities, cultures, and experiences to assure the projects will deliver the right information.

Over the years, I have had few experiences that have brought me as much satisfaction as watching this group of people develop into not only highly skilled and capable individuals but also productive, successful leaders. None of them came into the job with international experience, yet today they have no reservations about engaging and leading very diverse teams in new cultures. They routinely lead people and develop effective teams around the world. They are also sought out by site staff groups and often pursued for their expertise and leadership. The breadth of this group's impact and ability to lead multiple projects across multiple continents is of significant value to Lilly.

Everybody Wins

Leaders produce results by working through people. An effective leader understands and ensures the team completes the task and the customer is satisfied. He makes sure the team finishes strong and that they pay appropriate attention to important details. The leader also resolves issues and removes obstacles for the group. He ensures that issues hindering team performance are addressed and resolved. He does this through his expertise and by engaging others in defining issues and coming up with appropriate solutions. Part of the results of an effective leader is that he makes people better. It is important that leaders develop people around them by applying the principle of replication that brings people to new levels of competency and capability. As a result, everyone is a winner, the team is successful, individuals grow in ability, and the leader has achieved the results through working with people and making them better. In short, the leader has guaranteed that everyone wins!

Leadership Takeaways

- Ultimately, the leader must be successful in leading a team or organization to produce meaningful and measurable results.

- Behaviors a leader should demonstrate for *Producing Results* include

  o Complete the task—finish strong

  o Resolve issues

  o Make people better

- Leaders act with conviction when confronted with a problem and seize the opportunity to possibly create the team's finest hour.

- Effective leaders often ask questions instead of giving answers.

- Leaders understand that making people better is one of their key roles and responsibilities, and embracing this challenge can truly have a significant impact on people's lives as well as on the business.

13

Become a Strategic Innovator

Good thinkers always prime the pump of ideas. They always look for things to get the thinking process started, because what you put in always impacts what comes out.

—John C. Maxwell

The fourth dimension of the Leadership Model may be somewhat less intuitive. Leaders need to develop the ability to manifest *Strategic Innovation*. This characteristic involves focused innovation that drives critical change. The change brought about by strategic innovation should bring new capability to the organization or bring a change in paradigm regarding the business. Leaders who can do this can anticipate the future. They can look at technology, enterprise, and world systems and understand cause-and-effect relationships. They grasp systems and "if this ..., then ... could happen" relationships. As a result, they can formulate models and make proposals to the organization for new approaches and methods. They can challenge existing paradigms with thoughtful, deliberate analysis and make offers to rethink previously held positions. This ability can allow leaders to anticipate events and take appropriate action to benefit from an opportunity or prevent problems from occurring.

How does a leader develop such skills? By implementing the following behaviors.

Learn the Business

Earlier I discussed the importance of leaders understanding systems and processes. When leaders commit to the enterprise and develop a detailed understanding of their team as well as business functions, roles, and responsibilities, they can identify opportunities for improvement. They can challenge paradigms from a knowledge perspective and engage team members in meaningful dialogue about current practices and approaches. Through this process, leaders develop an understanding of history and perspective regarding the business. The intent here is not to become the expert but rather to secure and engage in a level of understanding about the business so that leaders can identify improvement opportunities and paradigm shifts.

If a leader does not understand the business, she will have trouble engaging team members and facilitating potential paradigm shifts. In addition, she will struggle to identify or facilitate a change agenda for the team to drive systemic improvement. When a leader does not actually understand the business, then old practices continue with business as usual. This leads to missing opportunities for improvement. People can believe that the current methods are the optimum methods because their leader fails to challenge them. If this happens, people do not see their leader as a change agent, nor do they believe the business can or needs to be changed. The status quo is thereby maintained.

While asking great questions and demonstrating a real desire to learn, a leader develops a good understanding of the business. She creates a unique experience for the people she is leading. The team believes she is engaged, interested, and knowledgeable. As a result, conversations become deeper and probing can occur to challenge thinking and explore opportunities. This exploration also sets a tone for the team to understand the business and seek to understand the existing paradigms. Consequently, an entire team can become energized by the leader who endeavors to learn the business. This is nothing but positive for an organization.

In the early 1990s, Bob Cole was leading the Lilly Clinton Bulk Pharmaceutical Manufacturing group. The business challenges were enormous as Ceclor, the primary product manufactured in the facility, was the largest selling antibiotic in the world at the time. It was the gold standard for antibiotics, and it was broadly used by medical professionals throughout the world. The Clinton manufacturing site was continuously running at capacity. Lilly depended on this product as its number one selling product to generate the revenues needed for corporate growth, research, and development. The pressure was enormous to supply the market and never run short. As the leader of manufacturing, Bob became an ardent student of the production systems and processes being used. He clearly understood the technology and the roles of the scientists and engineers overseeing these daily. He also wanted to understand the underlying business practices, methods, and decision-making processes going on in his manufacturing area.

Bob applied system thinking to understand the business. He gathered people such as Dr. Bernard McGarvey, who was a passionate practitioner of Senge's principles of system thinking, to discuss and explore possibilities. This work led to a manufacturing model called the C4i Loop Map, which has been the operating principle throughout Lilly manufacturing sites for over twenty years.

The C4i Loop Map model provides clarity and understanding for the manner in which manufacturing should run the business, make decisions, and resource initiatives. This model brought clarity to every level of the organization and became a part of the corporate manufacturing culture for discussing priorities and making decisions. It represented a systems-thinking perspective and led people to consider other system interactions and dependencies. It also became a building block for many other significant system developments. All of this exploration and discovery started because Bob and others set out to learn the business.

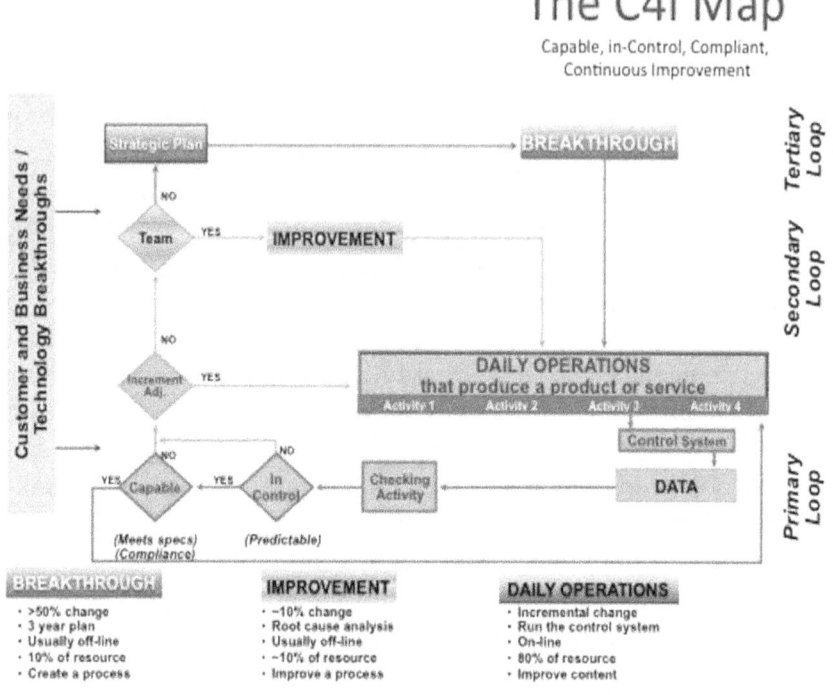

The C4I Map

Capable, in-Control, Compliant, Continuous Improvement

Dale Martlage was a director at Lilly's Clinton manufacturing facility in the late 1980s and early 1990s. To many, Dale's presence at Clinton seemed strange and even out of place. He was a trained architect and had previously been involved in the design and development of the Lilly Corporate Center, working closely with Richard Wood, CEO and president of Lilly, and other senior executives. At Clinton, Dale was responsible for several administrative functions but specifically oversaw the Performance Excellence Program (PEP), which was the precursor to the modern-day Six Sigma movement.

I had taken an assignment as a performance excellence facilitator, overseeing the role-out of the PEP across the large manufacturing facility. It was during this time that Dale and I developed a relationship and began having a number of unique conversations. Dale had an incredibly active mind that was constantly thirsting for understanding and exploring new concepts and ideas. He continually wanted to know why things were the way they were. He wanted to understand systems and relationships and read books, such as Peter Senge's *Fifth Discipline* as well as other books on the power of conversation.

Through our discussions, we identified a problem endemic to Lilly in nearly every level of the organization. Lilly had digressed into such a consensus-driven management style that the organization often appeared to move at the speed of a glacier when making decisions at

> Ideas are scary.
> They come into the world ugly and messy.
> Ideas are frightening because they threaten what is known.
> They are the natural born enemy of the way things are.
> Yes, ideas are scary and messy and fragile, but under the proper care they become something beautiful.
> —*GE Commercial*

virtually every level. The world was changing, and this method was ineffective and ultimately dangerous to the future if continued. We began exploring what experts had to say about how we fundamentally interact with each other and how cultures communicate. We discovered that sociologists and psychologists explained that all language functioned on a similar pattern of interaction in conversations. All conversations involve awareness of some topic or subject being given by one party to another, followed by questions or clarification of the information. Conversations then evolve to possibilities being generated by one or more individuals involved in the conversation. These possibilities are often characterized by statements such as "what if we ..." or "how about we ..." or "could we ..."—statements that transition the conversation into dealing with the awareness received. Finally, conversations move to action, which leads to some decision based on the awareness and possibilities generated. Studies had been done and validated that this is a pattern in human cultures across the world. Dale then asked, "What could this possibly mean for Lilly?"

As we looked carefully at Lilly's culture, we saw meetings and teams continually discussing and sharing awareness with each other but rarely taking action. At the time, it was common practice to have meetings to simply review what had been discussed at the previous meeting. This became maddening, and we decided to have a conversation around what could be done to change this cultural practice.

Dale worked with me to develop a methodology called Conversational Checkers to transform not only the way Lilly held meetings but also conducted business on a one-on-one basis. We developed key concepts and put tools together to train and facilitate conversations in a constructive manner to drive toward action and reduce the seemingly endless debate. Dale introduced the tools and concept to the Clinton Lead Team and proposed that site senior management try an experiment that used the tools for a set period of time. The proposal was to make a concentrated effort to apply the concepts of Conversational Checkers to their weekly team meetings. As the facilitator, I would primarily track conversations and provide timely feedback on how well participants followed the new methodology.

The experiment was eye-opening to the entire team as they began to realize how undisciplined their conversations and meetings had become. They quickly saw how their discussions rambled and topics were often left unresolved and then even abandoned after lengthy debates. People admitted leaving team meetings frustrated and having a sense of hopelessness. Slowly, though, the group began to apply the disciplines of the Conversational Checkers model. As they did, a transformation started to happen not only in team meetings but also in one-on-one conversations. People became more aware of what was going on in their conversations and how to move them forward. They consciously moved from awareness to possibilities and then to action.

As I tracked the discussions and provided feedback, it became readily apparent to all that we were making decisions and things were getting done. The team became much more conscious of a topic and deliberated around the intent of their discussions and, as a result, the Clinton Lead Team became much more efficient as a leadership team for the site.

Dale was leading this renovation of team dynamics and conversation. He saw a need and understood that change was needed, so he explored human conversation and culture. His creativity and ability to think differently about a problem led to the development of

Conversational Checkers and the subsequent dramatic improvement in Clinton Lead team performance. This was an excellent example of *Strategic Innovation* in which he made a new offer and shifted an entire paradigm of thinking by a group of people. Dale's ability to make this happen was linked to the confidence he had built with his supervision and his peers. He also effectively communicated the need and clearly described a proposed solution, Conversational Checkers—a new paradigm of conversation.

Be a Student of the World and Build Linkages

This may sound esoteric, but a leader who makes it a priority and passion to study the world can learn many things that are transferable to his business and team world. Senge emphasizes that the world is made up of complex systems, and we can learn from these interactions and relationships. A leader who wants to strengthen his ability to produce strategic innovation can learn much by studying others outside his immediate sphere. Leaders who do this often read voraciously, including books, magazines, and material found on the Internet. They put themselves into a position to be exposed to new thought patterns and ideas. This can be facilitated by going to conferences or seeking out conversations with interesting people who have different experiences and thought patterns about the world. Effective leaders value diversity of thought and perspective.

Leaders who are eager to learn from the world create alliances of learning that include finding others who are intrigued with exploring and understanding the world. For example, consider Dale Martlage and his work to develop Conversational Checkers. Dale built a relationship with Dr. Stan Marshal. Their relationship represented a bit of an odd couple. Dale was an architect by training and had worked in corporate engineering designing new buildings. He also had worked in administration at our Clinton manufacturing site in western Indiana. Stan Marshal, on the other hand, was a Distinguished Research Fellow at corporate Lilly, which was about as deep as a researcher could be in the Lilly Research organization. His life was about discovering new medicines, and he had been magnificent at that role throughout his very distinguished career, which included being listed as an inventor on over thirty-six patents. Together, Dale and Stan formed a dynamic relationship. For several years they engaged in conversations exploring organizational effectiveness and improvement opportunities. They were passionate about improving their organization and explored together what others had learned and published. They invited others to join them, and together they formulated the use of Conversation Checkers in both the worlds of research and manufacturing. Their relationship also led to other discussions and collaborations on improving organizational performance.

Regarding the importance and power of diversity, Dr. Carol Kinsey Goman of the Troy Media Corporation may have said it best:

> Experiments at the University of Michigan found that, when challenged with a difficult problem, groups composed of highly adept members performed worse than groups whose members had varying levels of skill and knowledge. The reason for this seemingly odd outcome has to do with the power of diverse thinking. Diversity causes people to consider perspectives and possibilities that would otherwise be ignored. Group members who think alike or are trained in similar disciplines with similar bases of knowledge run the risk of becoming insular in their ideas. Instead of exploring alternatives, a confirmation bias takes over and members tend to reinforce one another's predisposition. (Gorman, 2010)

When a leader understands and utilizes the power of diverse thinking, he unlocks the enormous potential for change. Exploring the world and using diverse experiences to build new linkages to the business can be a very effective manner for changing paradigms. It opens up the leader and his team to considering new possibilities. When a leader does this, he creates a bigger view of the world for his team and stretches them to re-examine past practices and methods and consider new alternatives. As a result, people working on a team come to believe the leader is broadening them and opening their minds to new ways of thinking. They recognize that the leader, and now the team, have the ability to connect previously unlinked ideas. Together, they discover new opportunities.

Dr. Kinsey also has made this very relevant point:

> Over the past 25 years, I've worked with a variety of very talented leaders, and one thing I know for sure: Regardless of how creative, smart and savvy a leader may be, he or she can't transform an organization, a department or a team without the brain power and commitment of others. Whether the change involves creating new products, services, processes—or a total reinvention of how the organization must look, operate, and position itself for the future—success dictates that the individuals impacted by change be involved in the change from the very beginning. (Gorman, 2010)

Feed the Creative Mind

He once said that had he not been a scientist, he would have been a musician. "Life without playing music is inconceivable for me," he declared. "I live my daydreams in music. I see my life in terms of

> Children astound me with their inquisitive minds. The world is wide and mysterious to them, and as they piece together the puzzle of life, they ask 'Why?' ceaselessly.
> —*John C. Maxwell*

music. ... I get most joy in life out of music." These were the words of the brilliant scientist Albert Einstein, who played the violin throughout his life. Music was not only a relaxation to Einstein; it also helped him in his work. His second wife, Elsa, gives a rare glimpse of their home life in Berlin. "As a little girl, I fell in love with Albert because he played Mozart so beautifully on the violin," she once wrote. "He also plays the piano. Music helps him when he is thinking about his theories.

He goes to his study, comes back, strikes a few chords on the piano, jot's something down, and returns to his study." (Pais, 1982)

The creative brain is not always as quickly associated with scientists or engineers as it is more commonly associated with artists, actors, and musicians. However, creativity comes from all types of people and often surprises us when an idea suddenly appears and sprouts in our mind. Often these ideas are stimulated by something experienced, observed, read, or a conversation we have with someone. An idea's birth could come from something as inconsequential as a sound or smell that triggers a thought and creates a linkage to another thought. An idea is generated. These ideas take hold of us, and we often incubate them for a period. We play with the idea, rolling it over, looking at it from different angles and perspectives in our mind. We eventually build mental models or theories from the idea. We often test the idea with others and tear it down. We then rebuild it based on input from others, new ideas, and empirical data found or generated. Eventually, we take action to turn the idea into reality. There are a number of models of creativity, but all have this basic fundamental embedded process.

The steps of stimulating an idea are fascinating and exciting. From the description above, it appears that many things, including all our five senses, can stimulate an idea. However, what is going on in our thought process that causes our brain to connect concepts and link them together with a thought that eventually can give birth to an idea?

A number of years ago, I was working with Dale Martlage on this problem, and we coined a term for it: *slippage*. By *slippage*, we do not mean to imply that one's mind slips out of gear. Rather, we use the term to describe thought processes that lead to the generation of an idea.

Think of your knowledge base. Each person has experiences and knowledge that he or she has gained throughout life. These experiences and knowledge are unique to every individual, yet we all have some level of common beliefs and knowledge. For example, we all come to an early understanding as a child that fire will burn and cause severe pain. On the other hand, as we interact with people of more diverse backgrounds, our variation in experiences and knowledge become greater. When I worked in China, I came to realize that my set of experiences and knowledge were quite different from many of my Chinese colleagues. My experiences and knowledge were neither good nor bad but different from the Chinese on particular topics. As an example, my experience has been that road signs and traffic signals were to be absolutely obeyed, while my Chinese colleagues' experience has been that they are mere suggestions and are generally optional to the driver. Our separate experiences led to different beliefs about road signs, and, as a consequence, we manifested different behaviors in our driving habits.

In the concept of slippage, each individual has a wide variety of experiences and knowledge on a vast array of topics. Visually you might think of each subject in the brain as a three-dimensional plane with an XY plane and a vertical Z plane. The size of the XY plane represents the breadth of knowledge and experience with a given topic. The depth of the plane, the Z axis, represents the depth of knowledge and expertise on the topic. So, a person could have a relatively broad understanding of a theme, represented by a large XY plane, but not in-depth knowledge and expertise of the topic. Everyone's experience is unique for each subject. For example: if someone says the word *boat*, because of my experience of growing up in the Midwest and limited knowledge of boats, I would possibly visualize a small speed boat or row boat. However, another person hearing the same word might visualize a cruise liner because she has been on one or more cruises. She may be able to describe in great depth the workings of a particular cruise ship she was on and how it functioned and all the amenities that were available to guests. And all this was generated from one word, *boat*. We both have a concept of a boat, but the breadth and depth each of us has are quite different.

As people interact together, we find we have different experiences and knowledge from one another. Our sights, sounds, and experiences through life are all laid down upon these planes of experience and knowledge. These planes provide context to our life and inform our interpretation of the events around us as well as the information we receive. Occasionally, an experience occurs that is so new and so different that we have no context for interpreting it. This can lead to confusion, but it also generates wonder and drives us to look for answers. These moments can stimulate creativity.

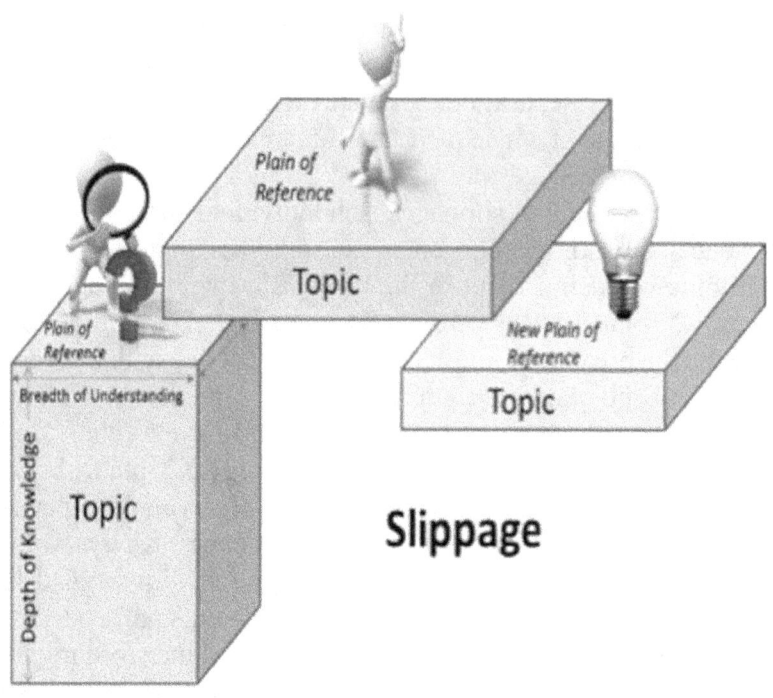

Another situation that occurs is similar to our boat example. People begin to talk about a problem or an opportunity with each having a different context in the form of experience and knowledge. We often think that the deepest knowledge base for a specific subject is the most important perspective. However, it can often be someone with less depth of knowledge on one topic but broad understanding and/or depth of another seemingly unrelated topic who is able to bring linkages and relevance and ultimately increase knowledge and understanding. Broader understanding sometimes produces breakthroughs, and whole new ideas are generated.

The following is a real-life example of the slippage phenomena.

Everyone knows what Post-it notes are: They are those great little self-stick notepapers. Most people have Post-it Notes. Most people use them. Most people love them. But Post-it Notes were not a planned product.

No one got the idea and then stayed up nights to invent it. A man named Spencer Silver was working in the 3M research laboratories in 1970 trying to find a strong adhesive. Silver developed a new adhesive, but it was even weaker than what 3M already manufactured. It stuck to objects, but could easily be lifted off. It was super weak instead of super strong.

No one knew what to do with the stuff, but Silver didn't discard it. Then one Sunday four years later, another 3M scientist named Arthur Fry was singing in the church choir. He used markers to keep his place in the hymnal, but they kept falling out of the book. Remembering Silver's adhesive, Fry used some to coat his markers. Success! With the weak adhesive, the markers stayed in place, yet lifted off without damaging the pages. 3M began distributing Post-it Notes nationwide in 1980—ten years after Silver developed the super weak adhesive. Today they are one of the most popular office products available. (The Great Idea Finder, 2006)

Spencer Silver had a paradigm regarding a good adhesive. This paradigm was based on his vast knowledge and experience in creating adhesives. His plain of reference for adhesives was both extensive and deep as related to our Slippage model.

Arthur Fry may have had as equally in-depth knowledge as Spencer Silver regarding adhesives, but his breadth of understanding the need for adhesives was different from Silver's. Silver's experience had been that good adhesives are required to bond things together so they cannot be separated. Thus, his frame of reference was to pursue very strong bonds that were inherently impossible or very difficult to break. There was nothing wrong with this plane of understanding and experience. It was simply his frame of reference. Arthur Fry, on the other hand, had another frame of reference and understanding. He understood the need for temporary adhesion and the ability to adhere objects gently and temporarily together. The perspective was a paradigm shift regarding the use and purpose of adhesives. It took Fry recognizing this opportunity because his plane of understanding and experience was different than Silver's. Fry was able to build the link between Spencer's failed adhesive and the value of a weak adhesive. Classic slippage, as we call it. Like tectonic plates shifting across each other, a linkage was built between ideas and frames of reference. This shift occurred in such a manner that an entirely new idea was birthed to meet a need that one of the individuals didn't realize existed. This is creativity.

A leader can feed the creative mind in a number of ways. She may read classic works of literature, take up painting, attend theaters, or take cooking lessons. The possibilities are limitless, but broadening your perspective and knowledge through exposure is enlightening.

Several years ago, my family took me to a business known as Wine & Canvas. Each night, typically forty to sixty people come to Wine & Canvas and learn to paint under the tutelage of a professional artist. The artist is at the front of the room and leads everyone through painting a picture. I had never painted before, but I immediately became enthralled with the process. The instructor guided us through the layout of the painting to assure proper proportion and placement of objects. She next taught us brush strokes and how to mix colors. She then progressed to teaching us about layers, and showed us how to work with the painting by applying layers of paint and color to create various effects and texture. Art suddenly became a more understandable process that was not just reliant on some "mystical" special skill that some have while others don't. It became something I could participate in and enjoy. Over time, my paradigm shifted, and I had a new frame of reference about painting. I now look at artwork differently. Not only do I enjoy the subject matter, but I now look for subtle signs of the artist's techniques for creating certain effects.

This experience directly supports Peter Senge's premise that the whole world is made up of complex systems that interact. As a leader, the more we develop understanding of these systems and broaden our planes of understanding and knowledge, the more we can then make linkages between what may appear on the surface to be unrelated domains. Arthur Fry certainly did this when he connected the domain of an apparently failed adhesive with the domain of church music. The result was the birth of a whole new product by 3M—Post-it-Notes.

Possibly no man in history more epitomizes this concept of feeding the creative mind than Leonardo da Vinci, the ultimate Renaissance man. Leonardo was a writer, sculptor, inventor, painter, architect, mathematician, engineer, musician, anatomist, geologist, cartographer, and botanist. All historical accounts regarding Leonardo indicate that he embraced all these fields with zeal and determination to learn, understand, and master them. He has been described by Helen Gardner in *Art through the Ages* as a man of "unquenchable curiosity" and "feverishly inventive imagination." She goes on to say that the scope and depth of his interests were without precedent and "his mind and personality seem to us superhuman, the man himself mysterious and remote" (Gardner, 2010). Marco Rosci (Marco, 1977) states that "while there is much speculation about Leonardo, his vision of the world is essentially logical rather than mysterious, and that the empirical methods he employed were unusual for his time." Leonardo blended all his interests and used his understanding of human anatomy to make him a better painter and sculptor. He used his knowledge of art to influence architecture and his interest in engineering and mathematics to invent.

Maybe we are not destined to be the next Leonardo, but by feeding the creative mind, we broaden our understanding and experience new planes of reference. By broadening our understanding, we open up possibilities we may have not seen before. We then can create links to new ideas and concepts that, in turn, stimulate more creative thought. When people work with a leader who does this, they draw energy from his enthusiasm to learn. They believe he has insight and perspective that can help them be successful. They seek out this type of leader and engage with him in driving change. Simply said, they see the leader as a change agent.

Dream and Continue Being Awed

Previously I talked about the importance of learning the business and opening up possibilities by being a student of the world and learning how to build linkages. I also looked at feeding the creative mind with the intent that all these work together to unlock the power of *Strategic Innovation* in leaders. While some of these behaviors may have seemed a bit esoteric, this final behavior may seem even more mysterious or bizarre. In my view, the effective leader needs to *dream and continue being awed.*

> When a person starts to talk about their dreams, it's as if something bubbles up from within. Their eyes brighten, their face glows, and you can feel the excitement in their words.
> —*John C. Maxwell*

I will always remember taking my six-year-old daughter, Lauren, to Disney World for the first time. When we walked into the Magic Kingdom for the very first time, she froze, pointed, and said, "Mommy, there's Cinderella!" She was in awe. To me, one of the most exciting things to see in a child is that sense of awe when he or she experiences something for the first time. For some children, this awe can ignite something deep inside that can change their destiny, even birth a dream. Many scientists, engineers, astronauts, actors, and writers can point to some distinct moment that changed their life—a time of awe at a new discovery or awareness. It may have been looking through a microscope for the first time and discovering the vast world of the microbe or sitting in a planetarium for the first time as the lights are lowered and the ceiling becomes transformed into millions of stars. It may have been triggered by the reading of a classic piece of literature or floating above the earth in an airplane. Such events triggered wonder and awe and ultimately led to new possibilities. People began to dream of what could be.

The leader who wants to be a *Strategic Innovator* needs to continue being awed and having dreams. If you are not captivated by anything anymore—if you don't have times of wonder—then you may be bored. I believe that we often stop being awed because we stop asking questions. We quit being inquisitive as to why things are the way they are. We become complacent and accept the status quo. We do not explore new frontiers; we do not want to pursue new knowledge and understanding. We become satisfied with our current plane of reference and perspective. The danger with not being awed anymore is that we can stop growing intellectually, emotionally, and spiritually. We stop having dreams.

Individuals who seek awe are continually looking for new things and new discoveries in life. They have passion. They are not satisfied to simply let the world go by but continue to ask questions, discover, and be surprised. Earlier we discussed the importance of being a student of the world and building linkages. As we become a student, we open up ourselves to wonder as we experience new cultures, new ideas, new challenges, and new paradigms.

In *Emotion* magazine, psychologists Griskevicius, Shiota, and Neufeld wrote an article entitled "Influence of Different Positive Emotions on Persuasion Processing: a Functional Evolutionary Approach." In it they wrote, "awe, unlike most other positive emotions, has been shown to increase systematic processing, rather than heuristic processing, leading participants who experience awe to become less susceptible to weak arguments." In other words, awe actually enables and fosters system thinking while also providing an obstacle to poor reasoning. (Griskevicius, Shiota, & Neufeld, 2010) That's quite a benefit.

When a leader allows herself to be awed, she creates significant experiences for her team and other colleagues. Those she leads as well as other co-workers will often experience her probing questions as she seeks to understand. They may even have her ask them to consider unusual ideas or approaches. This type of experience can create energy as the leader and team collaborate to discover a new understanding and generate new ideas. This kind of dialogue and emphasis on discovery can create moments of wonder where the leader and team step back together and take in a new idea or discovery and let the potential ramifications sink into their psyche. This can even lead to a new vision for the entire organization.

> Without leaps of imagination, or dreaming, we lose the excitement of possibilities. Dreaming, after all, is a form of planning.
>
> —*Gloria Steinem*

It may be uncommon for a CEO to tell her board that she has a dream, but many CEOs have laid out visions that may have been born from a dream. Unfortunately, other leaders have put out an annual mundane offering of "do the same" with minimal to no breakthrough potential for their organization. However, one of the best examples I have seen of sharing a dream has been that of Jeff Simons, president of Elanco, Lilly's Animal Health Division.

In the spring of 2014, Jeff Simmons walked on to the stage at Lilly Corporate Center and sat down on a box in front of several hundred Lilly associates at Lilly's first TEDx event. Several hundred more employees watched around the world on closed-circuit TV as Jeff began telling a story. He described in detail the scene of him sitting in a hut in a burrow outside Nairobi, Kenya. There he listened to a man named Wilson describe his shame of failing to provide food and care for his family and dealing with the impact of malnutrition and disease on himself and his family. Lying on a bed, behind a white linen cloth, Jeff could hear the heavy breathing of the man's teenage daughter who was fighting for her life—a victim of disease brought on by malnutrition. Jeff said he felt overwhelmed by the scene and realized the young girl was essentially the same age as one of his daughters back in Indianapolis. He explained to the audience that he had made a commitment. "If hunger was going to be my cause and our company's cause, then I must go see some of the twenty-five thousand who die every day from hunger. The experience was horrific; it was life-changing."

He then took us in his story to a home four blocks to the east from the Lilly Corporate Center. He told us how he sat at a table with a single mom and listened to her tell of her struggles to put proper food on the table for her family. She described the internal turmoil of knowing that she was often sending her ten-year-old daughter to school hungry. She was unable to give her proper foods to meet her nutritional needs. Through tears she said to him, "the worst part of the day is when she walks down that sidewalk to go to school, and I know she will not do well."

Jeff then shared his awe moment with those of us in the auditorium and hundreds of others sitting in conference rooms worldwide. "As I walked to the car in my hunt to understand kids and hunger, I found another parent's shame, but I also found my hunger. I sat in the front seat of my car, and I couldn't start the car. I just sat there. I closed my eyes, and what overcame me was that hunger is not a cause, it is not a Power Point slide, it is not just a disease—it is wrong!" With a crowd across the world watching and listening mesmerized, he went on, "If I am going to do one part in my story, it is that I am going to do everything in my power to make this wrong right! Because some mother living four blocks from here is not going to send her child to school feeling that way!"

Jeff then changed direction and talked about another kind of hunger. He asked a critical soul-searching question: "What makes you hungry?"

He went on. "Hungry people live different lives. Hungry people have freedom and contentment in their souls. They don't care about political correctness; they don't care about Power Point slides or meetings or calendars, and they don't worry about work-life balance. Those lines get blurred because they are living life like they never lived it before. They are living life like it was meant to be lived, and the vision doesn't come from the website or the walls of this company. The vision is so in their heart that they are restless until it is achieved, and it's crystal clear to them."

Jeff spoke from his heart that day, challenging the audience to pursue their hunger. He talked about how "hungry people's productivity is way beyond the norm, and their stamina is way beyond the norm, and their influence and creativity are way beyond the norm, and it has never been easier for them." He continued, "We need hungry people in this company!"

He talked about how the Elanco organization has undergone a transformation and the employees have taken on the "movement"

(Jeff's words used to describe it) that they call ENOUGH: The Fight for a Food-Secure Tomorrow. For over sixty years, Elanco has been successful selling products globally to commercial animal health businesses. The products have helped fight disease primarily in poultry, swine, and cattle operations and most recently in companion animals also. The business has been steadily successful. However, over the last eight years, the employees of Elanco have discovered that their hunger is to fight hunger in the world. Employees see themselves as part of something bigger than just producing a product to make a profit. Of course, profit is important, but to be part of a movement means being part of something bigger than the individual. Employees now speak of a greater mission and purpose. They speak of being part of a movement—a movement that can change the world!

> Innovation distinguishes between a leader and a follower.
>
> *—Steve Jobs*

These were not the typical words of a CEO or president of a company. Nothing was said about operating expenses, sales numbers, or net income. People in the auditorium sat listening transfixed on Jeff Simmons that day. They followed him through his story and, at the conclusion, rose to their feet in unison in thunderous applause. Yes, they were inspired, but in talking to people after the meeting, the common thought was that they wanted a leader who spoke of new possibilities, who spoke of a dream, who challenged others to join them in changing the world—and Jeff had met that desire.

Jeff manifested *Strategic Innovation* by studying the world around him and allowing himself to be awed by the overwhelming reality of hunger in the world. This wrong gave birth to a dream. The idea was birthed that Elanco was about more than just making animal health products, but it was also a crucial part of a much greater fight to eradicate hunger in the world by securing a sustainable supply of meat, milk, and eggs.

When a leader like Jeff Simmons manifests *Strategic Innovation*, he will be seen as a change agent, and others will seek him out for his perspectives, wisdom, and engagement. People want leaders who can drive change, and people will follow leaders who can clearly articulate a vision and want to engage them to help achieve that vision. Jeff Simmons is this type of leader. And the impact of this kind of leadership can be seen in the results. In the last several years, Elanco business has gone from a perennially $500 million to $600 million a year business to sales well over $3 billion in 2017. Sales at Elanco have more than tripled, and growth of Elanco has been three times greater than the rest of the animal health industry. In 2014, Elanco agreed to acquire Novartis Animal Health, making Elanco the second largest animal health company in the world.

Recently one of my colleagues who had transferred to the Elanco Division a couple of years ago shared his feelings openly. "Before I transferred into Elanco," he said, "I was planning on retiring in a year or two. Now I am so energized and excited by the organization and what we are about, I may work another seven to ten years." When leadership effectively shares a dream and creates a picture of a potential new reality, people become engaged, motivated, and refreshed. People see new possibilities and opportunities to be part of something very special and maybe even world changing.

> There are those who look at things the way they are, and ask why. ... I dream of things that never were, and ask why not?
>
> —*Robert Kennedy*

Looking Back

A wrap-up is in order. We covered a good deal of ground in this chapter. We delved further into the concept of *Strategic Innovation* and the importance of a leader who is able to lead change effectively. A leader can strengthen his own abilities in this area by assuring he has a solid understanding of the business he leads. He can do this by asking questions and probing with his team to understand the history, practices, methods, and thinking inherent within the organization. From a basis of understanding, the leader can begin to challenge the organization to consider new possibilities. While doing this, the leader can expand his plane of reference by becoming a student of the world. Becoming a student requires being inquisitive, asking questions, networking, listening, and discovering the world around him and often outside of his norm. Jeff Simmons did this when he traveled to Africa to sit in a hut with a father. Leaders also need to feed their creative mind by exposing themselves to new experiences that are sometimes completely outside of their comfort zone or skill set. They look for new ways of stimulating their thinking. As they expand their understanding of the world, they open up themselves to new discoveries. These discoveries lead to awe moments where their paradigms may be challenged or their current knowledge transformed. These experiences give seed to dreams, and dreams become the shining light on a hilltop that provide direction for creating a new reality that could change the world. When leaders do this, people see them as change agents and will follow them.

Leadership Takeaways

- Leaders who manifest *Strategic Innovation* understand systems and "if this …, then … could happen" relationships.

- Changes brought about by *Strategic Innovation* should bring new capabilities to the organization or bring a change in paradigm regarding the business.

- Behaviors to strengthen *Strategic Innovation* skills include:
  - Learn the business.
  - Be a student of the world and build linkages.
  - Feed the creative mind.
  - Dream and continue being awed.

- When leaders broaden their understanding, they open up new possibilities for themselves, their teams, their other colleagues, and their organizations as a whole.

14

Destructive Behaviors to Avoid

People may hear your words, but they feel your attitude.

—John C. Maxwell

Throughout this section, I have focused on leadership behaviors that can create the right results and experiences for others. These behaviors ultimately build confidence and credibility in the leader as well as reinforce the leader's command and respect by others. These actions also ultimately help the leader achieve the desired results by mentoring people to achieve success. Moreover, these behaviors constitute the very essence of a change agent. I must, though, briefly address the "dark side" of leadership behavior.

In our Behavior Model, we established that behaviors create results and both behaviors and results create experiences for other people that lead to the formulation of beliefs. When a leader behaves "badly," she creates experiences for others that formulate beliefs. These beliefs can often be negative or destructive to the team. Moreover, as our Behavior Model suggests, beliefs lead to behaviors, and consequently we may get behaviors by team members that are not conducive to success. Often leadership's reaction is to blame team members for their negative or ineffective actions. Leaders can begin a downward spiral when they tell team members that "the beatings will continue until morale improves," or something to that effect. By creating more negative experiences for the team, the beliefs of the organization can become more hardened or negative. The team's behavior may even become less effective and less successful.

The Behavior Model is simply the description of a human interaction system that involves reinforcing loops of behaviors. Behaviors create results and subsequent experiences for others. These new experinces lead to new or reinforced beliefs. These beliefs then lead to behaviors that create positive or negative experiences for others, and the loop continues.

So, what are some *negative* behaviors for leaders, and what are their potential consequences? Fundamentally, the leader must constantly be conscious of the impact her behaviors are having on the team and other individuals they impact. For illustrative purposes only, the following is a short list of behaviors a leader should avoid. I have grouped them into themes: *The Victim, The De-Valuer,* and *The Quitter.*

What Not to Do

The Victim

Some leaders adopt a victim mentality. They see negative feedback and results, failures, and all else that goes wrong as something happening to them. They view themselves as victims, seeing all that's turned out poorly as going against their best intentions and actions.

Leaders must avoid acting as victims. A victim attitude can result in feelings of powerlessness, incapability, and inevitable doom. Leaders must never be seen as adopting a victim mentality because it will not only minimize their effectiveness but translate to their entire organization. It is quite ugly when an entire organization adopts this mentality. The culture becomes poisoned, and people tend to readily point fingers of blame and complain about what has been done to them. Ultimately, productivity and effectiveness suffer. To avoid acting as victims, leaders should avoid the following behaviors. I call them the "Don'ts":

- Don't blame others—look for solutions!

- Don't whine—it just makes you look weak!

- Don't make excuses—accept responsibility!

- Don't pass the buck—own it!

The De-Valuer

The leader who is late with fulfilling commitments or always late showing up at meetings devalues people and their time. He sends a clear message that he and his time are more important. And if such leaders take credit from others, they destroy trust.

So, if leaders want to avoid acting as de-valuers, they should avoid these behaviors:

- Don't be continually late—be prompt!

- Don't over commit and under deliver—fulfill commitments!

- Don't take credit from others—celebrate success!

The Quitter

The leader who acts as the quitter gives up and accepts the status quo. He stops trying to grow personally and succumbs to the routine.

To avoid becoming a quitter, leaders need to do the following:

- Don't be content and merely accept the status quo!

- Don't stop learning and growing!

- Don't become bored and unengaged!

- Don't yield to routine and become robotic!

- Don't give up no matter what!

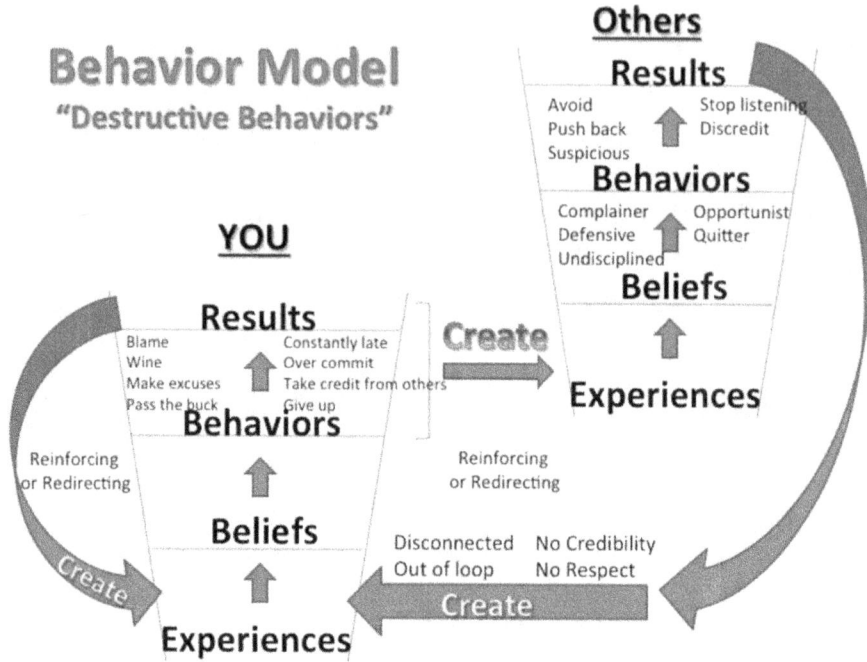

Probing Further

Let's examine just a few of these negative behaviors to understand their potential impact on others and the corresponding beliefs and behaviors they could create.

A destructive leader can fall into the habit of continually pointing fingers, making excuses, blaming others, or being unaccountable. Through this experience, her team may believe she is a complainer. They also may believe the leader is quick to pass the buck or throw someone under the bus. As a result, team members may become cautious when working with her. They may avoid her or withhold information. Trust erodes.

Leaders must understand that the team is not the only group observing their behavior. Upper management is paying attention too!

Consider also that a leader who constantly makes excuses or blames others creates this type of culture on his team. People will often begin to act as the leader does. They too will start making excuses and blaming others. Before long the entire team has created a poor reputation for itself.

I have worked around organizations filled with blamers and excuse-makers. I have found that this type of negative culture is always influenced by leadership. Organizations suffering from this condition were very difficult to work with, and I often made efforts to minimize interaction with them or avoid establishing any dependency on them.

Organizations filled with this type of culture can also hinder their company's growth potential in a number of ways. One way is by pushing other companies or investors away. Others simply don't want to deal with this negative cultural behavior. They perceive that it simply isn't worth their effort to interact with such an organization. I have sat in numerous meetings where decisions were made to not sign contracts with companies for their sevices or goods simply because of their negative culture. It was decided that it was simply too difficult to work with them. It is my opinion that many, if not most, leaders do not appreciate or understand the impact of their company's culture on sales and other opportunities.

Another impact of a negative culture is on recruiting of new talent. Candidates can pick up on the vibe in an organization by listening and asking the right questions. Few people, no matter how good the job appears, want to enter a poisonous negative culture.

Another negative behavior by a leader is to be constantly late not only in attendance but in fulfilling commitments. Things happen, and a leader may have to reschedule a meeting or renegotiate the timing of fulfilling a commitment. However, each time this happens, such leaders make a withdrawal from their people's emotional bank account. When this becomes a pattern, people begin to develop beliefs about their leader. These beliefs can be that he does not value them or their time. People can also come to believe that he considers himself and his agenda more relevant than theirs. Even worse, the team can come to believe the leader is simply not interested in them.

A variety of behaviors can result from these beliefs, including avoidance of the leader and disengagement. Communication can dry up between the team and the leader. The leader stops getting updates and becomes disconnected from the team. When this happens, the team and senior management lose confidence in the leader. This all results in a steady decay in the leader's credibility and respect.

An individual I'll call Bill was a colleague of mine many years ago. He was a very passionate leader who threw himself into his work. Unfortunately, he regularly failed to meet commitments to his team and his management team. He was consistently late to meetings and often arrived disheveled and out of breath. He was passionate, but he developed a persona around himself. The belief by his team and management was that Bill was disorganized and could not prioritize himself, let alone his team. This belief resulted in his being pigeon-holed in a position for many years and finally in his removal from leadership responsibilities. The unfortunate thing was that Bill was an extremely bright individual who had many excellent insights and ideas. However, the persona regarding him became the overriding pervasive view, and he never understood it or took action to change it.

Let's look at one last example of negative behavior by a leader. If a leader "retires in-place," they create incredibly negative experiences for a team. Retiring in-place includes becoming content with the status quo, ceasing to learn, acting bored, and just going through the routine day in and day out. It can signal surrender and succuming to the struggle. Now granted, we have all dealt with times of frustration, maybe even to the point of wanting to throw in the towel and quit. However, the behavior I am talking about is a consistent behaviorial pattern that represents complacency, surrender, or satisfaction with the way things are.

This type of behavior can have numerous adverse impacts on a team. One negative effect is that it may create a false sense of security. People may believe that everything is satisfactory when it is actually far from it. The team can think they are performing optimally while disregarding continuous improvement. This can stop the team's growth and can breed complacency. The team can begin to act like the guys in a buggy whip factory who are very proud of the quality of their buggy whips but have not noticed that very few people buy buggy whips anymore. One day they wake up, and they are completely out of business. Leaders must continually push themselves and their teams to be better.

Leaders must work constantly to keep their team engaged and not overwhelmed by situations or problems. If the leader gives any sign of hopelessness or giving up, morale can be destroyed and the team's energy, effort, and focus can be quickly lost. If this happens, people regress into survival mode and become consumed with their own situation.

Earlier we shared the dialogue from the movie *Apollo 13* in which Gene Kranz emphatically tells his staff of engineers, "People, let's work the problem!" As a leader, he kept his people focused and never gave any indication that he as their flight control leader had given-up and considered the situation hopeless.

Another example comes from *Star Trek*. I am thinking of the Kobayashi Maru. If you are a "Trekky," you will most likely know the story of the Kobayashi Maru. It is legendary in the *Star Trek* film series and was talked about throughout various episodes. While the series is science fiction, the situation speaks to leadership. Screenwriter Jack B. Sowards created the Kobayashi Maru to be a training test for young Star Fleet cadets at the Star Fleet Academy. The test occurred in a simulator, which was an exact replica of a starship command bridge. The simulation involves a scenario in which a distress signal is received from a space ship called the Kobayashi Maru. The ship is in the Klingon Neutral Zone (for non-*Star Trek* fans, the Klingons are the bad guys). The ship is rapidly losing power, hull integrity, and life support. With no other help nearby, the cadet acting as the ship commander in the simulation is faced with a decision: he can attempt rescue and potentially provoke an all-out war, or he can abandon the Kobayashi Maru and prevent war but leave its crew to die. If the cadet chooses to rescue the crew, the simulation progresses quickly. The cadet is notified by the bridge officers that they are in violation of the treaty. As the ship enters the Neutral Zone, Klingon starships appear quickly to intercept. Attempts to contact the Klingon ships are met with only radio silence. Then the Klingon's open fire on the Star Fleet ship, destroying it and its entire crew, including the cadet. It is, of course, only a simulation, and no one actually dies, but the primary objective of the simulation is to put a cadet in a no-win scenario to assess his or her response to failure and death.

The primary character in many of the *Star Trek* films is Captain James T. Kirk. He has the reputation of being the only cadet to have ever successfully beaten the Kobayashi Maru simulation and rescue the ship. It turns out that Kirk admits in the film *Star Trek II: The Wrath of Kahn* that he beat the no-win scenario by reprogramming the simulation so that it was possible to rescue the stranded ship and crew. Despite having cheated, Kirk was awarded a commendation for "original thinking." In justifying his action, Kirk declares to a colleague, "I don't believe in the no-win scenario" (Sowards, 1982).

Today's leaders should not give-up, because if they do, the team often follows and acquiesces to the inevitable based on the leaders' behavior. Leaders, like the fictional Kirk, may want to consider the Kobayashi Maru scenario. Rather than giving in to what appears to be inevitable, try redefining the rules when playing with a rigged game. Leaders often need to redefine the problem and step outside of conventional thinking to help their team be successful. The situation may appear to be a no-win scenario, but it need not stay that way. Leaders can change their thinking and work the problem, which may require redefining the problem or doing the unorthodox.

I have touched on only a few examples of negative behaviors by leaders. These and others should be consciously avoided because, as we have seen, experiences and subsequent beliefs created by negative behaviors will resonate throughout the team and perhaps even the entire organization. Wise leaders continually ask, *What kind of experiences am I creating for others around me?* Moreover, *Will these foster the beliefs and subsequent behaviors I want to create in my team?*

Leadership Takeaways

- When leaders behave badly, they create experiences for others that often formulate negative beliefs.

- Behaviors every leader should avoid include becoming …

  o The Victim

  o The De-Valuer

  o The Quitter

- Wise leaders continually ask, What kind of experiences am I creating for others around me?

Part 5

The Essential Character Traits

15

Trust

The first job of any leader is to inspire trust. Trust is confidence born of two dimensions: character and competence

—*Stephen M. R. Covey*

In the parts of the Leadership Model covered so far, I have described fundamental values that are critical for success. These have been important values of the Lilly culture for many years and were handed down from the Lilly family. They are part of the Lilly ethos. I have also explained the dimensions of leadership and the importance for a leader *Creating Confidence* among a host of people, including management, peers, and staff. I have described how credibility leads to confidence: if someone has confidence in another individual, he or she believes that person can be trusted.

I then talked about the dimension of *Demonstrated Command*, which establishes the need for leaders to develop an inherent understanding and level of mastery of the business they have responsibility for leading. A good leader puts in place systems and measures to assure the enterprise is in-control and functioning appropriately. When a leader demonstrates command of a particular area, he or she is respected.

Next, I discussed the absolute importance of a leader ultimately *Producing Results.* The leader must engage and enable his or her people to be successful. This means providing direction, resources, and coaching. The leader works through people by elevating them to even higher levels of performance and capability than previously exhibited. In doing this, leaders make people better and create a mechanism for sustainable results. As a result, people see their leader as an achiever—someone who can assure the team assures the desired outcomes.

Finally, I unpacked the dimension of *Strategic Innovation*, in which we considered the importance of a leader anticipating change and future needs. I emphasized the importance of bringing forward new offers to the organization and creating new possibilities. Ultimately, the leader may shift the entire paradigm of an organization. When a leader does this, she is seen as a change agent.

I followed up the dimensions discussion with a look at how a leader's behaviors impact her team. I introduced the Behavior Model from the OZ Principle that provided a context for the discussion around specific leadership behaviors. I used the Behavior Model to explain how leaders create experiences and impact their team and others. Leadership creates beliefs in the organization, which ultimately characterizes the culture.

As we have explored these areas, I hope it has become evident that all of the dimensions and behaviors in the Leadership Model are mutually supporting and have a significant impact on one another. Take, as an example, the incredible confidence and subsequent credibility that Pete Vanevenhoven created with his team and upper management. This trust was firmly linked to the results he had achieved throughout his storied career. These combined to support his offerings of new products and paradigm shifts as a strategic innovator. If Pete had not produced results consistently and created the confidence of peers and upper management, he would have had a very difficult time obtaining buy-in and support for some of his new ideas and proposals.

Also consider Bob Cole's demonstration of command and control of his manufacturing areas and how it impacted the confidence people had in him. Bob's long record of producing sustainable results for multiple organizations positively impacted their confidence. Their confidence led them to follow him when he was given the nearly impossible task for rebuilding the K105 parenteral manufacturing building.

All the dimensions of leadership work together and collectively define a leader.

There are still, however, some fundamental *Essential Characa-ter Traits* that are critical for leadership success. These traits are part of the fabric and makeup of an individual. They define and give dimension to our personal character. These traits govern our thinking, our perspective, and our reaction to events and situations. They are driven by deeply inherent beliefs that we have developed through a variety of experiences in our lives. The foundations of these beliefs are usually laid by parents, family, and other key figures, such as pastors, counselors, teachers, and coaches. Ultimately, these beliefs mold certain characer traits that manifest in behaviors. However, leaders must be aware that the influence of stress and outside forces can cause them to behave in contradiction to their values and character, and this can ultimately compromise their integrity and send a very confusing message to their team.

The following are five essential *Character Traits* that are identified as success for a leader. There could be others, but in this section, we will explore these five traits as I believe they are absolutely fundamental to the success of a leader. As we discuss them, take note that all of these have been in play with each of the dimensions we have discussed.

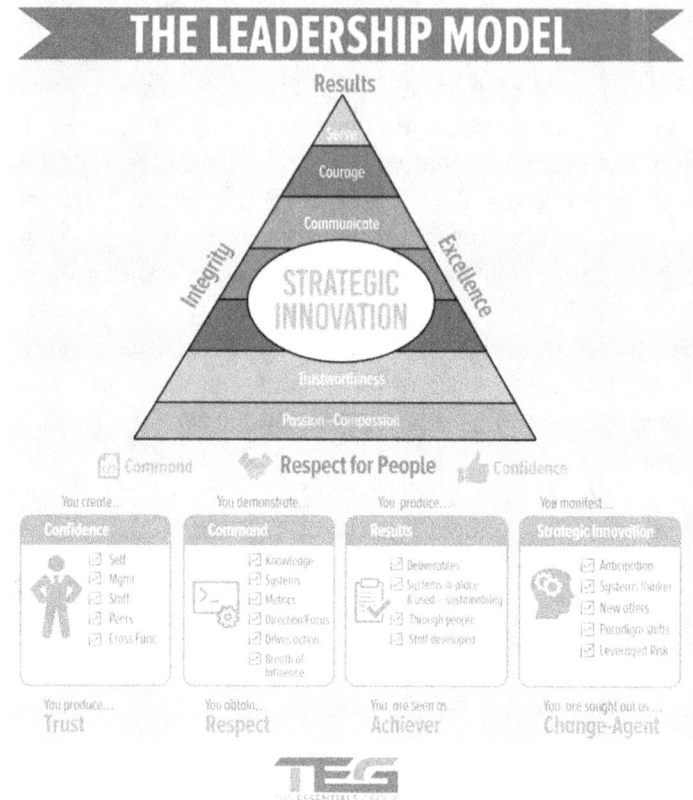

Risky Business

Jack Byrum was the Site Head for the Lilly Clinton Manufacturing Facility. He was a seasoned veteran at Lilly who had a reputation as a no-nonsense driving manager, one who insisted on absolute discipline in manufacturing execution. He had years of experience in managing manufacturing operations and was highly respected for his command of the business processes and systems. Senior management had very high confidence in Jack's abilities and history of producing results. Jack was leading the Clinton facility at its absolute peak of importance to Lilly. The company had withdrawn a promising drug called Oraflex from the market in the mid 1980s and was relying on their top-selling antibiotic, Ceclor, to provide the growth and cash flow to see it through the Oraflex withdrawl. The primary manufacturing site for this crucial product was Clinton, and Jack was the man responsible for making sure the supply chain was maintained.

In the middle of this intense period, Jack had assembled a talented staff that included exceptional leaders, such as Dale Martlage and Bob Cole. Each of these individuals had uniquely strong skill sets. Bob was strong in a disciplined approach to the daily management and leadership of manufacturing. His skills were very similar to Jack's approach and capabilities. Bob was all about execution in a controlled, disciplined manner, producing repetitive results day in and day out. Dale, on the other hand, while appreciating the importance of day-to-day disciplined production, was more about exploring and discovering new ways to conduct business. He embraced change and experimentation.

Jack recognized that he had a very talented staff with unique and contrasting skills. He drew on their strengths by providing the opportunity for each person to be effective and meet the needs of the corporation. Jack supported Bob in his day-to-day manufacturing leadership by reinforcing the need for disciplined execution in a controlled, capable, and compliant manner. However, Jack also understood the world was changing and that Lilly needed to adapt and change also. One of his most important decisions was to support Dale and the Conversational Checkers experiment with the senior management lead team. Jack was the leader of this team, which was responsible for management of the site. All major decisions flowed through this team. When Dale presented the concept of Conversational Checkers, Jack could have disregarded it as too risky or potentially disruptive. Jack had been with Lilly for nearly forty years, and it would have been easy and understandable for him to keep things at status quo. After all, this was his last assignment before retirement. Change may have created disruption, and disruption could create chaos, and chaos would put production capability at risk. It would have been easy for Jack to decline Dale's offer and play it safe.

However, Jack had confidence in Dale and understood that he had studied and developed a sound understanding of the dynamics of an effective team. Jack decided to support Dale's proposal to implement Conversational Checkers and became an ardent supporter and participant in applying the methodology to his meetings and one-on-one conversations.

Immediately, Jack began to see the impact of Conversational Checkers on his meetings. Conversations were more focused and stayed on topic. There was a sense of purpose associated with each discussion. The team developed discipline and systematically shared awareness on specific issues. They continued the disciplined approach as they moved into developing possibilities around this new awareness. Ultimately, they would make decisions and take the appropriate action in their conversations. The overall effectiveness and efficiency of the team improved, and the site was the benefactor. Jack took a calculated risk with Dale's proposal. He believed it was based on sound logic and would help resolve a major problem with his team. He did not reject it but rather fully embraced it.

Trust

We have discussed previously how creating confidence can lead to trust. Trust is vital to any meaningful relationship and its success, including in marriage, within family, and among friends, acquaintances, and co-workers. Obviously, different types of relationships will have various levels of trust, but trust is still common to them all. And the development and sustaining of trust requires attention and conscious, deliberate action.

A leader must be trustworthy and build a culture of trust in a team or organization to be successful. For trust to be engendered into a team culture, the leader must understand and practice this as a personal character trait. Let's explore some possible ways a leader can build trust in his team.

Be Open and Direct

The leader must display a level of openness to build trust. The openness I am referring to is the willingness to engage his team at all levels in meaningful dialogue. Having the courage to tell your team that you don't know something and want to hear their ideas and thoughts demonstrates humility and respect. It reinforces to your team that, as the leader, you do not necessarily have all the answers and that you respect, value, and embrace input from others. This sends a strong message of trust. Earlier I told you about a pastor who was transparent with his board about his own strengths and weaknesses. This action motivated his board to help him and brought the entire team closer together. This type of openness created a value and appreciation for each member's presence and talents. The same can occur with your team.

Another aspect of openness is sharing ideas and thoughts in their formative stages with others—to invite them to critique, respond to, challenge, and build upon a concept. An effective and secure leader allows people to add to or tweak an idea, much like a sculptor chips away pieces of rock with the constant intent to make it increasingly better. A leader must have the maturity and confidence that other team members are talented and can add significant value to an idea. This means not holding so tightly to an idea that the door is shut to all other possibilities. When a leader welcomes input, she facilitates others to take ownership for the idea. This gives the idea multiple sponsors, not just the leader. Multiple sponsorship has huge dividends when implementation occurs. Trust levels increase dramatically when a leader demonstrates the willingness to engage others and include them in the creation of ideas and the sharing of ownership.

Candor

In addition to engaging the team in open dialogue, the leader can demonstrate openness by being direct with individuals and the group. One way of doing this is to avoid sugar-coating messages. Effective leaders speak directly to people and demonstrate respect and value by laying out the need, issues, process, and so on. They create a culture of candor where people can speak plainly, question, and debate without feeling threatened. They invite people to openly evaluate an idea and dissect it in order to build on it.

I realize that a leader cannot always share everything because of business reasons or personal confidentiality. Bob Cole was one of the best leaders I have seen in this area. Bob worked at building trust with his people and developed a reputation for being straightforward and telling people the reality of a situation. When he could not tell people everything, they respected him and trusted that he could tell them what he could and that was good enough. I worked with Bob for a number of years, and the people in his organization always had high trust and confidence in Bob. As a result, they were extremely loyal to him. Bob created an experience for his people of openness and directness and, as a consequence, they believed they could trust him.

Support and Courage

Leaders build trust by demonstrating support to their people. Support can take on many forms, yet it does not entail the leader rescuing his people no matter what they have done or failed to do. People must be held accountable. Sometimes team members may find themselves involved in controversy if others disagree or challenge their decisions. Leaders must provide a careful review of this controversy and some appropriate coaching. This review may lead to a reversal of a previous decision or a need to correct a behavior, but it must be done in a respectful though firm manner that is always striving for personal and team improvement. The people involved must understand why a better decision could have been made and how they could have arrived at it. Even if things went horribly wrong, a leader can use the experience as a teachable moment to instruct and correct. Demeaning a person or team serves little value other than momentarily releasing the leader's frustration while serving to undermine trust and relationship. On the other hand, demonstrating support through coaching and constructive feedback, even when things did not go well, can send a message that the leader still values each individual and the team and intends for everyone involved to grow, learn, and improve.

When a tough situation arises, and the people feel their leader's support, their respect for their leader dramatically increases.

One morning I received a call from one of my staff who was leading a C&Q team on a major capital project. This employee was concerned. He wanted to talk to me about an interaction he had with another director. He explained that the director had asked him to sign and approve a document that had been improperly executed. The employee had refused to sign it and now was worried. He did not need my reassurance that he had done the right thing; he already knew he had made the right choice. What he really needed to know was that I backed him. We talked through the situation, so he was absolutely clear that I believed he was right to refuse to sign the document. Later, I approached the director involved and spoke to him about the matter, supporting what my staff member had done.

An employee must know that his leader will support him when pressure is applied from the outside. He must have the assurrance that he will not be left standing alone.

Nothing can destroy trust faster than for a leader to fail to provide explicit support for her team when it is merited. This may, at times, require her to demonstrate courage, especially when her show of support could create personal risk to her career. Courage of this kind can only occur if a leader has burned into her very character the value of standing up and supporting her people when others are upset and opposed. It only occurs if she values truth and trust more than personal gain. It can become a defining moment in a leader's career to demonstrate support for her team and individuals under adverse conditions. The leader may have to navigate carefully through the opinions and views of others, but if the situation goes well, she will find that her team will follow her to hell and back. Her support and courage will foster an abiding sense of respect and loyalty.

Enable, Empower, and Follow

At the TEDx event mentioned earlier, Jeff Simmons laughed and said that he spent most of his day chasing after his people. Trust is reinforced when a leader lets his people take initiative and lead. When a leader does this, he is saying, *I have confidence in you, I respect you, and I support you.* He is also saying, *I don't have to be driving this effort because you've got it. I trust you. Go for it!* Leaders who have a dream and are successful in communicating that vision can measure their success by the level others engage in that dream. When leaders successfully engage people so they buy into a vision or dream, leaders can then steer them when needed and make appropriate corrections or tweaks as necessary. Unlocking the energy and creativity of an organization can be extremely powerful. When accomplished, leaders can often be more about simply making sure their teams stay directionally correct to meet the vision. In this type of situation, the role of the leader can become more about coaching, steering, providing resources, and helping remove obstacles.

Leaders who do this are establishing that the success of the team or organization is not limited to their personal ambitions or abilities. They reinforce respect for people and a desire to see people grow and develop the skills to lead. The impact of this style of leadership behavior is that it builds trust among people as they develop new skills and experience personal success from their leaders. A leader who does this can also model what being a good follower looks like to the rest of his team. He can take assignments, follow-up in a timely manner, and support other members of the group. The whole time he does this, he can act as a coach and teacher to the employee who is leading as well as to the team. So, acting as a follower does not mean surrendering the role as the overall leader. Rather, the role takes on the coaching and teaching dimension of leadership. The leader still bears significant responsibility and the ability to steer the team and influence the outcome, but he can carry out most of what's needed through his team due to the culture of trust he has created.

Irish Stakes

Bruce McDonald was a project manager for a new biotech manufacturing facility at Lilly's Kinsale, Ireland, site. Bruce epitomizes the essential trait of *Trust* possibly more than any leader I have met at Lilly. He has enormous capability to engage people and empower them to take responsibility and lead. We will describe later the rocky working conditions for this project, but simply stated the Kinsale management team did not trust the GFD management team, and the feeling was mutual from the GFD team. This animosity translated through both organizations at every level. At the beginning of the project, nearly every discussion and every meeting were contentious with sometimes harsh words exchanged, including even slightly veiled threats. Bruce sat in on many of these meetings and provided a calming voice. He was open and direct with people regarding what he saw, but he always remained calm. He refused to become embroiled in petty arguments from either side but often worked behind the scenes listening and discussing concerns, always bringing people back to the mission and focus. When people needed support, he would work with them to find a solution. He never ran from a challenge but constantly kept everyone on task and focused on the mission. He also let people do their job and lead in their area of responsibility. He built a strong, collaborative relationship with his group leaders, and together they coached and steered their respective teams.

Slowly, the culture began to change on the project. Trust was built, and as the project progressed, Bruce continued to demonstrate openness and directness in his discussions with everyone associated with the project. He routinely pulled his team's leaders together with the leaders from operations and reviewed the project's status. Together they discussed issues, approaches, and methods. The old conflicts and tension gradually melted away, and people began to engage at a new level and were now working collaboratively to solve problems. The trust level continued to grow, and old alliances fell away while new ones formed around respect and trust. The whole time Bruce continued to support, engage, and enable his people to be successful.

The project finally moved to a state where Bruce would slip in to team meetings to primarily listen and monitor progress. As needed, he would offer up advice and direction, but the entire tone of the project had changed. His team was leading, and he was following closely and steering as needed.

Bruce understood the importance of trust to the success of the project. However, this trait was not foreign to Bruce since his very nature and character were to be open and direct with people and to provide meaningful support. He naturally engaged and enabled those around him and was comfortable and willing to lead from behind. He gently coached and steered by reinforcing his belief in team members as leaders and offering then advice and counsel. When Bruce has been involved in a team, he always elevates the trust level.

As a leader, you may have made fundamental mistakes that have degraded the trust level of your organization. You may be asking, *What can I do to restore confidence and trust?* Restoring trust requires time, patience, and continual effort. It can be restored, but it must start with you, the leader.

In your attempt to restore trust, you will likely encounter fear from those you have hurt. They become unsure of their relationship with you, your motives, and your behaviors. As a result, they can become defensive, stop communicating with you, and make decisions based on their personal protection instead of what is best for the team or organization.

So, what can the leader do? The first step to restoring trust is establishing that you are personally trustworthy. This may sound like Human Relations 101, and if it does, that's because it is that fundamental. People need to believe their leader can be trusted. The late Steven Covey introduced the metaphor of the emotional bank account in his best-selling book, *Seven Habits of Highly Effective People* (Covey, 1989). This concept established that we maintain a personal emotional bank account with anyone with whom we have a relationship, whether it is with our coworkers, family, or friends. This account begins with a neutral balance, and just as with any bank account, we can make deposits and withdrawals. However, instead of dealing with units of money, we deal with emotional units. The emotional units that Covey speaks of are centered on trust. When we make emotional deposits into someone's bank account, their fondness, trust, and confidence in us grows. As a result, our relationship develops and grows. If we can keep a positive reserve in our relationships by making regular deposits, there will be greater tolerance for our mistakes, and we'll enjoy open communication with that person. On the other hand, when we make withdrawals and our balance becomes low or even overdrawn, bitterness, mistrust, and discord develops in the relationship affected. If we are to salvage the relationship, we must make a conscious effort to make regular deposits into the account—that is, into that damaged relationship. People will view a leader as untrustworthy when the emotional bank account is running a deficit. If a leader is perceived as untrustworthy, the confidence others had in him degrades. When this happens with a leader's team, trust must be rebuilt; the emotional bank account must receive more deposits, not just for the team as a whole but for each member of the team.

In his *The 7 Habits of Highly Effective People*, Covey suggests six major ways to make deposits into a person's emotional bank account.

1. Understanding the Individual

Covey says, "seek first to understand, then to be understood." Typically, individuals want to be understood first. Then, if they have the patience and desire, they give others the chance to be understood. To build trust, however, leaders need to reverse this habit and build a new one. They need to seek to understand others first and then strive to be understood themselves. This puts the priority on others and their perspectives.

Still, understanding what others are feeling can be difficult. We must remove ourselves from our egocentric viewpoint and put ourselves into the minds and shoes of others. I say minds and shoes because we must try first to understand their thought patterns and empathize with how they feel.

One major fault when communicating with others can be thinking of what you are going to say next instead of listening. Truly understanding someone requires us to concentrate on what the other person is trying to say and not simply reloading, waiting to fire off our response.

2. Keeping Commitments

When we break our promises to others, we make major withdrawals from their emotional bank accounts. However, keeping commitments is not just relegated to promises. It also includes things such as arriving at work on time, keeping our appointments, fulfilling our duties, and living up to every word that comes out of our mouth.

3. Clarifying Expectations

There is nothing more frustrating in a relationship than not understanding what is expected of you. Although many of us wish we could be mind readers, we are not. And because each of us sees life differently and has different backgrounds and life experiences, expecting someone to just know what we think and how we feel is unrealistic and unfair. It's important that the people you are dealing with know exactly what is expected of them. Doing this will keep them out of the dark and allow them to confidently relate to you, knowing that what they are doing is in line with your expectations.

4. Attending to the Little Things

Little courtesies, kind words, and warm smiles are at the heart of the small things that brighten up a relationship. They show personal recognition and awareness of others. Within our relationships, if we want success, doing the little things will have a big, positive impact.

5. Showing Personal Integrity

Probably nothing is more damaging to a relationship than a lack of integrity. Since the emotional bank account is based on trust, regardless of what else you do, if there's no trust, all the rest is to no avail. Integrity means wholeness, completeness, or soundness. In the matter of personal integrity, it refers to soundness of moral character. Integrity is the rock-solid foundation upon which all successful relationships are built.

6. Apologizing Sincerely When Making a Withdrawal

Each of us is fallible. We all make mistakes. This is part of our lives and our learning process. Knowing when we are wrong and admitting our mistakes help prevent the wounds we have caused from festering in the lives of others. How we acknowledge our mistakes can actually facilitate healing. When appropriate, a sincere apology will keep your relationship accounts in the positive, allowing you to maintain the balance that has been created in your application of all of the previous steps.

The bottom-line is this: Leaders must demonstrate trust in others through their own trustworthy behaviors. A leader who demonstrates trustworthiness will be trusted by those who follow her.

Leadership Takeaways

- Character traits govern our thinking, our perspective, and our reaction to events and situations.

- A leader must be trustworthy and build a culture of trust in a team or organization to be successful.

- Approaches a leader can use to develop trust include
  - Being open and direct
  - Speaking with candor
  - Being supportive and courageous
  - Enabling, empowering, and following his team
- Fear is often the enemy of trust.
- Restoring trust requires time, patience, and continual effort.
- Leaders must manage the emotional bank account of their team.

16

Passion

You have to have a lot of passion for what you are doing because it is so hard. ... if you don't, any rational person would give up.

> —*Steve Jobs, 2007 (at the D5: All Things Digital conference, on stage with Bill Gates)*

Goooooood morning, research. We're going to have fun today!" The words blared through a bullhorn one early fall morning in 1991 in Building 98 at Lilly Corporate Center. Winston Stanley Marshall, PhD, was standing in the lab door with the bullhorn. He was the Distinguished Lilly Research Scholar for Eli Lilly and Company. After cheering on his colleagues, he walked through the labs and continued shaking his colleagues out of their seats and off their lab stools with his unexpected early morning greeting.

Dr. Stan Marshall was a brilliant research scientist who had already left an indelible mark on Lilly's history during his brilliant career. Stan, as he was called by his friends, had a very distinguished career at Lilly, holding many patents for various drugs and intermediate compounds. He had more than thirty years of experience with Lilly and had responsibility for a number of researchers throughout Lilly Research Labs. He and others, however, were concerned. Lilly Research had struggled to turn out meaningful new products for several years. There seemed to be a problem, and he wanted to get to the root of it and find a solution.

The Dead Poets Society

In the spring of 1991, Stan invited Dale Martlage and myself to join him in conversation to discuss the work we had been doing with Conversational Checkers at Clinton. This led to a series of meetings. Then one day we were invited to what I called Stan's version of the "Dead Poets Society." Deep in the basement of Building 98 at Lilly Headquarters, Stan Marshall had gathered a group of top research scientists. The group met each week after four o'clock in the afternoon. The doors were locked, and the meetings kept confidential for fear of senior leadership disapproval. If members arrived late, they would have to knock on the door and identify themselves before being allowed into

Carpe Diem lads, Carpe Diem.
—Robin Williams,
Dead Poets Society

the room. The purpose of the weekly gathering was to address deep issues within the organization and explore ways to get research moving again at Lilly. For several years the Lilly research group had struggled to bring forward meaningful new products, and these senior scientists who had known better days at Lilly were concerned with the trend. When I joined this group, I did not know the people in the room but later found out it was a who's who list of distinguished senior Lilly researchers. All were there for the same reason: to improve research performance and get Lilly research moving again.

Dale and I taught the principles of Conversational Checkers to this elite group, and they began employing the principles in their weekly meetings. Over several meetings, I acted as facilitator and provided feedback to the group regarding focus, clarity, and ability to drive action in their conversations. The team became increasingly comfortable with the process and became more efficient in generating possibilities and driving to actions.

Ultimately, Stan decided to expand the usage of Conversation Checkers to his broader staff, so Dale and I were invited to come to his team and teach the methodology and principles. This meant coming out from behind closed doors and trying something completely new with rooms of scientists. We arrived at his staff meeting and spent a little over an hour teaching Conversational Checkers. What happened next was fascinating as the room was filled with mostly introverted, introspective scientists who were not used to working closely with each other but instead had traditionally worked in tight silos of expertise.

These scientists were highly trained specialists who each had their field of expertise and who usually focused their work in their individual labs with their staff. These scientists applied the methodology slowly. They focused on listening to one another and began recording on paper questions and possibilities generated from the listening. Slowly the room became more energized as people began asking questions for clarification and then generating possibilities. The discussions eventually flowed rapidly, and the group saw an opportunity to have more focused conversations in the room around specific topics. They broke into several groups and continued sharing awareness about their work and generating possibilities. Then flip charts appeared, and the walls became covered with chemical formulas and ideas which were shared back and forth. Researchers could be heard saying things like, "I didn't know you were doing that" and "That could help me solve a problem" and "How about we do ..."

> It is your passion that empowers you to be able to do that thing you were created to do.
>
> *—T. D. Jakes*

Stan was smiling as he saw a new level of collaboration and communication beginning in his organization. He leaned over to me at one point and said, "Many of these researchers have never talked to one another, let alone shared ideas and possibilities." He was very pleased and adopted the methodology as an approach for his staff meetings moving forward.

Stan Marshall had a passion for excellence. As a leader, he strived to see his organization succeed and be effective. He had enjoyed tremendous success as a researcher, and he wanted to see his people succeed and be effective. So he took a risk. He created a conversation with other leaders and reached outside his organization to understand what others were doing.

An effective change agent helps shift paradigms and makes new offers to the organization. An effective leader "seizes the day" when there is an opportunity to improve himself and his team. He may even create the opportunity, as Stan did.

> Without passion you don't have energy, without energy you have nothing.
> *—Donald Trump*

Personal Passion

Earlier we shared Jeff Simmons' TEDx talk where he shared his personal "hunger" or passion. I believe a leader without passion is a manager. The leader without passion tends to go through life managing things, keeping them between the white lines on the highway of life, never deviating, always driving forward following the prescribed protocol and predestined route. Behavior of this type is not wrong, but it is management, not leadership. God knows we still need managers to keep the world in order and functioning, but in a world rapidly changing socially, economically, geopolitically, and businesswise, we need leaders who can discover and lead people to new realities and new possibilities.

For many years, the pharmaceutical industry was successful as a "gentleman's game." Each company had their niche of products, and each stayed within its market niche. This started to change in the late 1980s with growing international economies, regulatory changes in patent laws, and the vast influx of generic companies. Lilly found itself with layers of management teams that were successful at keeping business between the white lines of the pharmaceutical highway. However, the company now needed people to lead them creatively to new realities and new possibilities. They needed the very business model that had been successful for well over a hundred years to be redefined. This called for change. This would take risk taking. Most of all, it demanded leaders, not just managers, and leaders were not easily found.

Understanding one's personal passion is imperative for a leader because, in knowing her passion, she discovers her innermost drive, her heart, her hunger. At a very personal level, passion can even define her reason for being.

Jeff Simmons shared his passion for righting the wrong of hunger in the world. This passion personally drives him, and he has engaged his entire organization at Elanco to capture this passion. Together they have turned it into a deeper mission for the entire organization.

When people become passionate, they become driven and focused. They have a purpose for their actions and decisions. They make decisions through the lens of their passion. They make sacrifices that may be surprising to others but are entirely logical to them. Passion drives the Olympic athlete to get up at 4:30 in the morning to train in a swimming pool or to run fifteen miles. Passion drives the researcher to continue his quest to find a solution to a devastating disease such as cancer or alzheimers. Passion provides energy and drives commitment and persistence to try, try, and try again. Passion is driven by what could be or should be, and it burns deep within a person's heart, driving an internal unrest with the status quo. It drove Martin Luther King Jr. to not only proclaim on the steps of the Lincoln Memorial that he had a dream but to endure imprisonment, beatings, threats against his life, and attacks on his family. His dream was about what could be and should be, and he was committed to giving his very life to see that dream come true. This is genuine, life-changing passion.

Earlier I talked about the Behavior Model and walked through the relationship of experiences to beliefs, beliefs to behaviors, and how ultimately all this leads to results. People's passion are rooted in their experiences. For example, the African experience of Jeff Simmons in a hut with a man and his dying daughter greatly impacted him as did the story of a young mother crying as she sent her hungry daughter off to school. These spoke to the core of Jeff's being. He discovered within himself a rage at the injustice of hunger. As he stated, it became not a cause but a wrong that needed to be righted. This is when Jeff's passion was born. From this point on, his perspectives, decisions, and actions were altered. He made a personal commitment to spend the rest of his life doing whatever he could to alleviate hunger.

Jeff's experience aligns completely with my previous discussion on the importance of learning one's business and becoming a student of the world. These activities create experiences. These experiences, then, open up possibilities and a new understanding that formulate beliefs. These beliefs can be crystallized with deeper understanding and more awareness to create an uncomfortable feeling toward the present condition and status quo. This belief then begins to cook deep down in our very soul until it erupts into a passion for change and a commitment to take action. This passion gives birth to new behaviors that drive change and commitment.

So, what can a leader do to discover and instill passion into the team?

Explore and Understand

The passion of a leader or team does not have to be of such an epic challenge as the social injustice of hunger. However, in a similar manner when a leader takes the time and effort to explore and understand the current business practices and organizational performance, he can formulate a passion for change. The discovery of passion may also come from studying the world and realizing that there is a better way of doing business. The leader may realize that old paradigms locked into the organization may be antiquated and restrictive and have now served their purpose. They now need to be replaced by new ones. Passion, though, rarely comes from just understanding a need. It gives revelation of what could be or should be. The conflict between what could be and what is can grow into discontent with the status quo and ultimately give birth to the passion to transform the business and the people working in it. Sometimes this kind of passion can become world-changing.

While passion can and often does generate change, it can also clarify our commitment to existing positions and beliefs. A leader's passion may be around an existing organizational position, such as one involving quality, operational discipline, or safety. The passion may simply reinforce the existing tenant and direction of the team. This means the leader and team are aligned, and the current position is strengthened and supported. Not all passion must result in a change but rather may be more about commitment to continue a current path. Exploring and understanding the business may simply reinvigorate existing passion and direction.

Whether passionately driving change in the organization or reinforcing the current course, it is important that the entire team understand why they are changing or reinforcing the current direction.

Follow Success

Success creates passion because, as human beings, we embrace success, and our tendency is to desire and pursue more of it. Thus, we tend to continue doing what has made us successful, especially if we enjoy it. It is important for leaders to recognize what we are successful at and link that to the business. Bob Cole's passion was to see organizations operate with a disciplined approach that created sustainable results. He had been successful implementing disciplined operations at Lilly's manufacturing facilities. This passion was translated to the K105 project team's approach to the K105 rebuild. They applied a disciplined approach to the project that was instrumental in the overall project success. Leaders should recognize and learn from their past successes. They should build upon these successes to help new endeavors succeed.

Signs of True Passion

Finally, it is paramount that a leader *demonstrates* genuine passion. Erika Andersen, who blogs for *Forbes* on leadership, suggests that real passion requires honestly committing to something about which you feel deeply and staying committed through difficult circumstances. She goes on to offer the following as five indicators of a leader's true passion (Andersen, 2012):

- *Commit honestly* – Passionate leaders genuinely believe in what they espouse. People are touched and engaged by the genuineness of their passion.

- *Make a clear case without being dogmatic* – Passionate leaders convey the power of their belief without dismissing or belittling the points of view of others.

- *Invite real dialog about their passion* – Passionate leaders balance their passion with openness: they want to hear and integrate the views of others.

- *Act in support of their passion* – Passionate leaders walk their talk: their day-to-day behaviors support their beliefs.

- *Stay committed despite adversity and setbacks* – The commitment of passionate leaders is not flimsy; when difficulties arise, they hold to their principles and find a way forward.

Andersen is right. A leader's real passion involves personal commitment and provides a clear case for his passion. It also invites dialog and is open to various perspectives. Finally, the passionate leader walks the talk and demonstrates personal commitment to his passion by his behaviors, which includes the persistence to stay the course. When leaders behave in this manner, they create experiences for others that ultimately influence their beliefs.

So here too the Behavior Model is at work as leaders endeavor to communicate and live their passion to their team.

Leadership Takeaways

- It is imperative that leaders discover their personal passion, because in knowing their passion they discover their innermost drive, their heart, their hunger.

- When people become passionate, they become driven and focused.

- People's passion are rooted in their experiences.

- To discover and instill passion into a team,

  o Explore and understand: Discover a better way of doing business.

- o Follow success: Recognize past successes and build on them

- Recall Erika Andersen's five indicators of a leader's true passion:

    - o Commit honestly.
    - o Make a clear case without being dogmatic.
    - o Invite real dialog about your passion.
    - o Act in support of your passion.
    - o Stay committed despite adversity and set-backs.

- Real passion by the leader involves personal commitment and provides a clear case for the passion.

17

Compassion

Compassion doesn't weaken leadership, it makes it stronger.

—*Sechiquita Ratliff Marti*

Passion is an essential trait for leaders, but it has a dark side. It can drive people to behave poorly toward others, and this can have devastating results.

As I write this, the world is appalled at the acts of radical Islamic terrorist groups such as ISIS in Syria and the Taliban in Afghanistan as well as Boko Haram in Nigeria. These groups perform beheadings, torture, kidnap, rape, and sell women and children into slavery, all in the name of a radical, passionate interpretation of Islam. The world responds with outrage and tries desperately to contain their terror and turn the tide against these groups' expansion. Still, common to each of these groups is passion. The passion they exhibit is intense and driven. They will fight for their beliefs to the point of death. They will make whatever personal sacrifices are necessary to feed their passion, including acting completely outside the norms of civilized behavior. They are totally committed. This kind of unbridled passion can be extremely dangerous, and we often don't think of terrorists when talking about business leadership. However, each of these groups have dynamic, dramatic, totally committed leaders who have provided passion, direction, and focus for the behavior of large groups of people.

So, while passion in leadership matters, it must be balanced by *compassion*. Few books on leadership address this fundamental trait, but it provides a critical governor to our lives both personally and professionally. The leader who becomes obsessed by his passion to the point that nothing else matters runs the risk of running over people and leaving "dead bodies" all around them. Passion without compassion can be destructive.

John Baldoni, who is chair of the leadership development practices at N2Growth, a global leadership consultancy, has addressed the issue of compassion and leadership in the *Harvard Business Review* (Balboni, 2008):

> When it comes to leadership, passion is spoken about frequently, though primarily in the abstract, as in having a "passion for the job" or "passion for results." By contrast, compassion takes a back seat; it's considered a nice-to-have attribute, but few leaders speak publicly about it. In truth, if you want to deliver on passion; that is, use it as a lever to rally your team to achieve something sustainable, you must do so with compassion—by recognizing and demonstrating your belief that what people do matters.

Baldoni adds:

> Passion is often subjective. It is the zeal we feel when we are doing what we enjoy and when we see the positive effects it has on us as well as our team. Compassion, by contrast, is nurtured from within—but it doesn't have any effect until you apply it to others. It's no good being compassionate if you never do anything for anyone. Accountability matters in both passion and compassion. That is, you hold passionate people accountable for results for which they strive. And you demonstrate compassion by holding the

organization accountable for delivering on its promises to its employees.

Sensitive to People's Needs

Compassionate leaders value and understand the needs of their people. They navigate the boundary waters of work-life balance for their team, knowing when to push and when to back off. Sometimes a leader must intervene to pull back on the reins with their team to force them to rest. Several times in my career, I have had situations where I needed to compel a team of highly dedicated individuals to "shut it down" for a few days. I saw fatigue setting in and mistakes being made. I also needed them for the long haul and knew that their current pace would burn them out and render them nearly useless for the long road ahead. More than once, I have coached an employee to stop traveling back to an international project for a while because he or she had been away from their family so much that family stress was developing. The employee's commitment and passion for success needed to be steered and put in perspective. We were able to make adjustments and keep the project moving forward successfully. A compassionate leader is sensitive to his people's needs and values their work-life balance as critical for long-term success.

A leader must also keep in perspective that he is working with people who have not only needs but also desires and aspirations of their own. A compassionate leader recognizes people's aspirations and goals and works to help them develop skills and gain valuable experiences. Such leaders provide feedback and coaching and value the development of their people. They celebrate their people's accomplishments and encourage them when they struggle.

Coach Frequently

Leaders who are compassionate coach regularly, providing constant feedback to individuals and the team. They understand that leadership has a responsibility to enable others to succeed by putting them in the right positions and providing them the necessary resources. They also provide them with guidance and directions to assure success. Compassionate leaders understand the benefit of developing people through coaching. They follow the principle of replication and acknowledge that the organization will be much stronger if they can replicate skills and behaviors throughout their team by effective coaching and further enabling people.

A coach is someone who can give correction without causing resentment.

—*John Wooden*

Compassionate leaders do not ignore or minimize failures and mistakes but rather, with clear coaching, address them directly and in a timely manner. Problems often arise when these failures and mistakes go unaddressed and are allowed to continue. These problems can grow into major issues for the team and individual. Compassionate leaders demonstrate compassion by directly addressing issues long before they develop into major problems. This compassion prevents individuals from dealing with sometimes severe consequences from behavior or performance issues, which have been allowed to continue unaddressed for extended periods of time. By addressing issues early, the leader can redirect people in a non-threatening manner and coach them in the appropriate behavior and performance.

Link Passion and Compassion

Leaders should value compassion to the broader community. In this light, Baldoni (Balboni, 2008) suggests supporting volunteerism. Make it known that your organization will donate time and effort to community service efforts. Perhaps this focus goes to a local school or maybe a family shelter or a multiplicity of assistance efforts. Some organizations provide paid leave for people engaged in community volunteer efforts, which is wonderful but not always possible. What most organizations can do, however, is recognize a community need and make a commitment to serving it.

Jeff Simmons understood that the broader implication of his passion to fight world hunger involved extensive compassion to people around the world. This compassionate passion has translated into a number of efforts on numerous continents to participate in providing food to hungry people. Under Jeff's leadership, Elanco has created positions called "hunger ambassadors." Those who hold these positions focus on understanding hunger needs across the world. These hunger ambassadors look for ways to actively engage the Elanco employees in local and regional efforts to bring relief to hunger-ravaged areas. This

> I worry that business leaders are more interested in material gain than they are in having the patience to build up a strong organization, and a strong organization starts with caring for their people.
> —*John Wooden*

spirit of volunteerism and engagement in very tangible ways has served to strengthen the over-all mission of Elanco employees to overcome world hunger. It has made it much more personal as employees have traveled to regions worldwide to understand and participate in relief efforts. Now the focus of their passion has faces and names. No longer are people just chasing a hunger world issue, but they have identified with individual people struggling every day for food and come to realize this passion is about very real people and their families. Passion and compassion have become linked.

Calcutta Compassion

One of the best examples of leadership combining passion and compassion is the story of Mark and Huldah Buntain. Mark and Huldah are not celebrities; their names are not widely known. However, the people in Calcutta and the rest of India know the Buntains and recognize the impact they have had on millions of lives in that part of the world.

Mark and Huldah Buntain were a young married couple in their twenties with a young daughter when they boarded a ship in New York in 1954. They set sail on a three month journey to India to be missionaries for one year. They planned to evangelize and perhaps do a bit of volunteer work. However, upon arrival they saw a need so great that they ended up staying for the next sixty years. That trip turned into a lifetime of service to the people of Calcutta and throughout India.

According to Amitabh Singh, executive director for the ministry in Canada, it all started one day years ago when Mark Buntain was preaching in a church. A beggar walked in and said to him, "Preacher, first feed our bellies before you tell us that God loves us." Mark saw the need and responded to it. Calcutta Mercy Ministries was born, and it now feeds twenty-five thousand people every day. For the majority of those fed by this ministry, this single meal is the only one of the day. "They do not get any other food than the food we provide," explained Singh (Lee, 2011).

The Buntain's compassion and passion did not end here. They soon recognized they had to do more than just feed the poor. "Part of what we're doing here is: one, providing the fish because there's a crisis today, there's no fish. But you also have to provide them with the fishing rod," said Singh. "That is why they [the Buntains] got into education. When they started feeding they knew it wasn't going to change anything. They had to build a school." So, during the 1960s, the Buntains built several schools. In fact, they established a holistic inner-city outreach consisting of more than a hundred schools that have educated over one hundred thousand children. They also created over eight hundred churches and several Bible colleges, which added to their educational effort.

Mark and Huldah could have stopped their ministry there, but God had more plans. One day a little girl fainted in one of the classrooms. Mark rushed her to the hospital and there made a shocking discovery. In the room where the girl was admitted, there were two people on top of the bed, two under it, and rats running all around. After seeing this, Mark said, "I am not only going to feed a child, but I am going to educate a child, and I am medically going to treat a child." The Buntains and their ministry soon adopted the tag line "Building a better India by building better boys and girls" (Lee, 2011). So, the Buntains built a full general hospital that has treated 2.2 million people and provided free care to 880,000. Along with the hospital, they also established a nurses training center.

> Mark loved the poor. It didn't matter if they wore tattered clothes, were alcoholics, drug addicts, or lived on the street. He loved them and ardently believed that helping them fulfills Christ's commission and follows the example he set.
> —*Huldah Buntain*

In addition, the Buntains established laundry facilities that employ former prostitutes, and their non-profit ministry routinely employs over two thousand nationals and accepts the help of more than three hundred volunteers annually.

Although Mark Buntain passed away in 1989, Huldah and her daughter, Bonnie (and Bonnie's husband, James Long), still continue the work of Calcutta Mercy Ministries. The passion and compassion for the people of India continues, and the Buntains keep leading the way in meeting needs and improving lives.

***

Passion and compassion must always be linked together as they provide balance and perspective regarding priorities and people. Passion provides energy, focus, and drive while compassion provides context, perspective, and personal value.

Leadership Takeaways

- There is a dark side to passion. Passion can drive people to behave poorly.

- Passion must be balanced by compassion because passion without compassion can be dangerous.

- It's no good being compassionate if you never actually do anything for anyone.

- The leader can demonstrate compassion by ...
  - being sensitive to people's needs
  - coaching frequently
  - and linking passion and compassion.

- Passion provides energy, focus, and drive while compassion provides context, perspective, and personal value.

18

Communication

Speak in such a way that others love to listen to you. Listen in such a way that others love to speak to you.

—Anonymous

Earlier I told you about Bruce McDonald and how he developed *trust* in the IE42 Kinsale, Ireland project. Lilly had made a strategic decision to retask the Kinsale site from a bulk chemical manufacturing focus to becoming a primary site for biotech manufacturing. The site had to not only construct new facilities and install new technology but also had to retool its staff to support the new mission. Bruce's job was to oversee the design and construction of the new facility. He had responsibility for spending over $300 million to design and construct it. Because there was so much tension, Bruce was also responsible for making sure all the parties worked together cohesively. In other words, he worked to ensure they didn't kill each other.

When Lilly announced it was making such a sizable investment in Kinsale, the site management team exhibited significant concern regarding what approach to use in delivering the new assets. Some years before, the corporate engineering group had managed a major capital project at Kinsale delivering a new building. The project did not go well. The project manager had been instructed to deliver the new building exactly as designed with as little input or interference from the site staff as possible. That didn't happen. Conflicts between the site staff and the corporate engineering group created numerous problems.

Bob Cole, who was now the new corporate vice president of Engineering, performed shuttle diplomacy between Kinsale and the corporate engineering group, Global Facilities Delivery, who was tasked with delivering the new facility. One afternoon he walked into a conference room in Indianapolis filled with the GFD management team and proceeded to share a list of complaints and issues from the Kinsale management team. The list expressed why the Kinsale team did not

> The art of communication is the language of leadership.
> —*James Humes*

want GFD to lead the bio-tech project. Clearly, the project did not start with what was hoped to be a warm, collegial atmosphere between Kinsale management and GFD management. Bruce McDonald inherited this atmosphere when he was named the project manager for the IE42 project.

Bruce had been a successful GFD project manager for nearly thirty years, though the majority of his work had been in the Indianapolis area. On this project, he was responsible for getting all parties to work closely together to make critical decisions in a timely and efficient manner. The politically correct description was that this project brought with it significant cross-cultural issues combined with high visibility at all levels of the organization. Put more simply and clearly, the people working on the project really didn't like each other very much. So, Bruce began his task with the challenge of spending over $300 million to deliver a new technology to a site with a management team and staff who didn't want him there and didn't get along with one another. His job was daunting.

Realizing this, Bruce immediately began building key relationships with other leaders, such as the site owner representative who was responsible for representing the site in all decisions. They regularly met and developed a relationship of trust and mutual alignment on project scope and approach. This relationship proved to be valuable throughout the entire project as it enabled them to talk through numerous issues and represent a united position.

Bruce also assembled a strong leadership staff that led various elements of the project delivery process. He trusted his entire leadership team and maintained open communication with each of them. He sought out their input, and when the team was getting distracted, he brought everyone back to focus on the priorities.

He also held routine team meetings with members of his leadership team and site leadership to assure a clear understanding of issues and the project's status. Misunderstanding was the enemy, and Bruce worked diligently to assure everyone was dealing with facts and not assuming motives or creating "facts" out of thin air. He operated in a calm manner, always moving the team along by dealing with issues in a thoughtful, deliberate way and not letting them blow up by becoming bigger than they were.

One approach Bruce took was to bring in an outside consultant who focused on project dynamics and teamwork. The consultant hired was Sally Love, president of Paragon Worldwide Inc. She came to Ireland and held several workshops with the project team and site staff. She focused them on strengthening relationships, understanding, and reaching agreement regarding the overall objective of the project and how the culture of the project team should function. What happened was fascinating. People began to talk and listen to one another for the first time. They started realizing that, whether they were from Ireland or the States, they all wanted the same things, especially a cohesive, cooperative workplace that was an enjoyable place to work. These sessions created the space and time needed for the team to step away from the everyday noise and technical aspects and gather their thoughts. It also gave the space and time to check in with others and see where they were at emotionally. Sometimes stepping away and working on relationships will get you further than putting your head down and driving ahead with everyday tasks.

Bruce's efforts to build trust worked. The trust level began to rise among colleagues. As trust improved, conversations changed from substantial positional debates to thoughtful discussion and decisions. The staff even began spending more time outside of work together building relationships. At the beginning of the project, the culture was contentious, with ideological camps of people whispering in office corners and nodding toward other parties across the room. Over time, the team culture changed dramatically. It became an energetic, cooperative, and collegial environment.

Bruce McDonald understood the absolute importance of communication. He practiced outstanding listening skills while keeping everyone informed, and he directed the team appropriately to keep them moving along toward the goal. He would not let the team get stuck in time-wasting debates or distracting arguments. He set a tone for cooperation by living this example in front of his team over and over again. By his behavior, Bruce established that leadership was never about ego but about getting the job done well through a cooperative team effort.

What Bruce accomplished is still bearing fruit years later. I travel to Ireland frequently. What I found recently was that many of the same project team members are continuing with the design and construction of yet another even bigger biotech building called IE43. The cultural changes accomplished during the IE42 project live on today. When I now walk into the offices, it is typical to have Kinsale staff and other project staff members call out my name and run over to shake my hand and welcome me back to the site. People are working diligently alongside each other. Good, broad discussions are taking place. Work is getting done, but routine laughter rings through the halls. There has been no drama on the IE43 project but instead quiet efficiency and cooperation with colleagues, who trust, respect, and value one another. The IE43 project may simply be the best capital project Lilly has ever conducted, and they owe much of its success to the leadership and foundation that Bruce McDonald established on the IE42 project. That's a wonderful legacy as a leader to leave a company.

The Many Sides of Communication

Throughout this book, an underlying essential trait of the leader has been ever present but not yet brought into the light. I am talking about the essential trait of communication. Successful leaders must be effective at communication and also understand its critical importance not only upward and peer-to-peer but throughout the entire organization.

Communication can occur in many ways, and the message sent by the leader can either be informative, empowering, and energizing or in some cases debilitating, demoralizing, and confusing. Moreover, communication is not bound to words alone. It can and does occur in many different ways.

Some people think that communication is a skill and not necessarily a character trait. I understand this perspective and certainly agree there are skills associated with effective communication. However, I also believe that communication should be a deep personal commitment for a leader—something a leader must deeply value and strive to assure is integral to his team culture.

In addition to the importance of communication for a team's performance, communication as a character trait for a leader means that it is an integral part of who he is as a person. He assures his words, whether spoken or written, are clear, direct, and speak the truth. He seeks to understand before being understood by not just practicing strong listening skills but also valuing the opinions and views of others. Almost anyone can develop good communication skills. But communication needs to be a character trait that flows from deep within and is driven by a strong value for clarity and for bringing about understanding between people.

What are, then, the traits and sides of communication? And how can leaders make those their own? Let's spend some time addressing these questions.

Listening

Effective leaders practice excellent listening skills in communication to their people and the world around them. They endeavor to employ Stephen Covey's principle of "Seeking first to understand" (Covey, 1989). Effective leaders ask questions and seek to understand. They give people an opportunity to tell them what they know and what is going on. An effective leader follows up with more questions and applies active listening. She is always working to understand and create a dialogue with people.

Too many weak leaders think leadership is fundamentally about telling people what to do or expounding on their expertise. This type of behavior usually shuts people down or creates a tension of unnecessary conflict. There is an old saying: God gave us two ears and one mouth—use them in the same proportion! When a leader practices good listening skills to the world around her, she feeds her mind with new knowledge and understanding, and this can feed the *Strategic Innovation* dimensions. When this happens, it can lead to new ideas and possibilities. Listening to her people also reinforces her respect for the skills, knowledge, and talents of her team. When a leader actively seeks input from those around her, she actually builds the confidence of others. They come to believe that their leader is willing to listen to various perspectives and learn.

Steve (named changed) was bright and articulate and joined my group a number of years ago. We hired him because he interviewed very well and had an excellent résumé. He genuinely understood the field and was clearly an expert. However, when he began working with people and trying to lead teams, he began having problems. He constantly wanted to tell people what he knew before seeking to listen to them. And when he did listen, he was often resistant to others' views. He became combative in meetings, which led to disruption, and team dynamics virtually collapsed as team members became frustrated. His communications were essentially one way, with him being tell-assertive to everyone.

As a result of this behavior, Steve's team had little confidence in his leadership. Peers also did not respect him because they experienced his unwillingness to listen. He put in little effort to collaborate on projects. While he actually understood the field quite well and had good ideas, his communication and listening skills were essentially nonexistent. His leadership became completely ineffective.

After much unsuccessful coaching with him, we made the decision to go our separate ways. Steve had complete command of the field, but the confidence of his team, peers, and ultimately management was so degraded by his behavior that he could not be successful moving forward. He simply did not value effective communication.

Listening is a powerful skill for a leader. Demonstrating genuine interest in people's thoughts and ideas sends a powerful message of respect and value. In addition, when a leader asks questions, it allows him to probe for understanding and help his team clarify their thoughts and position. In other cases, the leader's questions can expose weaknesses in logic and the need for more data and thought. Asking questions and listening are potent communication skills for any leader to possess and use.

Earlier I told the story of Colonel Henry Knox and the retrieval of guns from Fort Ticonderoga during the American Revolutionary War. David McCullough, author of the award-winning book *1776*, described the interaction between Knox and General Washington (McCullough, 2005):

> It was Henry Knox who first suggested the idea of going after the canon at Fort Ticonderoga on Lake Champlain, an undertaking so enormous, so fraught with certain difficulties, that many thought it impossible.
>
> The capture of Fort Ticonderoga from the British by Ethan Allen, Benedict Arnold and a handful of Green Mountain Boys earlier in May had been sensational news, but the fort and it's captured artillery were abandoned. When Knox told Washington he was confident the guns could be retrieved and hauled overland to Boston, Washington agreed at once, and put the young officer in charge of the expedition.

McCullough went on to provide this insight:

> That such a scheme hatched by a junior officer in his twenties who had had no experience was transmitted so directly to the supreme commander, seriously considered, and acted upon, also marked an important difference between the civilian army of the Americans and that of the British. In an army where nearly everyone was new to the task of soldiering and fighting a war, almost anyone's ideas deserved a hearing.

This took place in a world where neither senior officers nor supreme commanders typically gave a junior officer the time of day, let alone listened to a proposal of such august boldness and high risk. As the supreme commander of the Continental Army, George Washington listened to his young officer propose his idea, acted on it, and thereby influenced the outcome of the war.

Listening matters.

Speaking

The most often considered attribute of communication is verbal communication, and it is vital in order for a leader to be effective. A leader must know his audience when speaking to an individual or presenting to a group. Many leaders have failed to understand this important principle: Know your audience. Over explanation or needless detail can create confusion or degrade confidence. Precise, clear communication that provides understanding, clarity of focus, and direction is vital. In addition, positive reinforcing words can provide stability. The leader must be truthful and speak honestly and directly about situations and people. People ultimately respond well to direct truths, even when those are painful to hear.

Furthermore, leaders need to use data and facts to support their positions. Emotion and opinion can only carry a person so far. Ultimately, someone will ask for data to support a direction or decision. Over the years, occasionally individuals have come to me challenging some aspect of our approach and guidance with the commissioning and qualification of new facilities. Invariably I have found their views unsupported by any facts or data but rich with opinion. I have ended many a debate by just saying, "Here is my data. I'd be more than happy to review yours, and we can discover together the differences." I have yet to have a person take me up on this challenge. Such individuals usually slip away because they simply have no data to support their opinion. My response is not intended to be rude or deliberately disengaging with people. However, at some point the data and facts need to be layed on the table to be examined and assessed openly. Without that, we can become nothing more than a debate club fueled by empty but persuasive rhetoric founded on emotion, personal preference, and opinion but little else. This is not a healthy way to run a business or to communicate.

Writing

In this day of almost instant communication around the world via email, text messaging, and tweeting, the ability to clearly articulate an idea is crucial. Many a leader has stuck their proverbial foot in their mouth by inappropriate or poorly timed messages. The successful

> Don't write so that you can be understood, write so that you can't be misunderstood.
> —*William Howard Taft*

leader must be able to properly articulate ideas in effective written or presentation format. Plans need to be clearly documented, systems described, and direction provided. Well-documented ideas and direction can influence the confidence of others at all levels, and this leads to credibility. In addition, excellent documentation contributes to a state of command and control. Well-documented systems provide clarity for expectations and practice.

I cannot overemphasize the importance of clear and concise written communication. Leaders can create incredible confusion by poorly worded emails or bewildering presentations. Many senior executives have become increasingly irritated with a lower-level manager who has marched, totally oblivious to his audience, through a fifty-slide presentation. I have seen senior management interrupt presenters and demand they get to the point. Unfortunately, this has often resulted in sometimes overly aggressive cross-examination, with the presenter being verbally fileted in front of the entire group by a member of senior management. While this is not a demonstration of good leadership by senior management, it is an entirely avoidable situation. Presenters should always carefully identify their audience and craft their message appropriately, regardless of the chosen media.

One final thought. Sometimes sitting on an email overnight may be the best thing a leader can do, especially if an issue is contentious. Thinking through the wording, the tone, and the intent is prudent.

Being Present

A leader can make a huge statement by his presence at key times in key places. Presence may be interpreted as either physical or emotional. The presence of American General Douglas McArthur on the beaches of the Philippines in World War II is a great example of this. There he announced: "People of the Philippines, I have returned. ... the hour of your redemption is here!" His presence and proclamation energized guerilla fighters across the island and fulfilled his previous promise. In a similar manner, a leader being at a particular place at a specific time energizes the people he is leading. Presence is a form of communication. It makes a statement of support, agreement, and commitment.

> A good leader should be visible, accessible, and approachable. A good leader should evoke inspiration, not fear.
> —*Richard Branson*

Leaders can also demonstrate presence by providing emotional support. They can do this by supporting an idea or initiative coming from their people. This support is especially important when there may be opposition or conflict. Leadership presence in the form of support for direction, ideas, and approach is vital for reinforcing confidence. When a leader takes a stand for an idea, a team, or an individual, they make a tremendous statement regarding their leadership ability.

Sometimes taking a stand may be risky for a leader's career, position with his management, or relationship with peers. Ground zero for the effective leader needs to be the core values of respect for people, excellence, and integrity. When these values are violated, ignored, or abused, leaders must take a stand or risk losing credibility and trust with their team, peers, and even management. Presence speaks volumes about a leader's commitment and strength.

I was a young engineer working in Technical Services supporting Elanco manufacturing at Clinton. It was my first job out of graduate school, and I had been in the group for several years. The room was packed with people, and the discussions had turned to a manufacturing problem. I had been studying the problem and collecting data on it for some time and had put together a proposal to make operational changes. These changes would require some adjustments to operating practices and the long-established way things had been done. I encountered resistance because my proposal meant changes to methods and approaches. Yet, the data I had accumulated was clear, indicating that changes were needed despite a long history of practice. As the discussion continued, it became more intense and heated. Pete Vanevenhoven, my boss, finally hit the palm of his hand on the table with a loud crack and stood up. He said, "The data clearly supports this approach, and we need to implement this now!" The discussion immediately turned more civil and began focusing on how to make the changes happen.

Pete was gregarious, outspoken, and demonstrative in his style. At that moment I knew he had my back and supported me as my leader. He did not do this just to help me personally, but he had seen the data and knew it was sound. He realized I had done the work and built the case. Convinced of my findings, Pete stood with me to support the proposal.

Networking

The other day my youngest daughter, Lauren, looked at me and said, "Dad, you have an extensive network of people." I thought for a second about that and realized I had not thought of it that way. Possibly due to generational differences, I had thought of my working relationships as my having a bunch of people around the world who were friends and associates who often talked and shared ideas. But her view was right. My network is large.

In today's business world, networking is essential to success. Networking provides access to others, ideas, and information. It offers a mechanism for understanding what others are doing and how they are doing it. Books and magazines are excellent tools for reading and understanding new approaches, but networking provides a vital, living, breathing community of people who can be used to test ideas and share learning. Successful leaders build networks within and outside their company. These networks can be safe havens to test ideas as well as opportunities for understanding what is new in the world. They also can be valuable when endeavoring to get support for a position or approach.

I have talked extensively about *Strategic Innovation*, and networking provides a valuable tool for the leader to see beyond her walls and learn the world. Leaders should build a network, not only in their field of expertise but also outside in areas of various interest. A robust network broadens their world of understanding and creates opportunities for slippage. Some idea or approach in an entirely unrelated field may trigger a new thought or possibility in one's own field.

A number of years ago, I was exposed to a software package developed by a company on the east coast and used in the construction industry. This small business had created a robust, simple tool that could help construction companies manage punch-list items in the field on job sites. The business had marketed this tool to a number of firms. Still, their primary customers were large government-run projects that did not seem to mind the high cost they had put on the software. Consequently, many other companies had not used the tool because of its premium cost.

I began having discussions with the CEO of the business, and he shared the tool's capability and how they had implemented it in the construction industry. I shared with him about the pharmaceutical business and educated him on the complex regulatory environment and how we constructed, commissioned, and qualified new facilities. Neither he nor his company had any experience with this industry. It quickly became evident to him that he was missing a huge business opportunity.

Over the next number of months, we worked together to help this company understand the pharmaceutical business needs. Consequently, their developers made small tweaks to the software. We then began using the tool as a primary part of our Construction Quality Assurance (CQA) program at Lilly.

I also worked with another colleague from Europe, and together we published several magazine articles on Construction Quality Assurance. These articles provided a context for using a CQA program and software tools for pharmaceutical and other industry projects.

So, through a network, a paradigm was changed. My paradigm shifted regarding the tools available, and the software company's paradigm changed regarding the markets they could explore. Multiple netorks impacted each other concerning Construction Quality Assurance.

Much has been written about building strong networking, and I will not try to delve into that here. One thing is sure, though, active networks are essential for successful leaders. Brian Uzzi and Sharon Dunlap wrote an article called "How to Build Your Network," published in the *Harvard Business Review* (Uzzi & Dunlap, 2005). In this article, they wrote:

> If you were to ask your colleagues, "Who was Paul Revere?" most would probably know the answer. He was, after all, immortalized in the Longfellow poem that begins, "Listen, my children, and you shall hear of the midnight ride of Paul Revere." Yet how many of your colleagues, students of American history aside, would be familiar with William Dawes? Both men rode on horseback from Boston on the night of April 18, 1775. Both sounded the alarm that the Revolutionary War had begun. Dawes rode south while Revere rode north, but the towns they traveled through were demographically similar. Both men came from the same social class and had similar educational backgrounds. But only Revere raised a militia, and only Revere's name became famous. What accounts for the difference? In large part, the type of social network each man cultivated.

Uzzi and Dunlap continued:

> Paul Revere was an information broker, a person who occupies a key role in a social network by connecting disparate groups of people. Because Revere targeted other well-connected people during his ride, his news spread widely and quickly, as explained in Malcolm Gladwell's *The Tipping Point*, for example. William Dawes was

not an information broker, so he didn't know which doors to knock on when he entered a new town. As a result, the information he carried was circulated within a small group of people instead of expanding outward.

The smart leader recognizes the importance and power of building a network of people. This network becomes a community for sharing, learning, and growing, which ultimately contributes to leadership success.

Standup and Be Counted

It was a beautiful fall afternoon. Fifty experts from around the world were gathered in a conference facility on the campus of Indiana University-Purdue University Indianapolis in Indiana. This group had been summoned to participate in a week-long conference to discuss and agree on approaches for executing Commissioning and Qualification at Eli Lilly. The company had a significant need to standardize and agree upon how to perform this work. Recent qualification failures on capital projects had led to significant cost overruns and the inability to qualify new manufacturing facilities. As a result, hundreds of millions of dollars of new production facilities could not be used for manufacturing products. A change was needed and needed fast.

Several months before this conference, I was asked to form a Commissioning and Qualification team as part of Lilly's Global Facility Delivery (GFD) division. The GFD group had direct responsibility for managing major capital projects around the world, and its failure to qualify new facilities was a significant problem. We quickly needed a standard approach that met regulatory requirements.

On the first day of the weeklong conference, I informed the experts in the room that this would be a decision-making week. I told them that we would review proposed methodologies, we would debate these methods, and we would ultimately agree upon the approach for the corporation. We would work as long as we needed each day, but we would have a recommendation for a path forward by the end of the week. This conference would define the future methodology for Eli Lilly and Company.

On the first day of the conference, I invited Frank Deane, vice president of Quality for Lilly, to be a keynote speaker and share his perspectives on the regulatory climate and issues. Frank gave his presentation, and then answered a few questions and sat down. Hours of presentations, discussions, and debates commenced. The entire time, Frank remained in the back of the room and listened.

The next day during ongoing discussion and evaluation, I turned around during an afternoon session to see Frank sitting in the back of the room, listening intently and taking notes. I was a bit surprised. I knew he was busy and consumed elsewhere with a number of pressing regulatory concerns and issues. This pattern continued for the next few days, with Frank slipping into the meetings and listening.

On Thursday afternoon during a break, Frank made a request that the next morning our group present to him and his staff our conclusions and proposals for the corporation. He said he would bring his staff to us at the IUPUI campus.

The next morning two of the delegates from across the world stood in front of the entire conference group, which had vice presidents and executive directors from Frank's staff sitting among them. For nearly two hours, they carefully reviewed our proposed new direction for Lilly. The team also answered a number of questions from Frank's staff.

At the end of the presentation, a dramatic moment of outstanding leadership occurred. The management team asked questions and clarified understanding. Then Frank Dean stood and went to the front of the large conference room and thanked all of the representatives for their hard work and effort to reach agreement. Standing in front of over fifty delegates from around the world and the entire corporate Quality leadership team, Frank made a simple but powerful declaration: "This is what we are going to do—across the world! Go do it!" Frank's declaration meant they were to return to their sites around the world and implement the new agreed-upon approaches, methods, and tools. Lilly would now have a standard, corporate-wide approach for executing commissioning and qualification.

Frank's action was an example of bold, decisive leadership. He communicated his intent clearly and directly. He spoke to a future state and showed his support for strategic innovation and a new paradigm.

He made it abundantly clear that he supported this approach and fully expected the recommendations to be completely implemented. Unfortunately, this type of behavior by leaders is not always common. I have left many meetings where the leader's position or direction was extremely unclear.

Frank's actions touched on many of the dimensions of the Leadership Model. He took a critical stand and clearly communicated direction and intent. And the results demonstrated the effectiveness of his actions. His definitive position and the ways he reached it led to Lilly saving over $600 million in C&Q cost over a ten-year period across capital projects.

Leaders clearly communicate by listening and providing clear direction and also taking a stand when needed to reinforce a position. Frank's actions established definitive expectations for Lilly and his staff worldwide. His leadership was critically supportive of the entire corporate initiative to change the manner in which Lilly delivered capital projects and assured qualification. And it had dramatic results.

Leadership Takeaways

- It does not take words alone to communicate; communication can occur in many different ways.

- Leaders must develop communication skills that include
  - Listening
  - Speaking
  - Writing
  - Being Present
  - Networking

19

Servant Leadership

Good leaders must first become good servants.

—*Robert Greenleaf*

In the Gospel of John, Jesus does a very strange thing. He gathers his disciples in an upper room for a dinner and then suddenly stands up, takes off his outer clothing, and wraps a towel around his waist. He then pours water into a basin and begins washing his disciples' feet and drying them with his towel. The image is socially awkward since the rabbi Jesus is the distinguished guest. He is the leader of the group, but here he performs a task typically relegated to a household servant or even a slave.

The moment becomes so uncomfortable for the disciples that finally one of them, Peter, speaks up and refuses to allow Jesus to wash his feet, saying, "No, you shall never wash my feet."

Jesus responds to Peter, "Unless I wash you, you have no part of me." Jesus goes on to say, "Now that I, your Lord and Teacher, have washed your feet, you also should wash one another's feet. I have set you an example that you should do as I have done for you. Very truly I tell you, no servant is greater than his master, nor is a messenger greater than the one who sent him. Now that you know these things, you will be blessed if you do them" (John 13:1–17 NIV).

Regardless of your religious views, the story of Jesus washing his disciples feet is powerful and poignant. He establishes not only an example of the desired relationship between his disciples but also establishes the desired relationship between servants and master. He modeled a relationship that was a complete paradox to the world order of his times—and ours as well. What he did even has application to today's leaders and their teams.

Principles of Servant Leadership

A great deal has been written about servant leadership over the years. The term was first coined by Robert K. Greenleaf in "The Servant as Leader," an essay he first published in 1970. In this work, Greenleaf established that

> The servant-leader is servant first ... It begins with the natural feeling that one wants to serve, to serve first. Then conscious choice brings one to aspire to lead ... (vs. one who is leader first...) ... [T]he best test, and difficult to administer, is: Do those served grow as persons ... (and become) more likely themselves to become servants? (Greenleaf R. K., 1970)

Larry Spears, president and CEO of The Spears Center and Servant-Leadership Scholar at Gonzaga University, identified the following ten characteristics of a servant-leader (Spears, 2005[1]):

> After some years of carefully considering Greenleaf's original writings, I have identified a set of ten characteristics of the servant-leader that I view as being of critical importance—central to the development of servant-leaders. My own work currently involves a deepening understanding of the following characteristics and how they

---

[1] Excerpted with permission from the author, Larry Spears, "The Understanding and Practice of Servant-Leadership," *International Journal of Servant-Leadership* (2005). Spears serves as senior advisory editor of IJSL, which is a joint publication of Gonzaga University and The Spears Center.

contribute to the meaningful practice of servant-leadership. These ten characteristics include:

Listening: Leaders have traditionally been valued for their communication and decision-making skills. Although these are also important skills for the servant-leader, they need to be reinforced by a deep commitment to listening intently to others. The servant-leader seeks to identify the will of a group and helps to clarify that will. He or she listens receptively to what is being said and unsaid. Listening also encompasses hearing one's own inner voice. Listening, coupled with periods of reflection, is essential to the growth and well-being of the servant-leader.

Empathy: The servant-leader strives to understand and empathize with others. People need to be accepted and recognized for their special and unique spirits. One assumes the good intentions of co-workers and colleagues and does not reject them as people, even when one may be forced to refuse to accept certain behaviors or performance. The most successful servant-leaders are those who have become skilled empathetic listeners.

Healing: The healing of relationships is a powerful force for transformation and integration. One of the great strengths of servant-leadership is the potential for healing one's self and one's relationship to others. Many people have broken spirits and have suffered from a variety of emotional hurts. Although this is a part of being human, servant-leaders recognize that they have an opportunity to help make whole those with whom they come in contact. In his essay, The Servant as Leader, Greenleaf writes, "There is something subtle communicated to one who is being served and led if, implicit in the compact between servant-leader and led, is the understanding that the search for wholeness is something they share."

Awareness: General awareness, and especially self-awareness, strengthens the servant-leader. Awareness helps one in understanding issues involving ethics, power, and values. It lends itself to being able to view most situations from a more integrated, holistic position. As Greenleaf observed: "Awareness is not a giver of solace—it is just the opposite. It is a disturber and an awakener. Able leaders are usually sharply awake and reasonably disturbed. They are not seekers after solace. They have their own inner serenity."

Persuasion: Another characteristic of servant-leaders is reliance on persuasion, rather than on one's positional authority, in making decisions within an organization. The servant-leader seeks to convince others, rather than coerce compliance. This particular element offers one of the clearest distinctions between the traditional authoritarian model and that of servant-leadership. The servant-leader is effective at building consensus within groups. This emphasis on persuasion over coercion finds its roots in the beliefs of the Religious Society of Friends (Quakers)—the denominational body to which Robert Greenleaf belonged.

Conceptualization: Servant-leaders seek to nurture their abilities to dream great dreams. The ability to look at a problem or an organization from a conceptualizing perspective means that one must think beyond day-to-day realities. For many leaders, this is a characteristic that requires discipline and practice. The traditional leader is consumed by the need to achieve short-term operational goals. The leader who wishes to also be a servant-leader must stretch his or her thinking to encompass broader-based conceptual thinking.

Within organizations, conceptualization is, by its very nature, a key role of boards of trustees or directors. Unfortunately, boards can sometimes become involved in the day-to-day operations— something that should be discouraged—and, thus, fail to provide the visionary concept for an institution. Trustees need to be mostly conceptual in their orientation, staffs need to be mostly operational in their perspective, and the most effective executive leaders probably need to develop both perspectives within themselves. Servant-leaders are called to seek a delicate balance between conceptual thinking and a day-to-day operational approach.

Foresight: Closely related to conceptualization, the ability to foresee the likely outcome of a situation is hard to define, but easier to identify. One knows foresight when one experiences it. Foresight is a characteristic that enables the servant-leader to understand the lessons from the past, the realities of the present, and the likely consequence of a decision for the future. It is also deeply rooted within the intuitive mind. Foresight remains a largely unexplored area in leadership studies, but one most deserving of careful attention.

Stewardship: Peter Block (author of *Stewardship* and *The Empowered Manager*) has defined stewardship as "holding something in trust for another." Robert Greenleaf's view of all institutions was one in which CEO's, staffs, and trustees all played significant roles in holding their institutions in trust for the greater good of society. Servant-leadership, like stewardship, assumes first and foremost a commitment to serving the needs of others. It also emphasizes the use of openness and persuasion, rather than control.

Commitment to the growth of people: Servant-leaders believe that people have an intrinsic value beyond their tangible contributions as workers. As such, the servant-leader is deeply committed to the growth of each and every individual within his or her organization. The servant-leader recognizes the tremendous responsibility to do everything in his or her power to nurture the personal and professional growth of employees and colleagues. In practice, this can include (but is not limited to) concrete actions such as making funds available for personal and professional development, taking a personal interest in the ideas and suggestions from everyone, encouraging worker involvement in decision-making, and actively assisting laid-off employees to find other positions.

Building community: The servant-leader senses that much has been lost in recent human history as a result of the shift from local communities to large institutions as the primary shaper of human lives. This awareness causes the servant-leader to seek to identify some means for building community among those who work within a given institution. Servant-leadership suggests that true community can be created among those who work in businesses and other institutions. Greenleaf said, "All that is needed to rebuild community as a viable life form for large numbers of people is for enough servant-leaders to show the way, not by mass movements, but by each servant-leader demonstrating his or her unlimited liability for a quite specific community-related group."

These ten characteristics of servant-leadership are by no means exhaustive. However, they do serve to communicate the power and promise that this concept offers to those who are open to its invitation and challenge.

Spears' summarization of Greenleaf's principles intertwine with much of what we have already discussed in our Leadership Model. He emphasizes the importance of listening intently to people. He goes on to expound on the importance of valuing people while being aware of one's own strengths and weaknesses. He also emphasizes the importance of leadership as collaboration versus authoritarian approaches to leadership. He continues with a discussion about servant-leaders dreaming dreams and nurturing those dreams. He even discusses the importance of foresight and being able to anticipate trends. The servant-leader values the growth of people much like our Leadership Model espouses respect for people. And the servant-leader accomplishes results through people working and growing together.

Robert Greenleaf recognized that organizations as well as individuals could be servant-leaders. Indeed, he had great faith that servant-leader organizations could change the world. In his second major essay on this topic, "The Institution as Servant," Greenleaf articulated what is often called the "credo":

> This is my thesis: caring for persons, the more able and the less able serving each other, is the rock upon which a good society is built. Whereas, until recently, caring was largely person to person, now most of it is mediated through institutions—often large, complex, powerful, impersonal; not always competent; sometimes corrupt. If a better society is to be built, one that is more just and more loving, one that provides greater creative opportunity for its people, then the most open course is to raise both the capacity to serve and the very performance as servant of existing major institutions by new regenerative forces operating within them. (Greenleaf R. , 2009)

What Servant-Leaders Do

With this background on servant-leadership, we return to our Leadership Model. Leaders can be effective when they act in the spirit of serving those around them. Leaders who act in this manner view their primary mission as serving and helping those around them to be successful. Servant leadership does not imply weakness but strength. This type of leader sees her role as enabling people to be successful as a team, as an organization, and individually.

Let's consider a few examples of how our Leadership Model and the essential trait of servant leadership can be integrated into it.

> The first responsibility of a leader is to define reality. The last is to say thank you. In between, the leader is a servant.
>
> —*Max de Pree*

Direction and Focus

A leader is serving her people when she provides direction and focus. How? Consider the alternative. A team that does not have direction is often confused and stress builds among team members. Sometimes debates become endless because there is no captain of the ship, no one to settle them down and get them on the right course. People can go off on tangents trying to do the "right thing" while not coordinated with others. This behavior adds to stress, repetitive work, and especially work done in conflict.

A servant-leader serves her people by providing clear direction and focus and by ultimately reducing damaging conflict and stress. No one enjoys a dysfunctional team, but everyone desires a well-functioning cohesive group united in focus and direction. Servant-leaders take this on as a way to serve their team. They are clear and concise, and they step in when necessary to resolve conflicts or confusion. A servant-leader is able to determine when conflict is constructive and when it is destructive. She takes appropriate action to facilitate or redirect conflict. The spirit or perspective of the servant-leader is, *I can serve my team because by doing so I can make the team more productive and ultimately successful.*

Work through People and Develop Them

A servant-leader understands that accomplishing work through people empowers and prepares them for future success. She realizes that she serves individuals by helping them develop skills and abilities. People who feel confident have less stress about their skills and abilities. When a servant-leader understands that she is serving her team in this manner, she is enabling people for current and future success.

Consider the old proverb: "Give a man a fish and you feed him for a day; teach a man to fish and you feed him for a lifetime." The servant-leader understands that developing people and accomplishing things through people serves them well because she has essentially taught them to fish.

Working with people means being available and giving time to people. It means coaching and listening and asking questions to help people discover solutions and work through them. This takes more time and requires patience. It may even mean letting people struggle at times so they can better learn and understand. If the leader makes all the decisions for his people, he does not serve them well. He can hurt his people professionally if they are not allowed to develop and strengthen their skills. I have seen this happen way too often.

One example of a failure to develop staff skills is in the area of decision making. I have seen leaders fail to develop their people's decision-making skills and then later be perplexed when these individuals get passed over for promotions or key opportunities. This pass-over is often because they have not demonstrated strong decision-making skills to upper management. The leader may have made all the decisions, but he has effectively crippled or stunted the growth of his people as a result.

My advice to young associates who work for a leader who will not develop them in their decision making or span of responsibility is to run and don't look back! Get out of that job and move on to someplace where you will be challenged and supported to grow and develop your decision making and leadership skills. A leader who refuses to put significant effort into developing his people is either too self-absorbed in his own career or too fearful and insecure to be an effective leader.

The servant-leader serves by valuing the individual's goals and aspirations as well as the organizational and team goals and objectives. The servant-leader endeavors to help both the individual and team be successful. Servant-leaders develop the individual to not only meet immediate team goals but also to improve his or her skills and capabilities for personal development. When servant-leaders approach their role in this spirit of serving the team and individuals, amazing things happen. Team goals are accomplished, and individuals become better employees with enhanced skills and abilities. Often in the process, individual team members develop stronger leadership skills. When leaders do this, they have effectively begun the process of replicating their skills in others. This creates a situation in which everyone wins, and they usually become better people.

Anticipation and Paradigm Shifts

In the dimension of *Strategic Innovation*, I discussed the importance of the leader anticipating the future and providing paradigm shifts. A servant-leader serves his team by constantly looking ahead and anticipating what may be coming to the team. There could be a change of direction by senior management or a change of scope on a project, but the leader is like the watch guard in the tower looking out for what may be coming. He explores and asks questions and searches out for understanding in trends or current thinking. He looks for ways to make the team more efficient and effective and sometimes wards off the wolves if there is any conflict. When the leader anticipates and looks ahead, he serves the group by preventing surprises that disrupt team unity and efficiency. He communicates what he can about changes and helps people adapt as necessary.

The servant-leader also looks for opportunities to improve the team's performance. Improvements can lead to complete paradigm shifts in the approach, methods, or organizational structure. The leader views this as an opportunity to keep the team effective, efficient, and relevant. Leaders who do this serve their team well and show respect and value to the team as well as to individuals.

Unfortunately, I have seen many situations where a leader has not driven continuous improvement, so the team has ended up surprised by changes in business needs or direction. The consequence has often been confusion, loss of trust, and the complete collapse of team unity and effectiveness. As leaders see trends changing, they must demonstrate thoughtful and effective communication to prepare their team. They must plan discussion and enter into a dialogue to facilitate transitions. Servant-leaders understand the human impact of change, and in an effort to serve people, they make an investment in time and effort to help people through the transition. Change management requires careful consideration and planning. I have seen this done well with excellent preparation and communication. I have also seen disasters.

I recently watched an organization decide to make a significant organizational change. The leaders were determined it would happen within a given timeframe and drove full speed ahead. They did this with very little preparation and minimal to no effort at communication. The connection with the people who were most impacted by the change was nearly nonexistent. The result was what you might expect. The short-term was disastrous. People felt unvalued, confused, and angry. Productivity nearly collapsed, and trust was deeply violated. Project performance slipped significantly. All of this could have been minimized if the leaders had just taken more time to plan, communicate, and understand how to effectively drive change. Instead, there was no semblance of servant leadership! The leaders did not indicate any spirit or attitude of serving the people through this change or intent to help them make the transition. They made insincere obligatory statements, such as "We know this will require adjustment." But they made no attempt at real engagement or dialogue with the people affected. They did not strive to build understanding, to listen, or to show any sense of genuine concern or compassion for people. As a result, many in the organization lost confidence in the leadership and felt their decisions were self-serving. Some of the best people left to join other organizations, productivity dropped, and overall performance of the business unit declined. Unfortunately, the leadership team still doesn't realize or acknowledge the long-term impact of their failure to act as servant-leaders and manage this change.

Simon Sinek is the author of *Start With Why: How Great Leaders Inspire Everyone to Take Action* (Sinek, 2009). Sinek has been fascinated by the leaders who make an impact in the world. In his book, he covers some remarkable patterns in how leaders think, act, and communicate. These patterns provided evidence for what Sinek labeled the Golden Circle— "a naturally occurring pattern, grounded in biology of human decision making, that explains why we are inspired by some people, leaders, messages and organizations over others." In essence, he discovered that effective leaders start with the why and not with the what or how. In the situation I described above, the leaders had failed to define the why for the organizational changes. As a consequence, the people affected were confused and angry.

Change is often difficult for people. It can mean old practices must be abandoned and new ones learned. Organization structure may be changed that requires new relationships to be established. Skills that were once highly valued may even become obsolete. Change can create real stress for people.

A number of years ago, I was part of a significant change effort at one of Lilly's manufacturing sites. Bob Cole was leading the area and spent significant time with the management team formulating a series of discussions with the staff. The focus of the preparation was on anticipating questions and concerns as well as formulating messages. All of this was to prepare people for the time when the change coming needed to be communicated. Eventually members of management held discussion groups with all our staff over a number of weeks. These meetings led to great discussions with the staff on why change was needed. Ultimately, when the change was announced, people accepted it and even thanked us for spending the time laying out the business realities. The paradigm shift was made successfully.

It may not always be feasible to spend such significant time preparing for a tough message, but never underestimate the value of spending time anticipating needs and helping people understand the why.

Getting Your Hands Dirty

On a cold, dark winter morning during the American Revolutionary War, General George

Washington rode out of his encampment and noticed a group of soldiers desperately trying to put a log on the top of a wall they were building. The only thing stopping them from throwing in the towel was a corporal, who was barking orders.

Washington asked the corporal why he didn't lend a hand. "Don't you see that I'm a corporal?" he answered. "I do," Washington said. The general then dismounted and helped the infantrymen put the timber in place. After completing the job, this commander and chief told the men that if they needed any help again, just send for him.

Why would Washington take time to help build a wall? Because the man who would become the Father of Our Country knew the war could not be won without the loyalty of his troops. And the way he created trustworthiness was through servant leadership. (Ramsey, 2015)

There are times when leaders need to come alongside their team and get their hands dirty. In doing this, leaders can support their team as well as truly understand the challenges the team faces. General Washington sent a clear message to his troops, who were trying to build a wall, that it was not beneath him to help. He clearly communicated that he was willing to do whatever was necessary to win the war. He showed great humility as a leader while his counterparts in the British army stood high on what the proper behavior should be for a superior officer. Washington also sent a clear message to the corporal that leadership means getting your hands dirty to help accomplish the goal.

As a director overseeing work across the globe, I found that I had the risk of losing perspective on the actual day-to-day challenges my people and their teams were dealing with in their jobs. So, over my career, I found one of the most important things I have done from time to time is to consciously reconnect with the actual work going on in the field.

In 2009, we were having some leadership resource issues on our large biotech project in Ireland. I talked with my boss, and we decided

I could temporarily run my group globally from Ireland as well as Indianapolis. I took a nine-month assignment living and working in Ireland at our Kinsale manufacturing site. I provided some day-to-day leadership support for our commissioning and qualification contractors and interfaced with the rest of the project team. These months were incredibly useful for me to reconnect with the teams in the field and help them identify and resolve problems. The time regrounded me and reminded me why we used some of our practices and methods to perform our work. It also generated a wealth of new ideas and opportunities for improvement on future projects. Finally, it allowed me to talk with project leaders around the world from a practical standpoint of having recently done the work in the field.

I realize not every leader will have this kind of opportunity to "get their hands dirty" by spending many months engaged in day-to-day activities. However, I encourage you to look for opportunities to demonstrate real-time support and engagement in the day-to-day challenges. Serve the team by helping solve a problem or provide insight or resources. When a leader does this, he has an opportunity to demonstrate genuine servant leadership.

The Larry Principle

At a Fellowship of Christian Athletes Leadership Camp many years ago, a thirteen-year old named Larry stood up to speak during an open mike night. He "was a five-foot-tall seventh grader from inner-city Kansas City and a hit with the campers. He was funny, lovable, charming, and outspoken. His contagious laugh and raspy voice made him stand out from the others, and he became the camp favorite." When Larry reached the mike, he spoke seven simple words: "If you ain't serving, you ain't leading!" Then he left the stage and returned to his seat (Britton & Page, 2007, pp. 67-70).

Larry aptly sums up the central point of this chapter. Leadership requires service. So, if you are not serving, you are not leading. Period.

Leadership Takeaways

- Robert K. Greenleaf in "The Servant as Leader" established that "The servant-leader is servant first … It begins with the natural feeling that if one wants to serve, serve first."

- Greenfield's ten principles of servant leadership are

  1. Listening
  2. Empathy
  3. Healing
  4. Awareness
  5. Persuasion
  6. Conceptualization
  7. Foresight
  8. Stewardship
  9. Commitment to the growth of people
  10. Building community

- Servant-leaders view their primary mission as serving and helping those around them become successful.

- Examples of how the essential trait of servant leadership can be integrated into the Leadership Model include

  o Direction and focus
  o Work through people and develop them
  o Anticipation and paradigm shifts
  o Getting your hands dirty

- Effective leaders start with the why and not with the what or how.

- Servant-leaders need to get their hands dirty, which involves serving the team by helping them solve problems.

20

Courage

Courage is not limited to the battlefield or the Indianapolis 500 or bravely catching a thief in your house. The real tests of courage are much quieter. They are the inner tests, like remaining faithful when nobody's looking, like enduring pain when the room is empty, like standing alone when you're misunderstood.

—Charles Swindoll

Throughout this book, I have discussed a number of essentials for effective leadership. However, the impact of courage—this final trait—must not be overlooked. Without it, pressure and fear can overwhelm a leader, and adversity will often become too much to handle. The desire to maintain the status quo will be the dominant mantra in the workplace culture that is resistant to change. In every example I have shared of outstanding leadership, courage is the trait that has been present in the background, enabling tough decisions and risk-taking and driving needed change.

Henry Knox showed incredible courage in bringing the artillery from Fort Ticonderoga in the dead of winter. Dr. Stan Marshall showed courage while taking a risk with new conversational techniques with his entire research staff. Nathaniel Bowditch stepped up and took the helm of the ship in a blinding storm and navigated it safely into harbor. General Dwight D. Eisenhower sat alone with his thoughts on a rainy night in Southwick House and made the decision for D-Day to commence. It took incredible courage for each leader to act.

Melanie Greenburg, PhD, explains (Greenberg, August 23, 2012):

> Courage is something that everyone wants—an attribute of good character that makes us worthy of respect. From the Bible to fairy tales, ancient myths to Hollywood movies, our culture is rich with exemplary tales of bravery and self-sacrifice for the greater good. From the cowardly lion in The *Wizard of Oz* who finds the courage to face the witch, to David and Goliath in the Bible, to *Star Wars* and *Harry Potter*, children are raised on a diet of heroic and inspirational tales.
>
> Yet courage is not just physical bravery. History books tell colorful tales of social activists, such as Martin Luther King and Nelson Mandela, who chose to speak out against injustice at great personal risk. Entrepreneurs such as Steve Jobs and Walt Disney, who took financial risks to follow their dreams and innovate, are like modern-day knights, exemplifying the rewards and public accolades that courage can bring. There are different types of courage, ranging from physical strength and endurance to mental and innovation.

I think there are four types of courage leaders need to have to be successful. Each type enables leaders to be effective in the Leadership Model.

The Courage to Act Despite Fear

Fear is a normal human condition. We all face fear at some point in our lives. The important thing is what we do with that fear, or rather what we let it do or not do to us. Fear is the behavioral response we have to a pervasive set of beliefs we have formed out of our past experiences. While fear can sometimes help us, it can also cripple us.

I have seen leaders paralyzed by fear. They have failed to make decisions because of it. This fear can be driven by concern over the disapproval of others, especially senior management. Sometimes the fear can be over the effort required to make a change. And then there's the fear of failure that plagues many leaders. In attempts to deal with fear, sometimes leaders play it safe and fail to make any decision, hoping the situation will simply blow over. When this happens, they miss the opportunity for significant change, leaving the status quo in place. Depending on the role a leader plays, giving in to her fear can even cause injustice and other wrongs to go unchallenged.

One ancient story of overcoming great fear is that of Esther, found in the Hebrew Scriptures in the book that bears her name. Esther lived in the Persian city of Susa with her uncle Mordecai in the 480s BCE. She had moved in with him following her parents' death. He raised her as his daughter. King Xeres who ruled the Medes and Persian Empire had exiled the previous queen after she had refused to respond to his command to appear before him and his drunken guests at a banquet.

After a period of time, King Xeres became lonely and his advisors convinced him to hold a type of beauty pageant to ultimately find a new queen. All of the young virgins were summoned to the palace and within the course of a year were prepared to individually meet the king. The king would then choose who would be the next queen. Ultimately, Esther was chosen as the new queen, and the king greatly loved her. But there was no straight road to this fairytale ending. A holocaust threatened to derail it.

You see, Esther was not a native Persian. She was Jewish, born to Jewish parents who the Babylonians carried into exile many years previously after the overthrow of Jerusalem. Esther had not divulged her national origin to King Xerxes.

However, one day her uncle Mordecai approached her in great distress. She asked him what the problem was, and he explained that the king had been convinced to issue a decree against all Jewish people in the Persian kingdom. They were all to be killed, every man, woman, and child. Esther was greatly distressed at the news, though she lived a life of unparalleled luxury. The king gave her a wonderful life, and she could keep enjoying it if she would just remain silent about her heritage. Mordecai pleaded with her to go to the king and ask him to stop the decree and spare the Jewish people. Esther had a decision to make. Would she risk her new life and possibly die for revealing her identity with fellow Jews? And if she went to speak to the king without him summoning her, she was also risking certain death. She knew that if the king held out his golden scepter when a person approached him, the man or woman would be welcome. If, on the other hand, he withheld his scepter, the individual would be killed. The king had not summoned her for over thirty days. What should she do? Should she play it safe and not risk death and keep her Jewish heritage hidden from the king?

Mordecai sent a message to her that said, "Don't think for a moment that because you're in the palace you will escape when all the Jews are killed. If you keep quiet at a time like this, deliverance and relief for the Jews will arise from some other place, but you and your relatives will die. Who knows if perhaps you were made queen for just such a time as this?" (Esther 4:13–14 New Living Translation)

After much prayer and fasting, Esther ultimately went to the king, despite her fear that he would not receive her or that she would fall under the death decree and die with her Jewish kindred. Upon seeing her enter the royal chamber, the king welcomed her into his presence. Esther asked that the king and the man, Haman—the one responsible for turning the king against the Jewish people—attend a banquet the next day. She had decided that this would be the time that she would reveal her request to King Xerxes.

The next day at the banquet, the king asked Esther what she desired. Queen Esther replied, "If I have found favor with the king, and if it pleases the king to grant my request, I ask that my life and the lives of my people will be spared." (Esther 7:3 New Living Translation) With this request, Esther identified that she was Jewish and that she was interceding for her people. She did this in front of Haman, the king's advisor who had instigated the plan to perpetuate a Jewish holocaust. Esther displayed incredible courage, the kind of courage that changed the destiny of an entire nation of people. Her act exposed Haman's plan and deceit, and saved the Jews from slaughter.

Leaders must be able to overcome their fears to act, even when it could mean personal loss or even death. Oskar Schindler had this kind of courage in World War II when he was credited with saving the lives of over 1,200 Jews from being sent to concentration camps and a horrible demise. He did this knowing that if he were caught, his life would be forfeited at the hands of the Nazis.

Maybe the decisions you are facing as a leader are not life-and-death, but you may still feel a great deal of fear. You may be fearful of failure and the professional and personal consequences. You may be afraid of facing resistance to change. Effective leaders must not let fear control them. Leaders with courage choose to act despite their fear.

Courage begins with our personal values—those deeply held beliefs. Personal values are the foundation of character and courage. Courage also comes from the confidence that the leader has fostered in her leadership.

When a leader feels that others trust her, she has more strength to make the tough decisions.

When a leader has invested the time and energy to really understand the business, then her analysis and path forward are clearer to her and others. Her courage grows.

And when she has been successful producing results in the past, she understands more clearly the pathway to success because she has been there before. Her courage increases.

When a leader has spent time looking at the future and understanding what is happening in the world, her courage to drive change accelerates. She knows the dangers and challenges ahead and acts with urgency.

Nurturing success in each dimension of the Leadership Model will ultimately build the courage to act decisively when needed.

Esther changed the destiny of the Jewish people. When they faced extinction as a people at the hands of sheer evil, she made a stand that could have ended her life. It would not be the last time the Jews would face this type of threat. To this day the Jewish people yearly celebrate the holiday of Purim, which commemorates God's deliverance of the Jewish people through Esther. Mordecai may have been right when he said, "Who knows if perhaps you were made queen for just such a time as this?" Leaders who are facing fears regarding tough decisions, even though they know they are the right decisions, should remember these words of Mordecai and apply them to themselves. Is it possible that you are in leadership for such a time as this?

Courage to Stand Up for What's Right

Leaders must also have the courage to take a stand when needed. The stand may be for a personal value, a principle, or a truth. It may be to stand against an injustice or outright evil in the world. The stand may even be against positions held by governments, companies, or even the prevailing culture. Taking a stand will often have a cost that will require courage.

William Wilberforce has been described in history as "the Washington of humanity." He led a two-decade-long fight in England's Parliament to abolish slave trading in the British Empire. Men like Abraham Lincoln and Frederick Douglas spoke of him reverently as the great pioneer and father of the abolition movement (Metaxaz 2015). But Wilberforce's decision to take on the abolitionist cause empire-wide did not come easily.

By a young age, Wilberforce had already become a powerful British politician in the 1700s. He had risen to great power and was highly respected. The culture in London and throughout much of Britain had become quite decadent. Slave trading was an accepted profitable practice with slave ships routinely taking thousands of slaves to the American colonies. Child labor was also a major problem in Britain, with poor children as young as five and six years old being forced to work ten- and twelve-hour days in horrendous conditions. Alcoholism was also rampant, as Eric Metaxas explains: "Everyone seemed to be addicted to alcohol, and there seemed to be nothing to help it. Members of the upper classes were perpetually drunk on claret—in fact, members of Parliament were often drunk during legislative sessions—and the lower class were drunk on gin." Prostitution was a serious problem as well. Says Metaxas, "It has been estimated that nearly 25 percent of all single women in London at the time were prostitutes with an average age of sixteen." (Metaxas 2015)

Wilberforce had been part of the political and cultural system. He had looked the other way, cynical about morality and faith. However, everything changed after a long trip across Europe with a traveling companion named Isaac Milner. During this trip, Milner shared his faith in God with Wilberforce. They discussed and debated over many days:

> To his credit, Wilberforce was intellectually honest, and he didn't shrink from robust debate.... By the time their trip together had come to an end, Wilberforce was in the unpleasant and difficult spot of believing that he had been quite wrong in his previous views and that Milner was right. ... Wilberforce found to his significant distress that he had come to believe with his whole mind that what he had been sure was false was in fact true: the God of the Bible existed, Jesus existed in history and was the promised Messiah, and the Scriptures were not silly old myths but truth itself. For someone of his social standing and prestige, he was in a curious and uncomfortable position. What to do about it? (Metaxas 2015)

Wilberforce was entrenched in British politics, which, at the time, was dirty and vile. His social circles were no better. And now he saw that his political and social worlds were in critical conflict with his new beliefs. He began to recognize the injustice, pain, and suffering that he had previously walked by and simply ignored. He saw the conflict between Scripture and the moral depravity of his time. He considered leaving politics, retreating from everything, and escaping to a monastery.

After much soul searching, prayer, and discussion with ministers regarding his path forward, Wilberforce wrote in his diary, "God Almighty has set me two Great Objectives: suppression of the Slave Trade and the Reformation of Manners." Wilberforce had now established his values and mission. With the phrase "Reformation of Manners," he meant the reformation of society and culture. Metaxas explains that Wilberforce now "saw all society was broken and in need of reform." These "Great Objectives" set the direction for the rest of his life. (Metaxas 2015)

Wilberforce was a change agent. He saw the world around him and could not let it stay the same. Injustice was everywhere, and it weighed heavily on him. He decided to take a stand. He did so with the fear of impacting relationships and risking the loss of power, influence, and position.

His fear was well founded. British society did not embrace his mission. He was challenging economic forces that had greatly profited from slave trading as well as child labor, prostitution, and alcohol sales. He knew he could not yield to his fears, so he pressed on to lead an incredible social change in his world. For two decades he debated and lobbied time and time again with the members of Parliament. He was rejected over and over again, but still he pushed forward, driving with all he had to change the direction of the British Empire.

After decades of struggle in Parliament. Wilberforce finally saw an Abolition Bill passed by the House of Lords and the House of Commons in 1807. His battle continued for twenty-five more years to eliminate any element of slavery within the British Empire. He had changed the direction of a nation and impacted countless lives in the process.

The leader who has established personal values as well as organizational values that are aligned has a solid foundation for the courage to act. When these values have been internalized, they establish what is important, what is vital. William Wilberforce could not reconcile a British Empire that allowed slave trading with his personal values and faith as a Christian. He chose to act. This was the same type of courage that Mark and Huldah Buntain exhibited in India. They chose to act, to make a difference, to invest their lives in changing the lives of countless people in India.

Leaders who establish a foundation of strong values create a basis for decision making. Well-established values can help them find the courage to act. To not act becomes a personal conflict with essentially who they are as a human being. Wilberforce chose to not live with the hypocrisy of inaction.

> Man cannot discover new oceans unless he has the courage to lose sight of the shore.
> —*Lord Chesterfield*

Courage to Expand Your Horizons

Earlier I talked about how leaders must expand their horizons. They must continually grow and increase their understanding of the business and the world around them. Expanding one's horizon may require courage because what a leader may find might bring surprise and even make him uncomfortable. Things may not be exactly as he thought, and this can require change in views, opinions, and direction. It may even require an urgent response.

Pixar is a tremendous success story of perseverance in creating a new type of animated movie. After years of development and challenges with technology and investors, Pixar's Ed Catmull and his colleagues were finally triumphant with the blockbuster movie *Toy Story*. Its huge success and that of its sequels, along with the numerous other animated adventures including *Monsters Inc.* and *Finding Nemo*, have made Pixar the absolute leader in animation in Hollywood. Pixar's technology innovation revolutionized animation so much that it quickly displaced the old methods used by Disney animators. The day *Toy Story* was released to theaters the whole approach to animation in movies irrevocably changed.

The journey of Ed Catmull and the Pixar team is very interesting. Pixar had been owned by Lucasfilm and George Lucas, the producer of *Star Wars*, and then sold to Steve Jobs, the founder of Apple. Both Lucas and Jobs had a profound impact on Pixar's formation and development as a powerhouse in digital animation. Lucas brought the vision of using computer generated effects to take movies to a whole new level of visual impact and special effects, while Jobs brought incredible technical and business insight for Pixar. The company struggled for years to develop the technology of computer animation with the explicit goal of making full-length feature films that touched audiences with a visually impactful story. Pixar finally accomplished that goal with *Toy Story*, but Ed Catmull, the CEO of Pixar, was left unsatisfied:

> For twenty years, my life had been defined by the goal of making the first computer graphics movie. Now that that goal had been reached, I had what I can only describe as a hollow, lost feeling.

> As a manager, I felt a troubling lack of purpose. *Now what?* The thing that had replaced it seemed to be the act of running a company, which was more than enough to keep me busy, but it wasn't *special.* Pixar was now public and successful, yet there was something unsatisfying about the prospect of merely keeping it running. (Catmull 2014)

Catmull had reached a point that many leaders do after a significant prolonged effort to build something that achieved a major goal. That let-down feeling after the initial excitement of project completion led him to wonder what needed to happen next. He knew that the day-to-day managing of the enterprise would not be enough to satisfy him. Through this seeking process, he came across something that surprised him: "I discovered that, during the making of *Toy Story*, I had completely missed something that was threatening to undo us. And I'd missed it even though I thought I'd been paying attention." (Catmull 2014) He went on to explain that he had missed a significant tension that had arisen between his production managers and creative staff during the making of *Toy Story*. Everyone was so focused on getting the movie out that demands and relationships had been broken—so much so that some of the staff were considering not signing up for the next movie, *A Bug's Life.*

When Catmull began to investigate this rift in the organization, he quickly realized that it had been going on around him while he was completely oblivious to it. Pixar had put great emphasis on mutual respect between artists and technical people. Catmull assumed this same respect had been afforded to Pixar's production managers, but it had not. Now its production managers were viewed as second-class citizens who impeded good filmmaking.

Catmull had assumed that people were open to him and sharing what was really going on in the organization. News of this internal rift completely blindsided him. This revelation led him to shape his new purpose moving forward with Pixar. As Catmull puts it:

> But one thing could not have been more plain: Figuring out how to build a sustainable

creative culture—one that didn't just pay lip service to the importance of things like honesty, excellence, communication, originality, and self-assessment but really *committed* to them, no matter how uncomfortable that became—wasn't a singular assignment. It was a day-in, day-out, full-time job. And one that I wanted to do. (Catmull 2014)

Once he knew about the problem, he delved deeply into it, striving to understand the source of the problem and identify a solution. As a result, Catmull created a clear new vision and purpose for himself at Pixar.

Previously, I described Jeff Simmons' internal Lilly TEDx talk. Simmons shared that he went to Nairobi, Kenya to see hunger up close, to understand what hunger really looks like in our world, to put a face to starving people. He wanted to try to comprehend the reality that thousands are dying across the world everyday from hunger. As a result, he became a changed man and brought change to Elanco Animal Health. The company focus changed. It was no longer about just selling products. It was now about being a part of the solution to overcome world hunger. Jeff Simmons is a leader who has broadened his horizons. He went outside of his comfort zone to a hut in Nairobi to get face to face with hunger.

Leaders must overcome their fears and move into areas that are new and often uncomfortable. It is in these places that they can learn, grow, and often get new vision.

The dimension of Strategic Innovation requires exploration and learning. Many things can be done to foster this in a leader. However, when a leader has been successful, he must muster the courage to keep growing and evolving. Human nature can tend to cause us to keep doing what we have always done, especially when we are successful. Ultimately, though, a leader must overcome fear of the unknown and become a student once again. He must stretch himself beyond his current understanding and comfort zone.

For Ed Catmull, this meant building on the success of *Toy Story* by exploring and understanding the human dynamics at play in Pixar.

Consequently, he came to a new vision and understanding of how he could impact the future of the company. For Jeff Simmons, his exploration led to a new personal hunger that translated to his entire organization. He led Elanco into embracing a new mission to help solve world hunger.

Are you willing to get out of your comfort zone? To learn new things? To personally grow? What do you have the courage to step out and actually do?

Courage to Be Accountable—Even When Wrong

Accountability implies transparency and responsibility. Effective leaders accept accountability as a key element of their role. They don't default to being defensive but strive to promote clarity, accuracy, and candidness regarding personal and organizational performance. Leaders who are accountable create an accountability culture in their organization. But some people can perceive accountability as painful and even dangerous, especially when things have not gone as expected. This is just one reason that accountability requires courage.

Recall that on the eve of the Allied invasion of Europe during World War II, General Eisenhower prepared a statement of accountability for the distinct possibility of things going terribly wrong. He understood the risks associated with D-Day, and he understood that he must be accountable for his decision to proceed.

Throughout history we have had many examples of leaders who refused to be accountable. They have often been the first to point fingers of blame and divert attention. One such case of leadership accountability failure was the Deepwater Horizon fire and subsequent oil spill in the Gulf of Mexico in April 2010. Eleven people went missing and were never found. This tragedy is considered the largest accidental marine oil spill in the history of the petroleum industry. Following the spill, the British Petroleum CEO Tony Heyward made a number of controversial statements. On May 30th, he told a reporter, "we're sorry for the massive disruption it's caused to their lives. There's no one who wants this thing over more than I do, I'd like my life back." (USA Today, 1 June 2010) On May 31st, Hayward disputed claims that there were huge underwater plumes of oil suspended in the Gulf as had been reported by scientists from three universities. He said that there was "no evidence" that plumes of oil were suspended under the sea, and that because it is lighter than water, any plumes seen are just in the process of rising to the surface. (AFP, 2 June 2010) Each of these statements became public relations disasters. But more importantly, they represented Heyward's pervasive attitude of declining to accept any accountability for the events on the Deepwater Horizon rig and the consequences that followed.

Accountability has a profound impact on an organization. If leaders fail to accept accountability, they can create a culture of blame, excuse making, and acceptance of poor performance. On the other hand, accountable leaders are not only accountable for their own actions, as Eisenhower was on the eve of D-Day, but they expect accountability throughout their organization. Accountable leaders address performance issues in a direct manner. They accept their role to coach, mentor, and correct poor performance. Leaders who provide timely feedback actually demonstrate genuine care for their employees. They address issues in a manner that keeps them from becoming even larger issues and set patterns of behavior. Failure by a leader to address a performance issue only worsens over time. The employee's poor performance continues, and others in the organization can become frustrated at their coworkers' inadequate performance.

It is human nature to avoid blame and the potential consequences associated with being held responsible. Some leaders become consumed with diverting blame and making sure it does not land on them or their organization. They avoid any hint of accountability. Still, I have seen some of the greatest acts of leadership occur when leaders have stepped up and accepted responsibility for a problem and committed to resolving the issues. Often an organization and other leaders will rally around an accountable leader to help them resolve an issue. People gravitate toward people who are accountable and commit to take action. Serious problems arise, though, when no one accepts accountability.

Earlier I established that leaders also must hold people accountable for their performance and behaviors. Unfortunately, some leaders avoid this. They are driven by a fear of conflict and confrontation. When they give in to this fear, leaders and organizations can be held captive by the poor performance of others. This doesn't benefit anyone.

Unfortunately, accountability has been often viewed as an ominous thing, a foreboding cloud of judgment held over people and organizations. The fact, however, is that the goal of a leader should be to create a culture of accountability in an organization. This culture should be defined as one in which people openly embrace accountability for results. It should be a culture of open, direct feedback that is not based on personal attacks but on a goal of continually improving.

Ed Catmull created this in the Pixar culture with a concept he calls "The Braintrust." The Braintrust is a group of experts who meet routinely during the creation of each Pixar movie and provide candid feedback regarding the movie's development. The goal in this is to make the movie better. No one takes the feedback personally. Catmull expressed the process and goal this way:

> Everyone says quality is important, but they must do more than say it. They must live, think, and breathe it. When our people asserted that they only wanted to make films of the highest quality and when we pushed ourselves to the limit in order to prove our commitment to that ideal, Pixar's identity was cemented. We would be a company that would never settle. That didn't mean that we wouldn't make mistakes. Mistakes are part of creativity. But when we did, we would strive to face them without defensiveness and [with a] willingness to change. (Catmull 2014)

The Pixar employees have embraced this commitment to quality and are accountable to continually growing and learning together. This type of culture is empowering and makes accountability very real and results focused.

Building Courage

I have described four areas in which a leader must demonstrate courage. But how does a leader develop the courage to act? I offer the following ways you can use to develop the courage to face fears, take a stand, expand your horizons, and embrace accountability.

Define the Fear

What is it that you are really afraid of? Is it a fear of failure? Is it potential conflict? Or could it possibly be a fear of ridicule or something similar? Sometimes our fears are irrational or unfounded, but other times they can be very real and justifiable. Understanding exactly what you are afraid of can help you define an approach for overcoming the fear and moving forward with definitive, effective action.

Revisit the Values

Leaders must be true to themselves and their values. Values define what is ultimately important. They influence behavior, attitudes, priorities, and interactions. Values can be defined as broad preferences concerning appropriate courses of action or outcomes. They reflect a person's sense of right and wrong or what ought to be. A leader can find courage by revisiting his values and reestablishing what is important to him. Wilberforce could not reconcile his values with the practices and behaviors of the British government and culture. He made a courageous decision to act despite potential personal risk.

What are your values? Do they foster courage or undermine it in you?

It is also important for you to revisit the organization's values. If organizational behaviors or decisions are not in alignment with the organization's values, a leader can invoke these values as support for her stand. While at Lilly, I experienced several incidences where leaders courageously confronted other leaders about decisions that did not align with Lilly corporate values. The challenge was uncomfortable but effectively caused people to stop and revisit their direction and behaviors.

Seek out Counsel

When faced with any difficult decision, it is wise to seek out input from trusted colleagues and mentors. When fear is present, their counsel can help a leader gain perspective, identify better approaches, and test thought processes. A leader should identify those people who are trusted colleagues and mentors. They should be people who are leaders themselves and willing to speak with honesty and frankness.

Every leader should have these kinds of people in their inner circle. They are not necessarily defined by title but more so by character and reputation. Counsel from an inner circle of colleagues and mentors should be listened to, appropriately weighed, and processed.

Do you have such an inner circle? If not, who could you approach to start forming such a group?

Prepare Carefully

The reality may be that our fears are grounded and very real. There may be conflict, ridicule, or even the potential for failure, but we still must prepare for the reaction to a decision, for this is vital for success. Preparation helps leaders be more confident and ultimately have the courage to act. I have seen leaders take action without preparation. The result has often been significant conflict and resistance that they were unprepared to deal with. When this happens, people impacted by a decision become less confident in the leader because she often becomes defensive. When a leader is about to make a tough decision for an organization, I strongly recommend preparing the message and answers to potential questions. In addition, networking with key "thought leaders" who will be impacted by the decision could provide valuable insight as well as potential supporters. Preparation builds courage because preparation creates confidence.

Stay the Course

When a leader is taking action that requires courage it is important to understand that resistance, frustration and even anger are normal responses. Human response to change has been well documented and can be described by the following diagram. A leader must not run from conflict, anger or resistance but rather help people navigate through the process to a place of understanding, acceptance, and moving on. This requires "grit" to stay the course as well as dialogue and listening by the leader. It also may require some adjustments to approach as feedback is received. The willingness to listen and make appropriate adjustments to approach can actually build support because people feel that their feedback has been heard.

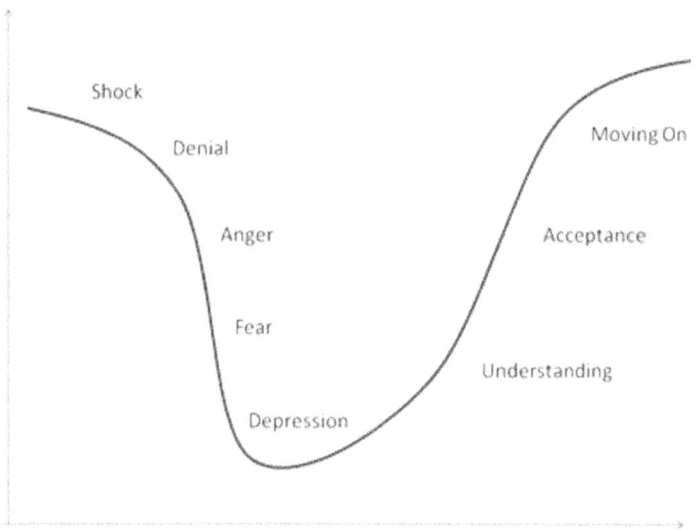

Commit to Listen and Learn

It may not sound as particularly courageous for a leader to expand her horizons, but more than one leader has refused to open her mind and heart to the reality of what is really going on in her organization. A popular TV show over the last several years has been *Undercover Boss*, produced by Steven Lambert. The show's format features the experiences of senior executives working undercover in their own companies to investigate how their firms really work and to identify how they can be improved. In nearly every show, a CEO working undercover is surprised to learn about inefficiencies, problems, and difficulties workers and customers face while working with their company. The reality is that once these issues are uncovered on national TV, these CEOs are compelled, as responsible leaders, to address the issues.

Ed Catmull could have been basking in the success of *Toy Story* after years of effort, but he was willing to look deeper at the Pixar organization. What he found was not good and required action. Jeff Simmons delved into really understanding the impact of hunger in our world, and it changed him and his organization. In each case, these leaders listened and learned. When a leader listens and learns, she builds understanding, and with understanding, she can develop the appropriate actions.

Some leaders can run from problems because they really don't understand them and have no idea how to take appropriate action. Courage to expand understanding can come from active listening and learning. A leader who chooses to become a student of not just her organization but also the world around her can develop the courage to confront major issues and challenges.

Create a Culture of Accountability

Accountability is best established when the entire organization embraces it as a cultural norm. Joseph Folkman in *Forbes* (November 14, 2014) shared details from a study he conducted on accountability in organizations (Folkman, 2014). When Folkman looked at exceptional leader behaviors, he found eight that were linked to personal accountability. Here is my summary of them.

Drive for Results

A lack of clarity in priorities and accountability leads to confusion. And conflicting messages dissipate accountability. So Folkman states, "If you want people to be responsible, then you must clearly define the results that you want them to deliver, and let them have a fair amount of control on how they deliver those results."

Honesty and Integrity

When leaders are open and direct with their people, they encourage people to reciprocate with openness and directness. Experiences create beliefs, which produce behaviors and corresponding results. Folkman asks people to examine their situation: "When your boss asks in a company meeting, 'how's that project coming?' do you honestly reply, 'we are really behind' or 'pretty good?' Those who are accountable have the courage to tell the truth. Leaders create the culture of openness and integrity."

Trust

Folkman's research found that, in cultures where the leaders were not trusted, the employees had the following issues:

- They were not confident that their efforts would be rewarded.

- They suspected the leader may take advantage of them.

- They constantly questioned the leader's motives.

- They were convinced that the leader would take credit for their accomplishments.

Obviously, these beliefs do not promote accountability. So what does? According to Folkman, "the three pillars that build trust are positive relationships, knowledge, and consistency of leaders."

Clear Vision and Direction

Absolute clarity of the organization's vision is paramount for success. Folkman asks, "How can you expect people to be accountable if they aren't absolutely clear about the organization's vision for where they're going and what needs to be accomplished? Clearly, you can't." He adds: "There is an old Chinese proverb that explains this issue well: 'The hunter that chases two rabbits catches neither one.' In organizations, people are often chasing multiple rabbits and they don't catch any of them."

Problem-Solving and Technical Expertise

People must be taught the skills and given the training also to be successful in their job. People cannot feel accountable if they don't feel capable or competent in their work. Leaders assure their people that they have the capability and competence, and this leads to accountability.

Communication

As Folkman states, "when a leader effectively communicates, others can understand what they are accountable for." Effective communication by a leader requires listening, asking, and telling—in this order!

Ability to Change

Folkman's research found a correlation between leaders being good at creating change in an organization and their having employees who operate at higher levels of accountability. Folkman establishes that "Leaders who are good at instituting change are effective at the following behaviors: accepting feedback, taking on challenges, innovating, spreading optimism, showing concern, and setting clear goals."

Collaboration and Resolving Conflict

Cooperation breeds accountability. Folkman asks, "Are you cooperating or competing with others in your group?" Once again, experiences create beliefs, and beliefs produce behaviors and subsequent results. A leader who fosters a highly competitive environment can undermine any spirit of collaboration. People and organizations can become pitted against one another. Peter Blow at Columbia University did a series of studies on this issue that showed that teams who collaborate and are cooperative are far more successful than those who compete.

When you examine Folkman's findings in light of the Leadership Model I have presented, you can draw a strong correlation. A leader who develops confidence creates trust, which is an important aspect Folkman describes. When the leader demonstrates strong command capability, he can provide the appropriate level of technical knowledge and guidance. A leader who achieves results provides clarity and focus. Folkman also emphasizes the importance of being an effective change agent, which aligns with manifesting Strategic Innovation within the model. Folkman's study essentially confirms that implementation of the Leadership Model and reinforces the establishment of an accountable culture within an organization.

Final Wisdom

Courage is an essential trait in a leader. Leadership is not for wimps. The vast challenges facing leaders in business, communities, and governments can be overwhelming.

I want to leave you with two final thoughts about the characteristics of leadership before we delve into Part 6 together. In addition to developing courage, a leader must have old fashion grit. By that I mean, the determination to stay the course. Sometimes a leader must slog through the resistance. How he does this matters. For instance, he needs to be patient with people as they learn and develop their skills. He must be consistent in message and supportive as people follow. He must be accountable and model the expected behaviors. All of this requires discipline and diligence and, well, grit.

Finally, every leader needs wisdom. When asked by God what he could grant him, King Solomon asked for wisdom. Scripture tells us that God was pleased with his request. Every leader needs wisdom. Wisdom transcends knowledge, experience, and skills. Wisdom is knowing when and how to act and respond to people and situations. Wisdom is about understanding people, situations, and events in a manner that a leader can formulate the appropriate optimal action. Wisdom can come from several sources, such as the counsel of an inner circle, but I have found that I should take the lead from Solomon and ask God for wisdom. Faith, prayer, and meditation can bring revelation, insight, and direction regarding decisions.

Leadership Takeaways

- Courage begins with our personal values—those deeply held beliefs.

- Courage must be developed to face fears.

- Courage must be obtained to take a stand.

- Courage is required to expand your horizons.

- Courage is required for accountability.

- To build courage:
    - Define the fear
    - Revisit the values
    - Seek out counsel
    - Prepare carefully

- o   Stay the course
- o   Commit to listen and learn
- o   Create a culture of accountability

- Apply grit.

- Seek wisdom.

Part 6

The Essentials of Identifying and Developing Leaders

21

The Essentials for Selecting Leaders

Choose your leaders with wisdom and forethought.
To be led by a coward is to be controlled by all that the coward fears.
To be led by a fool is to be led by the opportunists who control the fool.
To be led by a thief is to offer up your most precious treasures to be stolen.
To be led by a liar is to ask to be told lies.
To be led by a tyrant is to sell yourself and those you love into slavery.

—Octavia E. Butler

T hroughout this book, I have referred to the Leadership Model that I have used for a number of years to coach leadership behaviors. The model is a leadership system in which each dimension interacts to reinforce the others in a collaborative manner. This tool has been helpful in assessing the leadership strengths and weaknesses of people in and outside major companies. It has been used to frame conversations and explore opportunities for discussion about personal leadership abilities. The premise has always been that if individuals follow the principles of this model, they will have a high probability of becoming successful leaders.

In this chapter, I will address how this tool can be used to choose and develop leaders for an organization.

Explorers, Pioneers, and Settlers

Joel Barker introduced an interesting observation a number of years ago in his book *Future Edge* (Barker, 1992). Barker is a futurist. He spends his days exploring trends in culture, technology, business, and geopolitics. From his research, he can project future trends and opportunities. Leaders heavily rely on this type of reconnaissance if they are going to be Strategic Innovators and anticipate the future.

Barker shared in his book that through the first half of the nineteenth century, America could be demographically characterized by three groups of people: explorers, pioneers, and settlers. Explorers were the people who forged new trails and went where few others had gone. They were enticed by adventure and had a high level of curiosity for what was over the next mountain or around the next bend in the river. They always pushed farther and were often driven by the possibility of riches. They were often the hairy odd fellows in the town with a mule. They were socially awkward, and they stayed in town long enough to get supplies before pressing back into the wilderness to seek new adventures or riches. While in town, they always told stories about the incredible riches and the great adventures to be had over the mountains and down the rivers. Many dismissed these stories as wild exaggerations of crazy fools, but a few listened and thought and pondered about these claims of abundant opportunities and possibilities.

Slowly some people decided to go see for themselves if the reports of the explorers were true. Instead of going alone, however, they loaded wagons with supplies and even took their families. These people, the second group, were the pioneers. They wanted to go and possess the new land, to set up villages, and see what this new land had to offer. They wanted to exploit the land for its riches, or take this as an opportunity for a fresh beginning with nearly limitless possibilities.

The pioneers established the first settlements in America, which were rough villages and forts. They established the first structured commerce with explorers and trappers and Native American tribes. They brought some level of structure to the wilderness, though it was still primitive in many ways. More and more pioneers followed and pressed farther west.

As the expansion of America spread westward, the third group, the settlers, began to move from the east to the west. This group of people brought even greater order and structure to society. As they moved into the pioneer villages, the villages became towns, and the towns became cities with infrastructure for commerce, education, and religion. Libraries and churches were built. Courthouses were established, and roads improved.

Up until the latter part of the nineteenth century, a demographic map of the United States would have reflected the spread of these three types of groups. This remained the same until the railroads tied east and west together and made travel and migration much easier. An argument could be made that the fingerprints, though somewhat faintly, of this distribution of people still exists across the United States.

What does this have to do with the selection of leaders? you might ask. Well, let's see what the connection is as we explore how to use the Leadership Model to assess candidates for leadership.

Selecting a Leader

The selection of leaders is one of the most important tasks a member of management can ever perform. Unfortunately, many members of management are not effective leaders themselves. They may be tremendous managers but not necessarily great leaders. Over the years, I have often been surprised by the lack of process in the selection of leaders. I have asked people to describe their process for selecting leaders and have received responses ranging from blank stares to a general list of attributes usually pulled out of the air. Rarely have I seen a thoughtful, deliberate process defined. As a consequence, people have been selected for leadership who simply are not ready for it or do not have the essential core values or traits to be successful. In some cases, the people selected for leadership are simply not a good fit for the organization. In other cases, some people are just not leaders but excellent team players. As a result, there is often a very rough road ahead and sometimes absolute failure under these leadership choices.

Leaders and managers create experiences for their teams. The hiring of a new leader (that often occurs through a promotion) will create a huge experience for their team. This experience can be positive or negative, but it will be an experience nonetheless! When a management team selects a new leader, they are telling the rest of the team and organization that this is what they are looking for in a leader. The characteristics, values, and traits exhibited by this individual are representative for their next-generation leader. If this is actually understood, a management team should view this selection effort as extremely important and take great care in the decision. Unfortunately, too many times this has not been the case. People are selected without a clear understanding of their values and ability to function successfully in the leadership dimensions. Often when these decisions are made hastily, the organization and individuals pay a heavy price for years.

The following are some ways to leverage the Leadership Model to assist management in leadership selection.

Leader or Manager

When trying to select a leader for a team, it is important first to determine, What do we actually need—a leader or a manager or possibly both? Sometimes *leader* and *manager* are used interchangeably and that can create confusion. As I said at the beginning of this book, *leaders are people who know how to set vision, achieve goals, and inspire people to follow them and take specific actions.* Management, on the other hand, typically specialize in supervising teams and individuals around boundaries that have been set to achieve a task. Managers often focus on maintaining control and capability.

It's true that these two roles are not mutually exclusive. In fact, they are inexorably linked. Both roles are of vital importance, and many of the skills overlap between the roles, which is one reason that some people can be effective in both of them. Nevertheless, most of the time, it's better to find individuals who can either lead well or manage well, keeping the roles distinct and separate between different individuals and groups. Understanding what is the predominate need of the organization at the time should influence the leadership selection process. Questions to consider in this assessment include, Is a leader needed to establish a vision and accomplish a goal? Alternatively, Is a manager required who should focus on disciplined performance to standards with the primary focus on consistency and sustainable results? Both roles are incredibly important, but care should be taken to select the organizational need correctly.

As described above, the description of the leadership selection process has been highly varied and consists of all kinds of answers. Unfortunately, sometimes leadership selection comes across as though one is picking out a puppy. The organization wants someone who is friendly, easy to get along with, and easy to train. Are these really the essential qualities of leadership?

Moreover, if managers are the ones seeking to fulfill a leadership role, you must keep in mind that managers often want consistency as a safe zone. Essentially, they want a leader like themselves, someone they will feel safe around. Subconsciously, they often choose leaders and managers that look and act like them. This may work out fine if they want a manager, and they were particularly good managers. However, if they need a leader to transition the organization, choosing someone like themselves may be unwise.

In Joel Barker's model, choosing a settler to lead an expedition to discover a new land would not be wise. The settler would be great once the new land had been found and established but not well suited to explore and find the new land. Likewise, leaders must be carefully selected for their capabilities and the organizational mission ahead. Leaders typically lean more toward explorer/pioneer tendencies while managers tend to exhibit more settler/pioneer traits. Of course, there are overlaps in traits among these two roles, but understanding a person's predominate style and capabilities and then matching him or her to the needs of the organization are crucial to success.

Apply the Leadership Model

When a management team is selecting leadership, I propose asking a series of critical questions that can position the assessment appropriately regarding the candidate's readiness for leadership. Fundamentally, the past will often predict the future, so probing into past performance and approaches can be telling regarding the candidate's thought processes, values, and traits. No individual is perfect in every aspect of leadership, but the Leadership Model does provide an opportunity to assess a candidate's current capabilities and understand his or her strengths and weaknesses.

Core Values Assessment

The following questions regarding Core Values should be posed in interviews and discussions. When the candidate's answers are evaluated, it is important that the assessment be based on the candidate's demonstrated behavior, not just on his or her opinion.

- Has the individual demonstrated integrity by embracing the very highest standards of honesty and ethical behavior? Has she demonstrated exemplary moral character? If so, how and what are some specific examples of this behavior?

- Has the individual demonstrated a continuous search for new ways to improve the performance of the business? Can she or others provide examples?

- Has the individual embraced the interests and concerns of the people within the organization that she knows? If so, what is some evidence of this?

This assessment is focused on the essential, non-negotiable core values of *Integrity, Excellence,* and *Respect for People.* Your organization may have more or less of these core values, but failure at any one of these should raise concerns because these are foundational building blocks for the entire Leadership Model. If a candidate is weak in any one of these values, then concerns should be raised regarding the candidate's capabilities. These values should not be compromised.

Key Dimensions Assessment

I identified four critical dimensions in the Leadership Model: *Confidence, Command, Results,* and *Strategic Innovation.* In assessing potential leaders, each of these areas should be explored to understand the candidate's current strengths and weaknesses. Questions to consider could be:

- Is the individual credible with his peers and management? If so, what information supports his claim?

- Is the individual personally trustworthy? If so, how has he demonstrated this trait?

- Is the individual respected for his command of his current area of responsibility? How so?

- Has the individual achieved consistent, sustainable results? Can they be described and measured?

- Has the individual developed others around him? If so, how has he done this?

- Has the candidate demonstrated ability to drive change successfully? Can he motivate people to action?

These questions can provide insight into how the individual fits with the Leadership Model. Is the candidate prepared or a good fit for successful leadership? If we truly believe these are important dimensions of successful leadership, and our model is a reinforcing system in which each dimension supports the others, then understanding the candidate's abilities is imperative. Fundamentally, we are assessing whether the candidate is trustworthy, respected, an achiever, and a change agent.

It can also be valuable to probe into the behaviors candidates have exhibited in their past roles. Understanding past behavior can shed light on what kind of experience they may create in the future for those working under their leadership.

Essential Traits Assessment

Finally, when assessing candidates, you need to understand who they are in relation to the Essential Traits I described in the Leadership Model. These traits are vital to a leader's success and need to be understood concerning a candidate for leadership. A weakness in one of these areas could significantly hinder a leader's ability to fulfill his or her role and responsibilities. The following are a few questions to consider in the assessment:

- Have others viewed the individual as trustworthy, and does the candidate value trust as important?

- What is the candidate passionate about now? Does her passion align with the needs of the organization?

- How has she represented her passion to others? How does she live out her passion?

- How does the individual interact with others? Has she demonstrated the value of understanding others' needs, opinions, and passions?

- Has she shown acts of service to fellow employees by helping, supporting, or enabling others to be successful? Has she shown compassion to others?

These and other questions can help assess an individual's essential traits that reflect her character and define who she is as a person and potential leader.

I have sat in many meetings where potential leadership candidates were being evaluated. It became clear that there were multiple conflicting ideas of what we were even looking for in a leader. This led to confusion, conflict, and sometimes very poor decisions that became huge mistakes. By applying the Leadership Model to the assessment of candidates, everyone is working from a common reference point. As a result, everyone involved in the leader selection process can be aligned with a conventional model, as opposed to each interviewer having his or her own model or no model at all. Hopefully, the common model will create a focused, meaningful discussion around each candidate and his or her potential fit for the position.

One final consideration for Leadership Assessment is also to apply the Emotional Intelligence (EI) Model developed some years ago and widely available in books and on the Internet. Studies have shown that people with high EI have greater mental health, exemplary job performance, and more potent leadership skills (Bradberry & Greaves, 2009). Tools are readily available to measure an individual's EI score and could be considered as another source of assessment to complement the Leadership Model.

Leadership Takeaways

- Explorer, pioneer, or settler—each plays a vital role.

- Leader or manager—define what you need.

- Apply the Leadership Model: assess the capabilities of candidates in the areas of

  o *Core Values*
  o *Key Dimensions*
  o *Essential Traits*

- Past performance is a good predictor of future behavior.

22

The Essentials for Developing Leaders

Leadership development is person development, part of the lifelong learning process that everyone is involved in.

—*Robbin Chapman*

The Leadership Model has been successfully used for a number of years as a tool for evaluating an individual's current level of performance as a leader. The intent of the evaluation has always been to gather information for understanding leadership strengths and weaknesses. A meaningful conversation could then take place, with the model as the framework for discussion.

My organization consisted of people who had project leadership responsibilities for Commissioning and Qualification around the world. In these roles, they would travel to manufacturing sites in various countries, such as Ireland, China, France, Italy, the United Kingdom, the United States, and Puerto Rico. Their primary responsibilities were to establish teams and successfully lead those teams through the commissioning and qualification of a new or existing pharmaceutical facility. These teams were often diverse in experience and skill levels, and they were often located in cultures that required adaption and sensitivity to their nuances. The staff was leading these projects with little direct authority over the people they were leading. As a consequence, the organizational structure required them to be strong in their ability to influence and motivate large groups of people to agree on a plan and then follow it throughout the project.

We introduced the Leadership Model a number of years ago to help our staff understand what effective leadership looked like and to be conscious of areas they needed to focus on to be an effective leader. With the very diverse challenges of leading groups of people in a variety of cultures, we wanted the staff to operate with a common frame of reference regarding leadership and to understand the behaviors that support strong leadership. The Leadership Model has become a regular tool for performing feedback sessions with our staff. Typically, I would use a simple red, yellow, and green color designation to visually show staff my assessment. I used green as an indicator of a strength, yellow for areas needing continual improvement, and red for areas requiring immediate attention.

This use of the tool focused discussion on specific dimensions and individual strengths and weaknesses. I had a case where one of my staff was leading a project overseas. I had received feedback from the site management team that the confidence in this leader was waning. I shared this feedback with him and coached him in ways to improve his credibility on the job. The conversation occurred with a shared understanding of where confidence fit in the entire leadership model system. The individual understood clearly that credibility produced trust which led to confidence and that the lack of credibility would deeply hurt the confidence level of the staff as well as the management group. So the focus of my coaching was on how he could improve his crediblity.

The model provides a structure for conversations and coaching. It also provides a rich context for assessments and statements about leadership. It leads us to ask where feedback fits in the Leadership Model. And when that fit occurs, it guides us to ask, What can we do to react appropriately to the feedback we receive?

Another benefit of the model with our team was that it helped reset the leadership status with each group the leader led. My staff members were constantly changing locations and subsequently leading new teams. The tool emphasized that each group was unique, and though the leader may have excellent overall leadership skills, he needed to continually revisit his leadership status with each team on each project. Assessing leadership in this manner creates a non-threatening environment, and the model can be repeatedly revisited with the same leader in different situations.

Also, the Core Values are foundational to the leader's character. Likewise, the Essential Traits are the mortar of that foundation in that they reflect the essence of the leader and how she views her world and behaves in it. Finally, whether you are coaching an individual to improve her leadership or trying to develop your own skills, you should consider some fundamental questions.

- What are you doing to create confidence?

- Are you seen as credible? If yes, how do you know?

- Are you trustworthy?

- Do you demonstrate command of your field of responsibility?

- How are you increasing your knowledge and understanding of the situation, the business, the organization, and so on?

- Do others respect you for your insight and knowledge?

- Do others seek you out for your opinion and input?

- Have you produced measurable, meaningful results?

- Have you engaged others and made them a part of the success?

- Do you routinely celebrate team successes?

- Are you consciously developing people on your team?

- Do you take steps to expand your thinking and expose yourself to new ideas? How?

- Have you made any new offers to the organization?

- Have you identified the challenges your team may face in the short term and long term—over the next two months, two years, or even five years?

- Have you led a team through a significant change?

Open and honest evaluation of these questions and their answers can provide insight into leadership abilities and areas for improvement.

Leadership Takeaways

- The Leadership Model should be used for assessment and coaching.

- The model focuses discussion on specific dimensions and individual strengths and weaknesses.

- The model provides a mechanism for evaluating feedback.

- Each group is unique, and leadership status needs to be revisited for each team.

- When coaching or doing personal assessment, ask questions and gather feedback.

23

A New Kind of Leader

If we are to negotiate the coming years safely, we may need a new kind of leadership. To put it more precisely, we need the rediscovery of an ancient kind of leadership that has rarely been given the prominence it deserves. I mean the leader as teacher.

—Jonathan Sacks

Over five hundred people crowded into the ballroom at the Louisville Hyatt Regency Hotel on an early September morning to begin the third annual CES Conference. CES stands for "Consult, Expand and Sell." This conference had been held each of the previous three years. It has grown in popularity as a must-attend conference for improving skills in buying and selling and in using Internet platforms, such as Amazon.

Jim Cockrum went to the stage and was met by enthusiastic applause from attendees who came from all over the world, including countries such as Singapore and Australia as well as parts of Europe and the United States. Jim is the founder of the conference and the leader of a growing community of people around the globe who are using the Internet and platforms such as Amazon to acquire and sell goods. He has developed tools, methods, training, and coaching (MySilentTeam.com, ProvenAmazonCourse.com, and so on) to teach people how to be effective at finding inventory and marketing products. His methods have empowered housewives, schoolteachers, retirees, and many others from different walks of life to become financially successful entrepreneurs through their own online businesses.

Throughout this book, I have talked about leadership from the perspective of someone leading and influencing people to follow, and not just leading from an endowed title or position. An effective leader has followers who engage with her and are anxious to learn and accomplish great things together. The old corporate models looked at leadership as an appointed position with title, power, and responsibility. People were supposed to follow the leader because someone up the chain had given that person the leadership title. If people wanted to keep their job, they were expected to follow the leader even if she had low credibility, lacked respect, had no sign of previous success, or had never demonstrated an ability to improve anything. This recipe has been played out time and time again across corporations, and Lilly has

> A new kind of leader must be able to change an organization that is dreamless, soulless, and visionless. ... someone's got to make a wake-up call.
> —*Warren Bennis*

been no exception. The results have often been horrendous: failed teams, confusion, frustration, or, at best, obligatory submission. The paradigm I have presented describes leadership as less about a title and far more about a systematic approach to leading. Leadership includes work colleagues, volunteer organizations, informal groups, or even one's family. My point is that the *essentials of leadership* are applicable to all situations.

Jim Cockrum represents a new kind of leader in the twenty-first century. He is a leader who uses technology to effectively lead thousands of people across continents and time zones. These are groups of people who do not report to Jim or work directly for him, but they follow his lead and participate in a dynamic community. While using the Internet and tools such as Amazon, Jim is leading an entrepreneurial revolution. He and members of his community are going head-to-head and winning bids for inventory against big box stores like TJ Maxx.

They are making offers to companies across the world to show them how to market their products more effectively on Amazon. They are turning poor performing products into highly profitable ones. They have even become consultants to Amazon as well as to Amazon's clients. They are creating whole new business models for leveraging the power of the Internet for buying and selling products.

The wide-ranging use of technology in this approach was poignantly represented at the conference when Jim had Andrew Cavanagh join him on the stage. Jim and Andrew had been business partners for over five years, creating a revolutionary new business called OfflineBiz.com. They had developed this into a very successful, profitable business. However, Jim and Andrew had never physically met or even talked by phone. All their interaction and development had been electronic. In front of over five hundred colleagues, they met for the first time in an emotional display of gratitude and appreciation for what each had brought to their partnership.

The impact of Jim's program has clearly changed lives by providing financial freedom and independence through business success. Companies such as *Death Wish Coffee* and *Liberty Jane* have used his principles to expand their businesses, increase sales, and grow profits. Jim's approach has also created a community of people who support one another and openly and willingly share their successes and learning. A culture has been created of open sharing and giving back; members call it "giving value." This has been done by members helping each other be successful and to utilize their resources to improve the world.

For example, at this conference, Jason and Karen Tay shared the story of PremaTouch, a company selling all-natural coconut oil soap—an outstanding handmade soap that is free of SLS parabens and other harsh, harmful skin irritants. This soap is made by a non-profit organization called *Touch Nature: Kolbata.* This organization is helping women who were once sold into sex trafficking to develop skills to support themselves. This company provides these women with dignified, sustainable employment. The Tay's have used their leadership skills to create this organization and used Amazon marketing to position their company's products in the marketplace. They have invited people who buy these products to become part of a movement to help women coming out of the horror of sex trafficking. Here passion and compassion clearly unite.

Leadership Essentials at Work

Jim Cockrum's story is a good example of applying the essentials of leadership in the twenty-first century.

Many years ago, Jim left his job selling software to become an entrepreneur. He established some clear values that defined who he was and what he was about as a person and as an entrepreneur. He made a decision early on to do whatever he could to help others succeed. Having been the son of a minister, Jim recognized that many people who had given their lives to Christian service or other philanthropic efforts often had little financial reserves for future support. He made a value decision to help people reach financial independence and be free of stifling debt. These values helped shape his entire business and leadership approach. He published books, training materials, and educational videos, and made them readily available for free. He spent hours talking on the phone and answering questions for anyone who wanted his advice. He worked with people all over the globe, building a network of entrepreneurs, and exploring new business ideas. He learned and shared knowledge and slowly built a community of over a hundred thousand followers.

Jim's character traits have reflected his values. He has treated people with respect and demonstrated a servant's heart to the people all around him. As I watched him at the conference, he openly mingled with people during breaks. He gave as much time to those individuals just starting their business as he gave to those who had already built lucrative, successful ventures. He was always listening, providing insight, and giving advice. A leader's character reflects his values, and his were certainly those highlighted in the Leadership Model.

Jim Cockrum's success did not happen overnight, but as with many leaders, his has been a journey involving and bringing with him numerous people.

The First Dimension

In the first dimension of the essentials of the Leadership Model, we established that leaders must create confidence, which produces credibility and trust.

When Jim left his job selling software, one of his first entrepreneurial efforts was to put bubble gum machines in the entrance of restaurants. I'm talking about machines with a large round plastic container that held hundreds of different colored gumballs. He worked with restaurant managers to setup these machines and make sure they were refilled regularly. I don't know if he ever made a lot of money with this venture, but through it he built his confidence that he could be successful as an entrepreneur.

Jim moved on to other business endeavors and expanded his presence and abilities in the Internet worlds of eBay and Amazon. He networked with anyone he could to learn and share information. His presence and willingness to share with others quickly built confidence among many people in this field. They recognized his abilities and appreciated his openness and true concern for their success and well-being. Jim fulfilled his commitments and followed up promptly, which created confidence by others and resulted in being him viewed as highly credible in the eBay and Amazon world. Recently the watchdog service Internet Marketing Report Card voted Jim Cockrum *The Most Trusted Marketer Online*. Such leaders build credibility and trust and create confidence.

The Second Dimension

The second dimension of the essentials of Leadership Model emphasizes that leaders demonstrate command and produce respect.

As Jim became more successful in buying and selling inventory, he began teaching others the keys to his success. He continued to learn and be a student of others' successes and collaborated with many individuals and groups on various projects. He eventually wrote several books about his experience, including *Silent Sales Machine*, *Free Marketing: 101 Low and No-Cost Ways to Grow Your Business On and Offline*, and *Ten Years and Ten Lessons: Things I learned While Selling Millions*. Each book provided readers with valuable keys to becoming successful. For e-book buyers, Jim has updated the *Silent Sales Machine* book nine times, with consumers getting free updates each time so they can remain current.

He has become a world-class expert in Internet business and sales. He has created a training network with coaches and mentors to help new entrepreneurs become successful. Amazon has reached out to him and his organization on more than one occasion to consult with them on their platform and to receive valuable users' insight.

The result of all of this is that Jim is highly respected as an expert who truly understands his field. People want to follow leaders who are knowledgeable and have a command of their field. Jim would be the first to acknowledge that he is always learning from others and is not "the expert" but simply trying to get better every day and share what he knows. This approach and ability have brought him tremendous respect from people worldwide. They follow his advice and seek him out for his knowledge and insight. They are followers because he has high credibility and is respected for his demonstrated command of his field of business.

The Third Dimension

The third dimension of the essentials of Leadership Model establishes that leaders produce results. If they produce results and enable people to follow and take specific actions to produce those results in a sustainable manner, they are seen as enabling achievers. Ultimately, leaders must be able to show results for their leadership. Leading must move from theory, knowledge, and good intent to tangible results.

Jim Cockrum's track record is very clear. He has sold millions of dollars of products and services online in his own online businesses. He runs two successful online membership sites with over fifteen thousand paying members and has helped thousands of other budding entrepreneurs and businesses start or grow successful online businesses since he began in late 2000. Jim has appeared in the *Wall Street Journal*, *Men's Health* magazine, and *Entrepreneur* magazine. He has also hosted a weekly radio broadcast, *Creative Internet Income Strategies*, on eBay radio and has several successful book titles as well. He publishes a *CES Newsletter*, which is read by more than one hundred thousand people. Jim is clearly highly successful.

During the conference in Louisville, his success and results as a leader became even more evident as I talked with various people and heard their stories. One example is Carolyn from Utah who shared that fifteen years ago she and her children were living in a homeless shelter. When they finally moved out, she was barely making ends meet working for a school district. In 2006, she started selling her kids' old clothes on eBay, and in 2013 she bought Jim's "Proven Amazon Course." Applying it, she saw her online income double almost immediately. A few months later she lost her job in education and became determined to make selling on Amazon work even better for her and her family. By March of 2014, she had doubled her income from the previous year, and by August she was completely debt free. By March of 2015, she had doubled her income once again. She has become financially sound and credits the knowledge she received from Jim Cockrum and Kat Simpson (an associate of Jim's) as having changed her life.

In Carolyn—and so many others like her—Jim has seen one of his core values realized: to help people reach financial independence and become free of stifling debt. He has also extended this value to others through those he has helped. As Carolyn added, she is now helping a friend learn how to start an Amazon business.

Leaders achieve results through people and enable them to continue being successful and grow. Jim has a long list of people who have become empowered through his courses and coaching to create Amazon businesses. These businesses have provided financial freedom for families and supported numerous efforts to "give value back." Other examples of this include entrepreneurs funding clean water wells with World Help Organization, while others are providing sewing machines and teaching women in Zambia to sew and provide a living for their families. Still others are supporting orphans in Africa. And then there's the story I shared earlier of Jason and Karen Tay providing a means for women leaving the sex-trafficking world to support themselves. Leaders enable people, replicate success, and model values.

The Fourth Dimension

The fourth dimension of the essentials of the Leadership Model establishes that leaders are able to manifest strategic innovation. When they effectively do this, others see them as change agents—individuals who can anticipate future trends and opportunities and take action. Leaders are able to move their organization in a new direction as needed or as opportunities present themselves.

Jim Cockrum represents this dimension in his leadership. He has become a recognized thought leader for online business and has established new business models.

Earlier I spoke of Jim and Andrew Cavanagh's partnership that was separated by nine thousand miles. Together these two created an entirely new business model, OfflineBiz.com, that now has more than thirteen thousand members. This business provides a means for small and medium businesses to access the power of Internet marketing by leveraging the knowledge and capabilities of Offline Biz members.

> The new leader is a facilitator, not an order giver
> —*John Naisbitt*

Leaders listen, learn, and explore. They look for risk, trends, and opportunities. They make tough decisions when necessary to change direction, enter new markets, or pursue new opportunities. They lead their organization and collaborate with other leaders. Jim has consistently been in front of trends and opportunities from the start of his online business. He has shared his knowledge and helped others seize opportunities with him.

People pay attention to leaders who are trusted and respected for their knowledge and capabilities. People value leaders who can get results and have a track record of success. People take note when a leader has the insight and ability to propose new direction and make necessary changes to seize new opportunities. As a result, people follow them because they want to. They want leaders they see as trusted and respected, leaders who achieve results and can see far enough ahead to steer the organization effectively.

Jim Cockrum represents this new kind of leader for the twenty-first century. Ironically, Jim has only two full-time employees in his business, but he has thousands in his community who follow his leadership. These people collaborate with him as well as follow his coaching and mentoring. He listens to their ideas and feedback, explores new ideas, and acts to produce new products.

As we move deeper into the twenty-first century, corporate organizational models are being challenged and new approaches are being developed. These new approaches include outsourcing of activities that companies never considered outsourcing in the past. They also include collaborations between companies and strategic partnerships. Some of these partnerships create unique organizational challenges where people from different companies might be working closely together on collaborative teams. These new realities will call for more effective leadership.

Jim has led a community, not an organization in the sense of a corporate hierarchy. He leads a group of individual entrepreneurs from around the world, each with their own priorities and objectives.

As the corporate world evolves and old methods are abandoned, leaders may find themselves leading communities rather than traditional heirachial organizations. These communities will be made up of very diverse millennials and those coming behind them. These people have wide-ranging talents, multifaceted perspectives, and personal priorities that do not fit well with the long established heirarchial control structures typical in the corporate world. In fact, these groups value independence and entrepreneurism and have a fierce resistance to corporate bureaucracy. This is becoming the new reality. And leaders must be able to influence and lead such communities if they are to be effective and successful in the years ahead.

The View Forward

When I created the Commissioning and Qualification team at Lilly a number of years ago, I did not realize that leadership would be the primary challenge instead of technical knowledge. In essence, we were leading communities of people who reported through multiple organizations with different priorities and objectives. Leadership was the key to success as it is with many endeavors in business and society.

In this book, I have told the story of how I defined a leadership model to meet a significant business need. The purpose of this leadership model was to equip and enable people who were asked to travel the world and lead very diverse groups of people. The mission was to transform the manner in which Lilly had commissioned and qualified projects. When we started, the times were desperate for Lilly, with recent project failures and costly over-runs. However, slowly and steadily the tide changed and the teams needed were established. Leaders led teams to transform the manner in which we conducted business. We explored and learned leadership together. We made some mistakes along the way. We learned new skills and new ways of working together. And we celebrated successes together.

In these pages I have presented the Leadership Model as a framework for understanding a dynamic system. It defines core values, essential traits, and essential behaviors—all of which work together in the context of four critical leadership dimensions. This model has provided us with a clear and beneficial context for a meaningful analysis of leadership, discussion, and hopefully growing together to become the leaders we need to be and should be.

This Leadership Model has been successfully used throughout the world. My desire is that it will help you understand and appreciate the multiple dimensions and behaviors of effective leadership. I encourage you to use this model to help you explore leadership and eventually establish what you believe leadership should be and how it should function. If you take this journey, you will learn not only much about leadership but also as much, if not more, about yourself.

THE LEADERSHIP MODEL

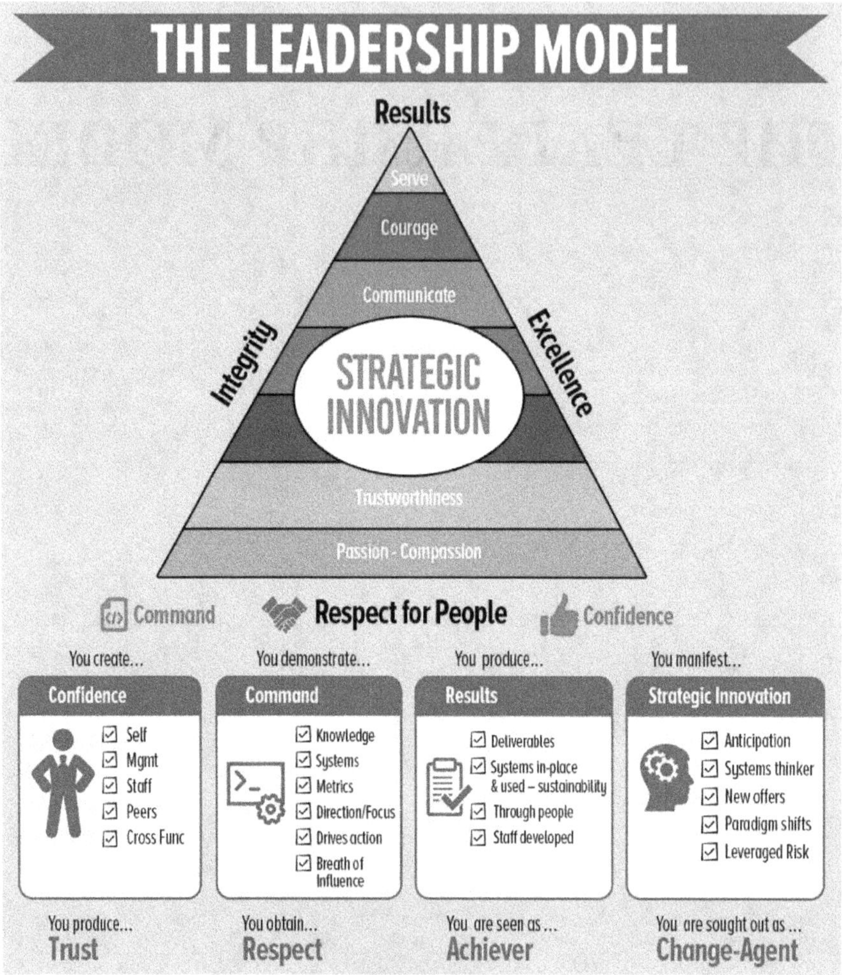

THE LEADERSHIP MODEL

Results

Serve

Courage

Communicate

Integrity

STRATEGIC INNOVATION

Excellence

Trustworthiness

Passion - Compassion

Command | **Respect for People** | Confidence

You create... | You demonstrate... | You produce... | You manifest...

Confidence	Command	Results	Strategic Innovation
☑ Self	☑ Knowledge	☑ Deliverables	☑ Anticipation
☑ Mgmt	☑ Systems	☑ Systems in-place & used – sustainability	☑ Systems thinker
☑ Staff	☑ Metrics		☑ New offers
☑ Peers	☑ Direction/Focus	☑ Through people	☑ Paradigm shifts
☑ Cross Func	☑ Drives action	☑ Staff developed	☑ Leveraged Risk
	☑ Breath of Influence		

You produce... | You obtain... | You are seen as ... | You are sought out as ...
Trust | **Respect** | **Achiever** | **Change-Agent**

THE ESSENTIALS GROUP

276

APPENDIX

Conversational Checkers

Often in this book I have referred to Conversational Checkers. Here I offer you more background and information into this model, its concept, its methodology, and its tools.

In the early 1990s, Dale Martlage and I developed this tool as a means for improving meeting effectiveness as well as individual one-on-one interactions. In the early '90s, many organizations were buried in a culture of consensus management. Decisions were based on the consensus won by teams of people, and the meetings and discussions turned into protracted debates in which focus was often lost and teams often failed to arrive at deliberate, precise decisions in a timely manner. This approach led to frustrated team members and sometimes missed opportunities for their company. There was nothing beneficial about the situation. Change was needed.

Dale and I began researching and studying communication. In the process, we discovered that experts in the field had recognized that all cultures and languages followed a similar pattern. This pattern consisted of an Awareness Phase where one party was providing another with some level of knowledge or information about a topic. After a period of questions and answers to clarify the subject, the conversations would often progress to a Possibility Phase in which the two parties would offer potential actions to take based on the awareness provided.

Finally, conversation often progressed to commitments to action (the Action Phase) about the awareness and possibilities generated. This pattern repeated itself in culture after culture, regardless of the language spoken. So, the question for Dale and I became, *What do we do with this knowledge about communication we now have?*

We realized that this pattern of Awareness, Possiblity, and Action (A-P-A cycle) was precisely the pattern we saw in many of our meetings, but with one critical exception: many discussions in meetings were getting caught in an endless loop of sharing awareness. We began tracking conversations in site Lead Team meetings and realized we had digressed to sharing enormous amounts of awareness—information in the form of presentations and roundtable discussions. We would sometimes generate possibilities, but rarely would we move to taking meaningful action that was driven by the awareness and possibilities we had discussed. This approach led to meeting after meeting and week after week of inefficient, nonproductive meetings. Something had to change.

As we talked about our team meetings and conversations, we used the analogy of an airplane flight. Our conversations were similar to taking off in a plane, flying around and around the airfield, and then landing without ever traveling anywhere else. We burned a lot of fuel and took up a lot of time but accomplished very little.

As we tracked conversations, we also discovered another pattern. We were undisciplined in keeping discussions on the topic and focused at the right level. We would get easily distracted as a team and go off on tangents in the middle of a conversation. This also contributed to our inability to drive to action. In our airplane analogy, we were changing altitudes quickly and getting airsick!

We took this awareness and developed the fundamentals of what we called Conversational Checkers. Meetings and conversations would move away from the old and inefficient approach to a new one that would have the following elements:

1. A defined objective that clearly establishes the intent and type of discussion to follow.
2. Awareness Phase: Someone may share a topic and appropriate information about it while the rest of the team

listens carefully and captures questions and possibilities on paper. Team members may not interrupt the presenter. He must be allowed to fulfill the Awareness Phase—in other words, to present all his planned information.

3. Clarification Phase: Team members may ask clarifying questions but must remain on topic. They may not move on to possibilities or stray from the topic at hand.

4. Possibility Phase: The team may now make a conscious effort to shift the conversation to creating possibilities. Often these types of conversations will be characterized by statements such as "What if ..." or "I wonder if ..." or "Could we ..." These possibilities should be recorded and tracked throughout the discussion.

5. Action Phase: Finally, the team should clarify possibilities and arrive at an action to take regarding the awareness and possibilities generated. During this phase, responsibilities are assigned and commitments made for delivery and confirmation.

A facilitator, often referred to as the Navigator, would be responsible for keeping the team on task. At the completion of the discussion, the team would review the process and assess conversational effectiveness. Each meeting would begin with a review of the previous commitments status.

The Conversational Checkers process would also include a clear understanding of the type of discussion needed. Conversations were defined as one of five different types, and it was paramount that the team remained on the "right" level during a conversation. Here were the five levels:

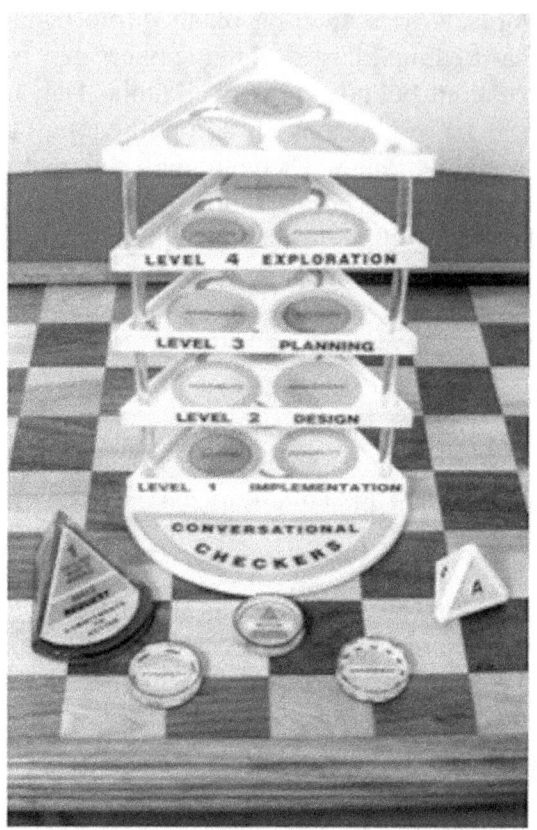

Exploration Level

This level of conversation is intended to reach beyond existing parameters or paradigms. Definition is given at this level. The intent is to explore new opportunities and encourage people to look for new possibilities. An individual should declare that she wants to have an exploration type discussion, and then participants should minimize rehashing already existing awareness and only use this level of conversation as a springboard for generating new possibilities. This may be the purest form of brainstorming. The key, though, is that the team should stay engaged at only this level of conversation. As the discussion proceeds at this level, as with every other level, the entire A-P-A, Awareness-Possibility-Action cycle must be used as the process for discussion. Someone will share awareness while others listen and take notes, once completed they can ask clarify questions and then move in to possibility generation. After a time of capturing possibilities and refining them the team moves to the action phase and focus on determining next steps.

Planning Level

The Planning Level is where "we place it or give it direction." The "it" is the particular topic we are discussing. At this level, discussion is about a topic already defined but which the group is trying to place strategically. Teams should not dive too much into detail at this level but instead have just enough specifics to provide direction for the next steps. The deeper detail work will be discussed at another level. As described above, the A-P-A cycle is the process for discussion.

Design Level

The Design Level focuses on content and detail around a topic. The discussion is at a different level of detail than the previous levels. This level focuses the conversation on specific features, so it is important that the appropriate people be in the conversation. A fundamental flaw we discovered was that some of the people having Design discussions around a topic were not qualified or capable of meaningfully contributing at this level. The details and content of a given topic should drive who should be involved in the conversation about them. The individuals engaged at this level should all be able to take action. As previously mentioned, A-P-A is used.

Implementation Level

This level of conversation focuses on execution or *giving force* to a particular domain. This level of conversation should occur after content, details, and direction have been given. Typical groups involved in this level are directly responsible for execution and implementation. A-P-A is the process.

Checking Level

A checking level conversation can occur at any of the above levels, but the intent is to check on the status of previous commitments and current progress. The intent of the group should be to focus the conversation on the status and progress of the Exploration, Planning, Design, or Implementation levels. Checking conversations are crucial and should be done consistently throughout the Conversational Checkers process.

***

Early on, it became obvious that groups were not always "flying" at the same altitude or level. An individual may have intended to have a Planning-level conversation, but invariably someone would dive into some level of detail that was at the Design level or even the Implementation level. Another person would respond to this comment and take it to a still different level. This constant changing of levels created frustration and made conversations very hard to follow. When this happened, people often shut down and disengaged from the conversation. In the end, little was accomplished.

Nevertheless, as team members became more used to the new approach and facilitators/navigators became more aggressive in its implementation, conversations stayed on track much more often. And when a conversation drifted from the appropriate level or directly violated the A-P-A cycle, the team leader would quickly redirect the conversation to where it belonged. Slowly, teams became more effective in their conversations using the Conversational Checkers methodology. Actions came more regularly from conversations. Progress was made on topics that before had been completely bogged down in debate. People began to feel their time was being used more efficiently and productively.

Dale and I also developed a tabletop Conversational Checkers Game that was used primarily in one-on-one conversations. An individual would request a conversation with another person, and they would pull the game onto the table or desk in front of them. One person would declare the conversation topic and the desired level at which he or she wanted to engage in conversation. The other individual had the opportunity to accept, decline, or counter the proposal. Once both parties were in agreement, a checker would be placed on the proper level of the "awareness" space, and the person who had requested the conversation would begin sharing awareness. The other individual would listen intently and make notes for follow-up to achieve clarification. Once the awareness had been delivered, questions could be asked to clarify the awareness and understanding. Either party could place another checker on the "possibilities" space when he or she was ready to move into exploring possibilities. Once this level of conversation was done, the conversation shifted to statements such as "What if ..." or "Could we ..." At any time, it was acceptable for either participant to slip back to awareness to clarify a possibility. Finally, someone would place a checker on the "action" space, and conversation would shift to defining specific actions at the appropriate level based on the awareness and possibilities generated. This A-P-A cycle would move the conversation forward in a clear, purposeful, and effective way.

This methodology was applied in a number of different venues throughout Lilly. It changed the conversation culture throughout the corporation and benefited the company, its employees, and ultimately all those we served, from vendors to customers.

Acknowledgments

I have had the pleasure and honor of leading an incredible group of people at Eli Lilly and Company. Together we created a Commissioning and Qualification capability that did not exist previously in the company. Today this capability is successfully used around the world and has conservatively saved Lilly in excess of $600 million over a ten-year period. Outside industry experts have acknowledged that the systems created by this group are among the best in the industry. They have also established that this team has consistently performed at worldclass levels for cost and deliverables.

The team's success has had challenges along the way, but with each challenge this group has risen to the task and made the needed adjustments. I have also seen individuals in this group develop new skills, and, as a result, they have become true experts in their field. However, I am particularly proud of the way this group of men and women have become outstanding leaders. Routinely they have traveled the world leading very diverse groups from sometimes quite different cultures to successfully commission and qualify new Lilly facilities. Some of these individuals are still a part of this group while others have moved on, but all have had a significant impact. We have learned and grown together, and I am truly blessed for having had each of them be a vital part of my journey.

This book is dedicated to this group of leaders:

Dave Kwilosz	Mohsin Ruhayel
Rebecca Ford	Keith Mimms

Rick Haggard
Dick Knight
Jason Hasenour
Kelli Goebel
Scott Hamm
R.J. Kulkarni
Brenda Meredith
Dan Franklin
Pat Callahan
Dick Reinhart
Dennis Naughton
Ivonne Mendizabal
Stig Bockman-Pedersen
Bob Woodrum
Samana Huggins
Leroy Raghunath
Tom Fletcher

Chris Donaldson
Gerome Avenoso
Bill Prather
Jim Miller
Jim Hufford
John Eickman
Rob Young
Chris Holewinski
Thao Phan
Nassir Ahmed
Dave Miller
Mark Minot
Daniel Harrison
Melissa Marcum
Kent Kyburz
Dave Fiedeldey

I offer special thanks to Shakeel Ahmad for asking "the question" on that fateful day.

Additional thanks go to Jim Cockrum, Eldon Kibbey, Dr. Don Osborn, and Mark Hodson for your feedback, mentoring, and friendship in the writing of this book.

A very special thanks to my editor, Bill Watkins, who has provided profound insight and wisdom in the editing of this work. You have mentored me, encouraged me, and guided me through this process. Your friendship is greatly valued. God bless you!

Finally, thanks to those colleagues whose stories I have shared in these pages. Each of you has had a profound impact on my leadership journey.

About the Author

Bruce Beck is a consultant and writer who lives outside Indianapolis, Indiana, with his wife Kathy. He worked for Eli Lilly and Company for thirty-four years, and his career included a number of roles supporting manufacturing and project delivery. In his last role, he led a corporate group responsible for developing the Lilly global commissioning and qualification program. This group was also responsible for the implementation of this program throughout the world for all new Lilly facilities.

Bruce has a masters degree in chemical engineering from the Ohio State University and a bachelors degree in chemistry from Asbury University. He has authored articles on construction quality assurance in magazines such as *Pharmaceutical Engineering*, *The Chemical Engineer Today*, and *Quality Progress*.

Today he is the president and founder of The Essentials Group, LLC (theessentialsgroup.net) that provides consulting for a variety of organizations. He focuses on individual and team effectiveness as well as providing insights on commissioning and qualification practices and program setup. He is passionate about helping develop leaders to reach their full potential.

The Essentials Group

TEG is a consulting firm dedicated to helping clients identify their organizational and personal keys to success. Once these keys are understood, TEG works with teams and individual leaders to improve performance and create innovative solutions. This involves personnel coaching as well as facilitating teams. We offer the following services:

- Workshops on leadership
- Individual leadership coaching of staff and teams
- Coaching for project delivery
- Coaching manufacturing effectiveness

We have extensive experience in manufacturing, project delivery, and leadership development, with a strong international background having worked in locations such as China, Ireland, Italy, France, Spain, Germany, and the United Kingdom.

Contact us today to discuss how we may help.

Visit us at

theessentialsgroup.net
or call (317) 703-9410

Works Cited

- AFP. (2010, June 2). BP Chief appologizes for "I'd like my life back comment".

- Ambrose, S. (1994). D-Day. New York, New York, USA: Simon & Schuster.

- Andersen, E. (2012, June 11). Passionate Leaders Aren't Loud- They're Deep. Retrieved from Forbes:http://www.forbes.com/sites/erikaandersen/2012/06/11/passionate-leaders-arent-loud-theyre-deep/

- Balboni, J. (2008, January 14). You Need Both Passion and Compassion to Lead. Retrieved from Harvard Business Review blog: http://logs.hbr.org/cs/2008/01/you_need_both_passion_and_comp.html

- Barker, J. (1992). Future Edge. New York, New York, USA: William Morrow.

- Bowditch, N. I. (1840). Memoir of Nathaniel Bowditch. Boston, Massachusetts, USA: Charles C. Little and James Brown.

- Bradberry, T., & Greaves, J. (2009). Emotional Intelligence 2.0. San Diego, California, USA: TallentSmart Inc.

- Britton, D., & Page, J. (2007). Wisdom Walks Sports. Novato, California, USA: New World Library.

- Grazer, B. (Producer), Broyles, W., Reinert, A. (Writers), & Howard, R. (Director). (1995). Apollo 13 [Motion Picture]. Universal Pictures.

- Catmull, E. (2014). Creativity, Inc. New York: Random House.

- Connors, R., Smith, T., & Hickman, C. (1990). The Oz Principle: Getting Results Through Individual and Organizational Accountability. New York, New York, USA: Currency Doubleday.

- Covey, S. (1989). Seven Habits of Highly Effective People. New York, New York, USA: Free Press.

- Derler, A. (2011, September 20). Bersin by Deloitte. Retrieved from Leadership Development in Support of Globalization: www.bersin.com/Blog/post/Leadership-Development-in-Support-of-Globalization.aspx

- D'Este, C. (2002). Eisenhower: A Soldier's Life. New York, New York, USA: Harry Holt and Company.

- Durando, J. (2010, June 1). BP's Tony Hayward: "I'd like my life back". USA Today

- Eisenhower, D. D. (1948). Crusade in Europe. London: Heinemann.

- Enron, Inc. (2000). Enron Annual Report 2000. Annual Report, Houston.

- Folkman, J. (2014, November 2014). The '8 Great' Accountability Skills for Business Success. Forbes Magazine .

- Gardner, H. (2010). Art through the Ages. Boston, Massachusetts, USA: Cenguage.

- Gorman, C. K. (2010, April 9). Seven Insights for Collaboration. Retrieved from ReliablePlant: www.reliableplant.com/Read/23929/7-insights-collaboration-workplace

- Grant, A. (2014). Give and Take. New York, New York, USA: Penguin Random House.

- Greenburg, M. (2012, August 23). The Six Attributes of Courage. Psychology Today .

- Greenleaf, R. K. (1970). The Servant as Leader. Atlanta, Georgia, USA: The Center for Servant Leadership.

- Greenleaf, R. (2009). The Institution as Servant. Atlanta, Georgia: Greenleaf Center for Servant Leadership.

- Griskevicius, V., Shiota, M., & Neufeld, S. (2010, April 10). Influence of different positive emotions on persusion processing: afunctional evolutionary approach. Emotion , 190-206.

- Lee, S. (2011, August 31). Calcutta Mercy Ministries: social justice through evangelism. Retrieved from Canadian Christianity: http://www.canadianchristianity. com/calcutta-mercy-ministries-social-justice-evangelism-1984

- Lewis, M. (2003). Moneyball: The Art of Winning an Unfair Game. New York, New York: W. W. Norton & Company.

- London: The Times. (2010, May 31). Embattled BP chief: I want my life back. The Times .

- Lytle, T. (2009, November 27). Enron, Huricane Katrina: Examples of Leadership Gone Wrong. US News and World Report .

- Marco, R. (1977). Leonardo. Sidney, Australia: Bay Books.

- Maxwell, J. (1999). The 21 Indispensible Qualities of a Leader. Nashville, TN, USA: Thomas Nelson.

- McCraw, T. K. (2000). American Business, 1920-2000: How it Worked. Wheeling, Illinois, USA: Harlan Davidson, Inc.

- McCullough, D. (2005). 1776. New York, New York, USA: Simon & Schuster.

- Pais, A. (1982). Subtle is the Lord: The Science and the Life of Albert Einstein. Oxford, New York, USA: Oxford University Press.

- Ramsey, D. (2015, February 15). Three Leadership Lessons from President George Washington. Retrieved from http://www.daveramsey.com/blog/3-leadership-lessons-from-president-george-washington

- Senge, P. M. (1990). The Fifth Dimension: The Art & Practice of the Learning Organization. New York, New York, USA: Doubleday.

- Sinek, S. (2009). Start With Why: How Great Leaders Inspire Everyone to Take Action. Westminster, London, United Kingdom: Penguin Publishing Group.

- Salen, R. (Producer), Sowards, J. (Writer), & Meyer, N. (Director). (1982). Star Trek II: Wrath of Kahn [Motion Picture].

- The Great Idea Finder. (2006, May 20). The Great Idea Finder. Retrieved from http://www.ideafinder.com/history/inventions/postit.htm

- Trapp, R. (2014, May 23). Successful Organizations Need Leaders At All Levels. Forbes magazine .

- Uzzi, B., & Dunlap, S. (2005, December). How to Build Your Network. Retrieved from Harvard Business Review: http://hbr.org/2005/12/how-to-build-your-network

- Wharton . (2009, February 18). A World Transformed:What Are the top 30 Innovations of the Last 30 Years. Retrieved from knowledge.wharton.upenn.edu/article/a-world-transformed-what-are-the-top-30-innovations-of-the-last-30-years/

Index

www.ingramcontent.com/pod-product-compliance
Lightning Source LLC
Chambersburg PA
CBHW071251220526
45468CB00001B/81